Karibu. Mauya. Wamkelekile. እንኳን ደህና መጣህ. Olandiridwa. Murakaza
Karibu. Mauya. Wamkelekile. እንኳን ደህና መጣህ. Olandiridwa. Barka.
Murakaza neza. Amohelehile. Siyalemukela. Luɔɔr. O amogelesegile.
Barka. Tukusanyukide.

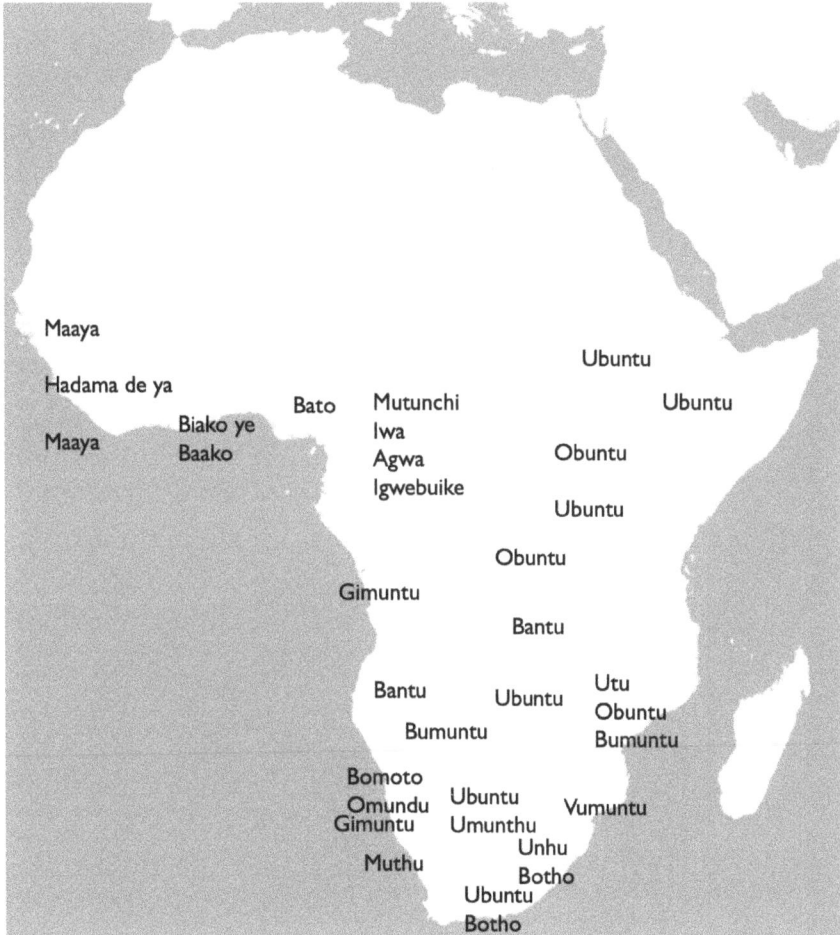

Maaya

Hadama de ya

Maaya

Biako ye
Baako

Bato

Mutunchi
Iwa
Agwa
Igwebuike

Ubuntu

Ubuntu

Obuntu

Ubuntu

Obuntu

Gimuntu

Bantu

Bantu

Bumuntu

Ubuntu

Utu
Obuntu
Bumuntu

Bomoto
Omundu
Gimuntu
Muthu

Ubuntu
Umunthu

Vumuntu

Unhu
Botho
Ubuntu
Botho

Names of Africa's philosophy

Authors

Rugare Mugumbate, Zimbabwe, PhD
Wilson Zvomuya, Zimbabwe, MSW
William Abur, South Sudan and Australia, PhD
Morena Jerkarman Rankopo, Botswana, PhD
Kabo Diraditsile, Botswana, PhD
Kgosietsile Maripe, Botswana, PhD
Phillip Manyanye Bohwasi, Zimbabwe, MPS
Edward Muzondo, Zimbabwe, MSW

Citation

Mugumbate R., Zvomuya W., Abur W., Rankopo M. J., Diraditsile K., Maripe K., Bohwasi P. M., and Muzondo, E. (2025). *Ubuntu in Social Services and Development in Africa: A Comprehensive Guide.* Harare: Zivo Publishers.

This book was prepared for lecturers and students of certificate, diploma, bachelor, master and doctoral courses for social workers, development workers, community workers, counsellors, psychologists, social welfare workers, social development workers, Indigenous workers, cultural service workers and social administrators.

Ubuntu in Social Services and Development in Africa
A Comprehensive Guide

First published 2025

Published by:

ZIV BOOKS

Zivo Publishing, Harare, Zimbabwe
At Zivo, we turn African stories, experiences, creations, relations and dreams into written literature.
https://zivo.africasocialwork.net/

International Standard Book Number (ISBN) | National Library of South Africa
978-1-77920-450-9 (print) | 978-1-0370-0235-9 (ebook)

Archiving and legal deposit: A copy of this book is held by the National Library of South Africa in accordance with the Legal Deposit Act 54 of 1997 of the Republic of South Africa. The Act was promulgated to provide for the preservation of the national documentary heritage through the legal deposit of published documents.

Typeset in Baskerville by Zivo Publishers. Pages: 378. Words: 98400. Dimensions: 15.6 x 2.18 x 23.39 cm. Size: 5.7MB (PDF), 7.6MB (ePuB).

Cover designer: Rugare Mugumbate. The picture shows a natural waterhole where humans, animals, plants and spiritual beings nourish on top of a flat rock. In Africa, the natural, spiritual, physical, environmental and human are interconnected in simple and complicated ways, a key lesson for social and development services.

Editor: Associate Professor Mabvurira, North-West University, South Africa
Decolonisation reviewer: Dr Rugare Mugumbate
Peer reviewers: Dr Abel B. Matsika, Weston Chidyausiku, Wilberforce Kurevakwesu, Lisa William (nee Samupita) and Dr Mathew Mabefam, Tendai Phillip Daka (student) and Primrose Mangwendeza (student). Each chapter published in this book was subject to review by peers who are experts in the subject area. The process was anonymous, that is, reviewers and writers were not disclosed to each other.

Subject areas: social services, social work, development work, social development, cultural work, indigenous work, decolonisation, counselling, community work, social welfare, social care and Ubuntu work.

English usage: The book used both British English and American English in line with publisher editorial policy to reduce the burden of writing for non-English authors, and to suit a global audience. Words and concepts in African languages, mainly Swahili have been included.

Writing, publishing and formatting style: Africa Social Work and Development (ASWDNet) Style

Chapter tour

Each chapter starts with an Introduction; Objectives of the chapter and Skills and competencies addressed in the chapter. Examples:

Objectives of this chapter

By writing this chapter, we hope to achieve the following:

- Share the basic and major ideas of African philosophy.
- Show that African philosophy exists in oral and written formats.
- Share the main African philosophers and their philosophical ideas (philosophies).
- Show that African philosophy is distinct, thriving and is different from other philosophies.
- Help students to value and be confident with Africa's gourd of knowledge.

Skills and competencies addressed in this chapter

By the end of this chapter, readers will be expected to have acquired the following skills and competencies:

- Applying philosophical knowledge to shape skills and make interventions more relevant to Africa.
- Valuing and using African philosophy and decolonising African knowledge and practices.
- Answer questions or assessments about the topic of this chapter.
- Create research questions and methods that are appropriate to the local context and values.
- Plan fieldwork, workplace-based and community-based learning that is contextual.

Each chapter ends with Guidance about using Ubuntu; Summary; Further and advanced knowledge; Questions for in-class assessments and examinations; Potential questions for research; Fieldwork ideas; Key terms and their meanings; and References and recommended. Examples:

Summary

- Each group of people has their own philosophy.
- Ubuntu is the overarching philosophy of Africa.
- Ubuntu shapes life and how social functioning is understood.
- In social work, philosophy shapes values, ethics, theories, methods – in short, philosophy shapes all we do in social work
- Africans value family, community, environment, spirituality, wholeness and decoloniality.

Further and advanced knowledge

- How to address the shortcomings of African philosophy.
- Is culture a result of philosophy or vice versa?
- What were the philosophies of Sankara and Biko?
- Who and what are the ideas of emerging African philosophers?

Potential questions for research

1. What African philosophy could you use to guide a study of family strengthening? Why?
2. Do a literature review or an indaba on the role of Abrahamic religion (Christianity and Islam) in colonising Ubuntu.
3. Design a research proposal using any of these research designs: African research methodology (ARM) (e.g. Khupe and Keane, 2017); Afrikology (Nabudere, 2011) or Indigenous research methodology (IRM) (Chilisa et al, 2017).

Fieldwork ideas

1. Visit a site for community development two or more times and create a mind map of their model.
2. Think about a person who helps others to achieve better social functioning in your family or community, visit, observe or call to ask them: Who gave them this role or authority? What motivates them to do what they do? What philosophies could be behind their work?

Table of contents

Illustrations

Tables

Figures

Pictures

Information boxes

Frameworks and models

Templates

Case studies

Authors

The authors have lived experience of Ubuntu, from three countries—
Botswana, South Sudan and Zimbabwe. They all have experience in social
work and development from outside their countries, through work or
education. All authors have experience in higher education and have
researched and published on different social services and development
areas. Other important experiences of the authors include advising
governments on policy and programming, initiating development
organisations, networks or social enterprises, consultancy on social
services, developing or reviewing journals, living or working in rural
communities, including refugee camps and working abroad.

Rugare Mugumbate

Dr Rugare Mugumbate is a Zimbabwean social worker who trained at the
School of Social Work, University of Zimbabwe and worked at the
Epilepsy Support Foundation and the Bindura University of Science
Education (BUSE) in Zimbabwe between 2003 and 2015. He has a Doctor
of Philosophy (PhD) from the University of Newcastle, Australia, awarded
in 2017. His research centres on disability as well as valuing and using the
African philosophy of Ubuntu in education, practice, research and
management. He is the founder and convenor of the Africa Social Work
and Development Network (ASWDNet) and is the Editor-in-Chief of the
African Journal of Social Work and founder and Editor of the Journal of
Development Administration. He founded the Epilepsy Resource Centre
Zimbabwe based in Harare and the Epilepsy Alliance Africa based in
Rwanda. Presently, he is a senior lecturer in the School of Health and
Society at the University of Wollongong in Australia and a Senior
Research Associate, at the Department of Social Work and Community
Development, University of Johannesburg, South Africa.

Wilson Zvomuya

Wilson Zvomuya holds an honours and a master's degree in social work
from the University of Zimbabwe. He practised social work in Zimbabwe
and the Kingdom of Eswatini before moving to the United Kingdom
where he continues as a practitioner. He authored several articles,
conference papers and book chapters on community health, social
development, environmental social work, child protection, Ubuntu social

work and indigenisation of social work and climate change since 2017. He also contributed to *Mutakunanzva weNhetembo,* an anthology of Shona poetry in Zimbabwe. He promotes indigenisation of social work and transformative approaches to social development and child safeguarding. He supports developmental social work where indigenous systems, resources and networks are at the core of all solutions to problems presented by clients for sustainable interventions. Through the Ubuntu philosophy, it is not too late for Africa and the world to realise meaningful transformation.

William Abur

Dr William Abur is a lecturer and researcher in social work at the Faculty of Medicine, Dentistry and Health Sciences, University of Melbourne, Australia. His research interests include refugee settlement, mental health, trauma, resilience, youth and family wellbeing, social work education and practice, participation in employment and sport, racism and discrimination and Ubuntu social work practice. He has extensive experience and skills in group work, casework, case management, community development, social work education, social research, counselling, and cultural training. He has worked in secondary schools, community mental health and settlement services. He has worked in refugee camps as a counsellor, trainer, and a manager for a counselling centre in Kenya for seven years.

Morena Jerkarman Rankopo

Dr Morena Rankopo has a Bachelor of Social Work (University of Botswana), Master of Social Work (MSW) (Dalhousie University) and PhD (University of Queensland). He is currently a Senior Lecturer and Coordinator of Graduate Social Work programs at the University of Botswana. He is actively involved in research on community development, community economic development, indigenous social work education and practice, disaster risk management, human rights, Human immunodeficiency virus Acquired immunodeficiency syndrome (HIV/AIDS), and gender and development. He has served in several national advisory committees on youth policy, population and development and children in especially difficult circumstances. He has over 25 publications including books, book chapters and journal articles in the areas of community development, indigenous knowledge, community home-based care, social protection, and poverty alleviation. His interests are community development, social policy, gender and development and community resilience. He is the Vice Chairperson of the National Gender Commission of Botswana which advises government on gender and development policies and programming.

Kabo Diraditsile

Dr Kabo Diraditsile has a BSW, MSW (University of Botswana)) and PhD (Waseda University, Japan). He is currently a Lecturer at the Department of Community Development, Botswana Open University. He is also a Research Associate at the University of Pretoria, South Africa. He has served as a lecturer of social work at the University of Botswana where he taught social research, social services planning, social policy and social welfare. His interests are in social policy, social work research, social work with youth and social development issues. He has researched and consulted extensively on youth empowerment programs in Botswana. To date (2024), he has published more than 30 articles in refereed journals; 10 book chapters; 11 published conference proceedings; 12 conference abstracts; and more than 40 unpublished conference proceedings. He sits on the editorial boards of 3 international journals. Knowledge dissemination and the interface between research and practice is an important dimension of his engagement. Over the years, he has devoted his career to applied research, using both qualitative and quantitative methods.

Kgosietsile Maripe

Dr Kgosietsile Maripe has Certificate in Social Work (CSW), Diploma in Social Work (DSW), BSW, MSW (University of Botswana) and PhD (Northwest University, South Africa). He is currently a Senior Lecturer in the Department of Social Work, University of Botswana, where he is teaching courses in the community practice stream and specializing in community resilience to disasters. He has researched on community resilience to disasters and the caregivers of children with disabilities. His other research is a tracer study for university graduates from 1998-2008. He published on disasters in communities – the role of practitioners, early warning systems, and poverty as a vulnerability factor to disasters. He has presented papers at national, regional, and international conferences on various subjects in social services. He has participated in international and regional trainings on leadership development, managing multinational peace missions, food security assessment, vulnerability capacity assessment and crises and mass disasters. He has experience with non-governmental organisations and government sectors and is a member of the National Disaster Management Technical Committee.

Phillip Manyanye Bohwasi

Mr Phillip Bohwasi is a senior social worker and a Founding Lecturer at the School of Social Work Africa University, Zimbabwe. He has a DSW and a BSW degree from the University of Zimbabwe. Mr Bohwasi holds a Master of Policy Studies degree jointly conferred by the University of Zimbabwe and the University of Fort Hare. He is a social entrepreneur and has worked in the field of community enterprise development specialising in small business and entrepreneurship development in Zimbabwe and working largely with women and youth community social enterprises and social entrepreneurs. He is a founder of several social development institutions and a board member of many including the Zimbabwe Association of Micro Finance Organisations (ZAMFI). He founded Zimbabwe Opportunity Industrialisations Centres (ZOIC) in 1998. He was the vice president of the National Association of Social Workers of Zimbabwe (1990 – 2000) and participated in the reforms that saw the development of the social work legal framework in Zimbabwe. He became the second Chairman of the regulatory body, the Council of Social Workers (CSW) Zimbabwe for 10 years from 2006-2016. His areas of research interest include building of strong social work institutions in Africa, indigenous social work intervention, social policy planning, community resilience building and social entrepreneurship.

Edward Muzondo

Mr Edward Muzondo holds a BSW and MSW from the University of Zimbabwe. He is currently a lecturer in the Department of Social Work at Eswatini Medical Christian University in The Kingdom of Eswatini, formerly Swaziland. Edward is a licensed social worker and an expert in behaviour modification using various Motivational Enhancement and Interviewing Techniques. His research interests are Ubuntu social work, employee welfare, mental health, disability affairs, Sexual and Reproductive Health Rights (SRHR) and drug and substance use.

Foreword

Karibu. Mauya. Wamkelekile. አንኳን ደህና መጣህ*. Olandiridwa. Barka. Murakaza neza. Amohelehile. Siyalemukela. Tukusanyukide. O amogelesegile. Luɔɔr,* Greetings reader and welcome. You might be a lecturer, a tutor, a student, a practitioner, or a researcher, we want to welcome you to this book which is available in different formats. Innovations in technology have resulted in many options for publishing. This book appears as a printed hard copy and a soft copy (ebook). We have provided all these options to ensure this book is easily accessible. In writing this book, our major aims were to address the lack of relevant textbooks in Africa and promote use of Africa's pieces of knowledge in social services and development. The authors' experience of having to use literature from outside Africa for their training was a motivation for this book. This book therefore addresses the needs of librarians who have very limited textbooks from Africa to order, lecturers and tutors who have limited options of African textbooks to use as their references during their lectures, lessons, tutorials or seminars and students who have very limited local textbooks to read. The important and major features of this book are:

- It focuses on a range of social service professions - social workers, development workers, community workers, counsellors, psychologists, social welfare workers, social development workers, cultural services workers, and social administrators.
- It is suitable at all levels of tertiary education - certificate, diploma, bachelor, master and doctoral.
- It is suitable for lecturers, tutors, students, researchers, and fieldwork educators.
- It focuses on skills required for practice in Africa.
- It is a decolonised guide.
- Focuses on the family and community, the individual is viewed through the family.
- It has chapters on philosophy, ethics, and theories in social services.
- There is a chapter on the diaspora of Africa.
- All writers are Africans.
- 90% of literature cited in this book is from Africa.
- At the end of each chapter, there are questions, activities, and ideas for assessments, research and fieldwork.
- A glossary of terms is provided at the end of the book.

- A list of used and recommended references is provided at the end of the book.
- A comprehensive index is provided at the end of the book.
- The book offers skills that could be applied anywhere in Africa and are transferable globally.
- It provides comprehensive guidance on how to use Ubuntu.

These are the several ways to use this book:

- List the book in the course or subject outline as an essential textbook or reference book.
- Give students specific pages or chapters as a reading in the course or subject outline.
- Use images and illustrations in your presentations
- Use case studies for teaching.
- Copy and use assignment and examination questions.
- Copy and use questions for research.
- Copy and use ideas for fieldwork.
- Use as a reference guide during fieldwork supervision.
- Use as a reference for literature review.

Appendices at the end of the book were carefully selected, and they provide detailed information about Ubuntu, including misconceptions, strengths and shortcomings; Umoja waAfrica (African Union) and research approaches, designs, and methods for Africa.

Acknowledgements

The authors acknowledge the support provided by the Africa Social Work and Development Network (ASWDNet) in the writing of this book, particularly resources on their website – www.africasocialwork.net. We also acknowledge the work done by Zivo Publishers in preparing the book for publication. The editors and peer reviewers did a fantastic job, especially by scaling the initial idea of this book from a narrow focus on social work to a focus on all social services and development.

Introduction

Social analysts, researchers and practitioners have all said the current direction of social services in Africa is biased towards welfarist and individualised services, yet Africa's social economic environment is characterised by mass poverty and communalism. In response to this reality, the authors of this textbook have come up with a pack of knowledge that promotes development of communities instead of welfare of individuals. The broad intention is to train social service workers who prevent and address the root causes of poverty instead of covering it up with relief, charitable and short-term interventions. If social services are based on tokenistic welfare, social control and foreign philosophies, then their intentions are to perpetuate colonisation and poverty. There is no doubt, the people of Africa have been yearning for social services that are grounded in their philosophical, cultural, historical, spiritual and aspirational existence. We consider this to be the first textbook that meets these yearnings for the study of social services in higher education in Africa. The book offers new insights into social services in Africa, and structures social service in a way that makes it truly African. An Africa-centred structure has been used – family, village, 'country', national, continental, and global.

Under normal circumstances, individuals, families, communities and society should function socially. If anything disturbs the functioning, they should be able to provide a solution. Social problems are situations or conditions where individuals, families, communities, and society fail to achieve functioning. If not addressed, social problems result in lack of human needs, poverty, failure to take on responsibilities, human rights violations, disability, death or passing of the same problems to future generations. There are many causes of social problems, including but not limited to:

- Philosophy breakdown (e.g. because of philosophical colonisation).
- Values conflict, that is, conflict that arise due to the interpretation of philosophy.
- Ethics conflict, that is, conflict that arise due to the interpretation of philosophy.
- Unexpected events, such as disasters, death and war.
- Dispossession of means of livelihood or production.

xxiv

There are many social problems that social services aim to address at seven levels. Examples are:

1. Family problems
   - Divorce
   - Unwanted pregnancy
   - Early adulthood (early sex, early marriage, early work, early out of home)
   - Lack of resources e.g. land to build a home
   - Lack of development
   - Failure to protect identity
   - Religious conflict
   - Having no child
2. Village problems
   - Disagreements about values or leadership
   - Failure to access basic needs – health (including mental health), education, food, land, shelter, security
   - Use of harmful substances
   - Religious ideas
3. Community problems
   - Disagreements about values or leadership
   - Failure to access basic needs – health (including mental health), education, food, land, shelter, security
   - Use of harmful substances
   - Religious ideas
4. 'Country', county or district problems
   - Lack of solidarity, communality, and collective
   - Lack of recognition by national leaders and institutions
   - Political conflict
   - Highly politicised environment
   - Dictatorship and oppressive systems
5. National problems
   - Dependence
   - Colonisation and new colonisation
   - Failing to perform responsibilities
6. Continental problems
   - Failing to enjoy human rights
   - Black race looked down upon
7. Global problems
   - Lack of agreement on sexuality
   - lack of agreement on rights

- o Dominance of local initiatives by global initiatives
- o Lack of income
- o Other countries recruiting workers from others and leaving them without
- o Other countries recruiting students from others, grabbing local markets for themselves
- o Aid

Social service providers work with individuals, families, communities, and societal institutions to:

- Identify social problems or potential for social problems to arise.
- Identify causes of social problems.
- Prevent social problems.
- Reduce or eradicate social problems.
- Reduce or eradicate the impact of social problems.
- Empower people so that they can prevent or deal with new or recurring social and political problems.
- Raise people's consciousness so that they can deal with their oppressive environment.

There are many social service providers who have been trained culturally. These include but are not limited to:

- Parents
- Older siblings
- Members of the village and community
- Grandparents
- Family mothers, fathers, aunts and uncles
- Family friends
- Cultural leaders
- Africa religion leaders

There are many tertiary trained social services providers, including:

- Social workers
- Development workers
- Community workers
- Counsellors
- Psychologists
- Social welfare workers
- Social development workers
- Cultural services workers
- Social administrators
- Political social workers

The types of social services offered at these levels by providers are:

- Agriculture services
- Production and resource extraction services
- Development services
- Marketing and exporting services
- Manufacturing and value addition services
- Infrastructure services
- Health services
- Cultural services
- Social assistance, social welfare and social security services
- National cultural, psychological and spiritual services
- Voting services political awareness
- Environmental services
- Food and nutrition services
- Spiritual services
- Housing services
- Health, public health and vaccination services
- Security, crime, law and order services
- Justice services
- Sexual reproductive health services
- Research services
- Refugee services

Chapter 1 is about African philosophy for social services. It is not possible to understand social work and development work without understanding philosophy because it forms the basis of every knowledge or every knowledge depends on it, that is, human knowledge starts with philosophy. Philosophy refers to the ideas that form the foundations of a people's knowledge, beliefs, values, ethics and practices. Philosophy can be oral, lived or written and can be ascribed to a society or an individual. Philosophy is also a discipline or an area of study, meaning someone can learn to be a qualified philosopher with a diploma or degree. Africans were philosophising before the academic discipline of philosophy was founded, just as they were social working and developing before the disciplines of social work and development were founded. Each group of people have their own primary philosophy – Black Africans, Pacific Islanders, Native Americans, Asians, Europeans or Arabs. Across the ages, some philosophies tried to conquer others, but as you will see in this book, philosophies are like sweet potato cuttings – if you cut and bury them, they will sprout. In this chapter, you will learn about African philosophy and philosophers. You will also learn about the uses of philosophy in social work and development work.

Chapter 2 is on Ubuntu values and ethics. Values and ethics are derived from a people's ideas and beliefs, that is, philosophies. Each group of people have their own. Values are about what a people place importance on while ethics refer to good actions or character acceptable in each society. Values and ethics are different sides of an anthill. Values represent the side on an anthill that is facing the sun. The side facing the sun makes the other side have a shadow. That is, values shape ethics. Families, communities and individuals may develop sub-values that are derived from their people's shared values. Social workers work with people, hence, their own values and the values of families and communities they work with are important. In this chapter, you will learn about African values and ethics that are derived from Ubuntu philosophy. You will also learn how values and ethics are used in social work.

Chapter 3 is about theories of social services. We have already learned that each society developed its philosophy from where their values and ethics are derived. Philosophies, values and ethics form the foundation of knowledge used in all disciplines. This knowledge is not complete without theories. Theories are the interpretation of philosophy, values and ethics to make them 'applicable' to a learning, practice or research situation. Not all philosophical, value and ethical knowledge needs interpretation, most of the time they are applied as they are. Theories can be oral (proverb, maxim, poem, song, idiom or other) or written (statement, a list of points, a paragraph, a few paragraphs, a chapter or book). They help us understand social problems and ways to prevent, reduce or eradicate them. In this chapter, you will learn about Africa theories that are applicable to social work and development work. You will also learn how we use the theories in social work and development work.

Chapter 4 provides the history of social services and social work in Africa. Now that we have covered philosophy, values, ethics and theories, we now turn to the history of social work in Africa. The development of social work in Africa has taken several related phases. These include customary indigenous phase, missionary phase, colonial-missionary phase, African philanthropists' phase, independence phase and indigenized-developmental phase. This chapter traces the five phases in the development of the profession. After the phases, we will provide information about social work institutions and publications in Africa.

Chapter 5 is on social services at different levels of society. This chapter summarises the different levels of social work and development work. The first level of social work is the family, and this level includes the individual. After the family, we have the village level, and this is followed by the community. The other levels are 'country'/district/county, national, continental, and global.

Chapter 6 is about *botho* (Ubuntu) as an organising precept for social services in Botswana. The chapter promotes Africa's perspectives in social services. This chapter presents an in-depth description of *botho* as a philosophy of social development that can strengthen social work theory and practice. The chapter encourages discussions and debates on *botho* and its potential impact on the international social work profession. The chapter is structured as follows. Following an introduction, the paper presents section two, which covers highlights, objective of the paper and skills and competencies addressed in the chapter. This is followed by section three which discusses *botho* as an African philosophy on positive human relationships. Next, is section four which talks about indigenous institutions, *botho* and social protection support systems. This is followed by section five which is the discussion on *botho* as a human ethic of care, social work, and spirituality. Next, is a section on Afrocentric models of social work education and practice. Finally, section six draws a conclusion and is followed by potential questions for research.

Chapter 7 is about Ubuntu and social development in Africa. This chapter focuses on developmental social work, particularly the process of achieving it using the Ubuntu perspective. Authors have included Ubuntu principles that foster development, the role of social workers in the process and challenges faced in the process. Ubuntu oriented approaches allow social work students and practitioners to implement appropriate interventions in Africa. Such interventions are capable of tackling poverty currently affecting most families and communities of Africa. Key definitions will be provided first, followed by theories and then the process of developmental social work before the Ubuntu bowl is presented. At the end challenges will be discussed, and questions for assessments, research and fieldwork provided.

Chapter 8 is the longest chapter. It is on community work and community development in Africa. This chapter introduces community work and community development from an African Ubuntu perspective. The chapter then defines community work and community development and lists their objectives, guiding principles and ethics. Theories of working with communities are provided. These are ujamaa, Ubuntu and the developmental approach that promotes social and economic development. Strategies and examples of community work and community development are provided, followed by the process and pillars of community work and community development. Readers will also find useful templates and detailed case studies. At the end of the chapter, it is expected that readers will have both theoretical knowledge and practical skills to conceptualize, plan, initiate, implement, review and close a community project in African contexts.

Chapter 9 is on doing Ubuntu social services with the African diaspora: It focuses on knowledge, values, and strategies. This chapter presented Ubuntu values and social work practice in migration and settlement with the African diaspora. The aim is to provide theoretical knowledge and practice skills in social work using the Ubuntu values as one of the ways of addressing social issues of African families, community and individuals while residing in diaspora. The Ubuntu values are essential and are observed by many African community groups and families as a way of maintaining their African heritage and practice. Therefore, social work students and social practitioners are expected to learn Ubuntu approach and practice to provide essential support services to African families, individuals and community groups. Ubuntu social work is distinguished as a social work practice that is theoretically, pedagogically, and practically grounded in African community knowledge and practice. This Ubuntu practice has been preserved as oral literature which has passed from generation to generation through storytelling, poetry, song, art, dance, and many other forms. Maintaining indigenous positive values, including spiritual values, can assist young people and their families to overcome many difficulties.

Chapter 10 is about training and fieldwork for social services. In this final chapter, we look at social work education and fieldwork. Education is a form of training which involves developing an educational philosophy, developing a training program, developing training methods, gathering training resources, selecting of trainees, delivering the training, assessing skills and knowledge gained and graduating. Within training there is a skill building method where trainees go to the field to observe, learn, and perfect skills. In social work, this is called fieldwork, placement, or attachment. Research refers to a process of setting a knowledge generation philosophy, identifying knowledge gaps, creating research methods, implementing the methods, collecting data, analysing, reporting, using the findings and reviewing it.

Useful and carefully selected appendices have been provided. The first one is on Ubuntu, and it provides detailed information about it. The second one provides detailed information about Umoja waAfrica, the African Union. The last one provides a list of research design, approaches and methods generated in Africa. At the end, carefully curated glossary and index are provided.

CHAPTER 1

Africa' philosophy for social services

Introduction

It is not possible to understand social work and development work without understanding philosophy because it is from philosophy that every knowledge comes from, that is, human knowledge starts with philosophy. Philosophy refers to the ideas that form the foundations of a people's knowledge, beliefs, values, ethics and practices. It can be oral, lived or written and can be ascribed to a society or an individual. Correspondingly, it can also be understood as a discipline or an area of study, denoting that one can learn to be a qualified philosopher and be awarded a diploma or degree. Africans were philosophising before the academic discipline of philosophy was founded, just as they were social working and developing before the disciplines of social work and development work were founded. Each 'people' (meaning group of people with a shared philosophy) has a primary philosophy – Black Africans, Pacific Islanders, Native Americans, Asians, Europeans or Arabs. Across the ages, some philosophies tried to conquer others, but as you will see in this book, philosophies are like sweet potato cuttings – if you cut and bury them, they will sprout. In this chapter, you will learn about Africa's philosophy and philosophers. You will also learn about the uses of philosophy in social work and development work.

Objectives of this chapter

By writing this chapter, we hope to achieve the following:

- Share the basic and major ideas of African philosophy.
- Show that African philosophy exists in oral and written formats.
- Share the main African philosophers and their philosophical ideas (philosophies).

1

- Show that African philosophy is distinct, thriving and is different from other philosophies.
- Help students to value and be confident with Africa's gourd of knowledge.
- Assessments that are suitable for the local context.
- Research questions and methods that are appropriate to the local context.
- Fieldwork, workplace-based and community-based learning which is contextual.
- Guide the use of the Ubuntu philosophy in social services provision.

Skills and competencies addressed in this chapter

By the end of this chapter, readers will be expected to have acquired the following skills and competencies:

- Applying philosophical knowledge to shape skills and make interventions more relevant to Africa.
- Valuing and using African philosophy and decolonising African knowledge and practices.
- Answer questions or assessments about the topic of this chapter.
- Create research questions and methods that are appropriate to the local context and values.
- Plan fieldwork, workplace-based and community-based learning that is contextual.

Understanding philosophy

A philosophy contains a people's deep thoughts and ways of looking at life, developed carefully and collectively over time. 'People' is used here to refer to those who share a common philosophy. Philosophy shapes how people think about the family, community, society, environment and spirituality. It shapes ideas about reality, existence, reason, knowledge, science, disciplines, religion, truth, race, values, mind, behaviour, justice, social problems, needs and even language. Values, ethics, theories and practices are derived from philosophy. In the hierarchy of knowledge, philosophy sits right near the top. To understand philosophy, we must understand

2

knowledge and its hierarchy. What we know can be organised in a hierarchy as shown in Figure 1. A society usually has one primary or overarching philosophy but there can also be secondary philosophies. Each continent of the world has an overarching philosophy of its own. Africa's overarching philosophy is called Ubuntu. Ubuntu belongs to all who inherited it, and it cannot be attributed to one individual founder, one community or one country. It is the philosophy of the Black people of Africa.

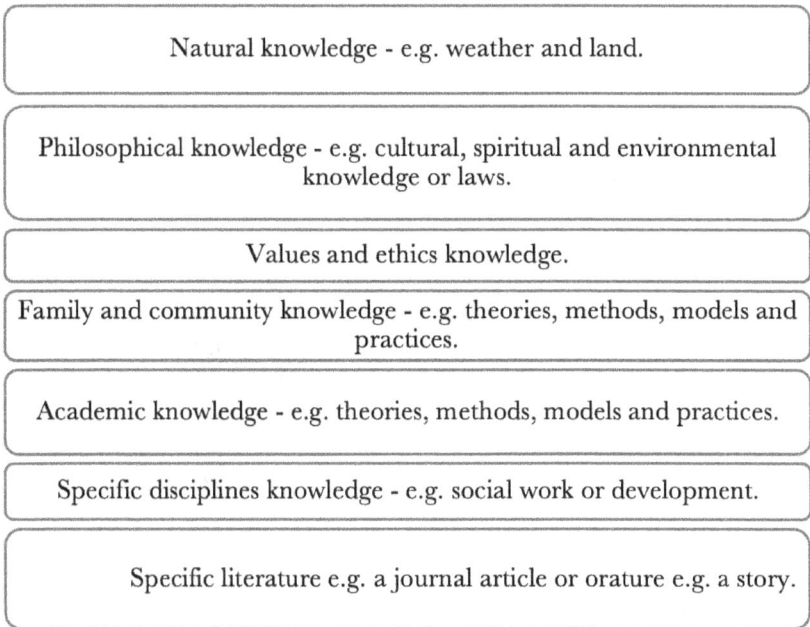

Natural knowledge - e.g. weather and land.

Philosophical knowledge - e.g. cultural, spiritual and environmental knowledge or laws.

Values and ethics knowledge.

Family and community knowledge - e.g. theories, methods, models and practices.

Academic knowledge - e.g. theories, methods, models and practices.

Specific disciplines knowledge - e.g. social work or development.

Specific literature e.g. a journal article or orature e.g. a story.

Figure 1: The hierarchy of knowledge

Significance of philosophy in social work and development work

Philosophy shapes how we think about social work, how we define social problems and the interventions that we put in place. Philosophy:

- shapes how we think about social work.
- forms the foundation of social work knowledge.

3

- shapes or religious beliefs and spirituality.
- shapes how we teach and learn social work.
- guides how we define social problems.
- shapes social work interventions and how we practice.
- guides behaviour of participants – individuals, families and communities.
- gives each social worker their social work philosophy.
- helps us distinguish what is indigenous to us from what is foreign or colonial.
- shapes how we view relationships with the environment.
- shapes our vision of social functioning.
- motivates philanthropy.
- defines being human.
- shapes relationships with others.

African philosophy makes social work and development work more relevant to Africa, it helps to decolonise. If we use a relevant philosophy, the social interventions done by social workers, welfare workers and development workers will strengthen, not weaken families, communities, society, the environment and peoples' spirituality. Each group of people has its own philosophy which shapes their life and how social functioning is understood. Therefore, it naturally follows that social work cannot be the same. You cannot uproot it from one people to another.

Ubuntu philosophy

The term Ubuntu is expressed differently is several African communities and languages but all referring to the same thing. In Angola, it is known as *gimuntu*, Botswana (*muthu*), Burkina Faso (*maaya*), Burundi (Ubuntu), Cameroon (*bato*), Congo (*bantu*), Congo Democratic Republic (*bomoto/bantu*), Cote d'Ivoire (*maaya*), Equatorial Guinea (*maaya*), Guinea (*maaya*), Gambia (*maaya*), Ghana (*biako ye*), Kenya (*utu/munto/mondo*), Liberia (maaya), Malawi (*umunthu*), Mali (*maaya/hadama de ya*), Mozambique (*vumuntu*), Namibia (*omundu*), Nigeria (*mutunchi/iwa/agwa*), Rwanda (*bantu*), Sierra Leonne (*maaya*), South Africa (Ubuntu/*botho*), Tanzania (*utu/obuntu/bumuntu*), Uganda (*obuntu*), Zambia (*umunthu/Ubuntu*) and Zimbabwe (*hunhu/unhu/botho*/Ubuntu).

- There is a misconception that African philosophy has one name, Ubuntu. No, it is known by several names, almost all the names have a common linguistic origin. The popular name in the literature is Ubuntu.
- There is a misconception that the philosophy is new and it started recently. No. It started thousands of years ago.
- There is a misconception that Ubuntu originated from the Bantu group. It originated from all groups of Black people in Africa - the *Bantu, Kush, Ba, Nile-Sahara, Khoi, Masarwa, Hadza* and *Sandawe*. These groups interacted since time immemorial and values and principles of Ubuntu are found among all of them.
- There is a misconception that Ubuntu started in South Africa (country) or Southern Africa (region). No. It was popularised in South Africa, particularly the name *Ubuntu* which is a Nguni used in Nguni languages like *isiZulu, isiNdebele, siSwati, siXhosa* and others
- There is a misconception that Ubuntu is inferior to western or eastern ways. No, it is not.
- There is a misconception that Ubuntu was discarded by Africans. No, it still shapes their life, knowledge and being.
- There is a misconception that Ubuntu is only about individuals and families. No, it also about communities, countries and nations and applies to continental and global issues.
- There is a misconception that it is about being respectful, harmonious, solidarity, compassionate, subservient or helpful only. These are aspects of Ubuntu at the individual. In addition, it is also about freedom, liberation, responsibility, and possession.
- There is a misconception that in Ubuntu, questioning is not allowed. You are not allowed to be critical or to oppose. This is not true. You can question, be critical, be radical and oppose in a respectful way.
- It is not applicable outside Africa. This is a misconception. Ubuntu has influenced *Kwanza* (the Black American holiday started in the 1960s) and it continues to influence mentoring programs outside Africa. It also influences management, leadership, and community work. The Ubuntu value of Sankofa, looking back to inform the present and future, is very much used by Black Americans who look back to Africa as their source of culture and personhood.
- It is not even a philosophy at all; it does not have philosophers like in western countries. Ubuntu is a philosophy with several

5

philosophers. Most of it exists as orature, unwritten philosophy but there is now a considerable number of written philosophers on Ubuntu.

- Ubuntu has no founders, how come? It does not need founders because by principle, Ubuntu is collective. Founders are found in individualistic societies.

- Others think it is a weakness for Ubuntu to be more collective than individualistic and yet others say Ubuntu does not respect individuality. This is not all true. Being collective is not a weakness but a strength. The individual has their space in African life, but their space derives from and is seen through the family and community.

- There is a misconception that it cannot be used in research, teaching and practice. This is not true. It has been used, is being used and is useful. The truth is African literature in general has been relegated to the periphery or discarded in favour of western literature.

- There is a misconception that Ubuntu is anti-women, anti-disability, and anti-children. Not true at all. When institutions for children, sometimes called orphanages were introduced in Africa by western missionaries and social workers, it was against the Ubuntu principle of child growth, development and protection in the family and community. It has not been realised that Ubuntu was right all along. Children do not belong to institutions, it's not in their best interest at all.

- There is a misconception that Ubuntu means going back to Africa's old life. Not at all. It means going to where we are comfortable in this age if we had not been colonised. Africa was never static, its culture and philosophy were dynamic.

- Ubuntu resulted in Africa's colonisation? This could be true, but we need to go further to say that anti-colonisation and decolonisation results from Ubuntu. You cannot be human without freedom, you cannot be human when you have been dispossessed - these were the Ubuntu ideals that motivated anti-colonisers, freedom fighters and pan-Africanists.

- If Ubuntu was useful, why is there still conflict in Africa? Why do we have dictators and corruption? Why is there gender-based or other forms of violence? But conflict, poor governance and violence exist even in countries that use western and eastern philosophies.

- Why are families sometimes individualistic and collective? because of colonisation. This is more prevalent in urban communities that were more westernised.
- Why are social vices like rape, even in the family by family members, so high in some African communities if we have Ubuntu? This is due to a family breakdown. With Ubuntu, families are the utmost places of safety. Family breakdown has many causes, among them urbanisation, westernisation, migration, foreign religious beliefs like Christianity or Islam and other issues like death as a result of the human immunodeficiency virus (HIV) acquired immunodeficiency syndrome (AIDS).
- What is the best choice, going back to Ubuntu or to westernise more? Westernisation is colonial, it has been shown in many countries to result in more social challenges. The best choice is to indigenise, meaning using own philosophy to solve our own challenges?
- What are the good examples of Ubuntu practice in Africa? When white people led by Christian missionaries and colonial administrators colonised Africa, they took away some children from their homes and put them in orphanages or children's homes despite advice from African elders, leaders and spiritual leaders that this was contrary to African philosophy, beliefs and practices. Years later, Africa is now dismantling the institutions because they have caused so much suffering - psychological harm, separation, loss of identity, loss of heritage etc (Kurevakwesu and Chizasa, 2020). Today, our elders, leaders and spiritual leaders have been proven right and the white missionaries and colonists, wrong.
- Ubuntu is against Christianity and Islam? No, it is these foreign religions that are against African ways of being. They are against African beliefs, identities and heritage. They are against African histories, values and beliefs. Ubuntu contains stronger values about life that are expressed in ways Africans understand. Foreign religions are mythical, mysterious, oppressive, difficult to understand and believe and unquestionable. As Chimamanda Ngozi said "Some of the early Christian missionaries across the African continent were very keen on destroying African art, carved African deities which they told the Africans, were just magic. I cannot help but really wonder what could be more magical than

the story of a man who dies and then magically rises again; a man who also manages to magically give his body as bread."

- There is a misconception that Ubuntu does not impact all African life. It does. It impacts African art, beliefs, theories, relations, knowledge, ways of doing social work, its literature and history.

Shortcomings of Ubuntu

- In urban areas, especially, and in African diaspora communities, Ubuntu has been eroded to varying levels but exists.
- There is not enough written literature on Ubuntu, most exist as orature. This has resulted in some people criticising it as vague.
- The application of Ubuntu in education, practice, fieldwork and research has not been adequately explored, clarified and exemplified.
- Available literature on Ubuntu is not easily accessible to schools, universities, students, practitioners, lecturers, and researchers.
- Not used that much by Africans in their professions (this is changing) but used in their daily lives. This is because of the colonial separation of education from real-life experiences.
- It is misused when people focus on 'a good human' aspects of Ubuntu such as being respectful and forgiving neglecting the more critical, structural, and transformational issues. This happened with the Truth and Reconciliation Commission led by Desmond Tutu and Nelson Mandela in South Africa. In the process, they did not allow for the return of land that was stolen from South Africans by white people.

Strengths of Ubuntu

- It exists in all Black African communities and is available in abundance as orature.
- It has international influence.
- It can decolonise and indigenise (or re-indigenise) at the same time.
- It exists in African language and culture.
- Ubuntu is an overarching philosophy, that is, it is broad enough. to be used in all disciplines, and aspects of life at all levels of society.

8

Characteristics of African philosophy

The characteristics of African philosophy are:

a. It originated with the first Africans and has been passed down through generations.

b. African philosophy belongs to the community, there are usually no individual philosophers. Individual philosophers have only expanded community ideas (Makinde, 2007).

c. African philosophy is largely not written, it exists in different non-written formats (orature) that are contained in African culture including languages.

d. At one stage it was colonised and the impact is still being felt today. Often, African writers, lecturers, teachers, researchers, librarians, reviewers and students know western or eastern philosophies more than their own philosophies. This is a legacy of colonialism.

e. African philosophy is decolonial in approach, rejecting colonialism, assimilation and individualism. African philosophy seeks to remove misconceptions created by non-African and pseudo-African philosophers.

f. It emphasises the similarities and commonalities between Black African people as opposed to viewing Black Africans as different, divided and separate people.

g. African philosophy searches for and reclaims a true African identity and rejects Europe's invention of Africa.

Historical development of African philosophy

African philosophy can be divided into four historical phases as follows:

1. The phase of indigenous communal philosophy which started from time immemorial. At this stage, for most communities, philosophy was not written. This is an unwritten oratory philosophy. The communities carry it forward and pass it down to future generations. It is contained in orature – rituals, music, dance, stories, proverbs, metaphors, ceremonies, laws, practices and rites. Communal philosophy answers many questions that first Africans had as they interpreted and interfaced with natural knowledge.

2. The colonial philosophy phase that was characterised by fundamental misconceptions made about African philosophy by European missionaries, ethnologists and ethnographers and indigenous African scholars. These people had a hidden agenda to show that Africans had no philosophy and were incapable of high-order thinking. They argued that Africa had no philosophy. Their thinking resonated with the general misconception of white people those days that they were superior to Black people (Makinde, 2007). At this stage, communal philosophy did not die although it was suppressed by written colonial philosophy.
3. The phase of reconstructive philosophy in Africa was marked by strong arguments that Africa indeed had its own philosophy. African thought was logical and Africans were capable of high-order thinking (Diop, 1991; 1964). This is also known as the reconstruction phase. Written philosophy increased but communal philosophy was not displaced. Colonial philosophy persisted during this phase.
4. The phase of renaissance philosophy can be described as the future stage where African philosophy shapes every aspect of life of Africa's people: education, justice, spirituality, ecology and others (Mbeki, 2004).

African philosophers

A philosopher is a thinker or person who has thought deeply about their people or society and made their ideas known, orally, practically or in writing.

Early philosophers

*   In Kemet, the area where Egypt exists today, Black people developed language, technology, engineering, science and philosophy (Asante, 2024). Kemet means black, which could be both black people and black soils of the Nile valleys. In their philosophy, the Kemet people defined the physical universe and spirituality (Asante, 2024). The most well-known individual philosopher was Imhotep who answered questions on volume, time, illness and death. Imhotep lived about 4700 years ago.

Philosophers from outside Africa were educated in Africa (Asante, 2024).

- Zara Yaqob (ዘርአ ያዕቆብ) (1399 −1468) was an Ethiopian teacher and philosopher born in Aksum, Tigray Province, Ethiopian Empire. He created the first *Hatata* (book of inquiry or investigation), basically, writings of his philosophy. Zara wrote his philosophy well before most western philosophers but as usual, his African ideas have been largely neglected. Zara was succeeded by his student, Walda Heywat who wrote *Hatata* 2.

  o On discrimination he said "All men are equal in the presence of God, and all are intelligent since they are his creatures; he did not assign one people for life, another for death, one for mercy, another for judgment. Our reason teaches us that this sort of discrimination cannot exist."

  o On creation he said: "If I say that my father and my mother created me, then I must search for the creator of my parents and of the parents of my parents until they arrive at the first who were not created as we [are] but who came into this world in some other way without being generated."

  o On ethics he proposed that if it advances humanity or harmony in the world, then it is ethical.

  o On religion he said the truth comes from observation of the natural world and not from religion.

  o On slavery he said "What the Gospel says on this subject cannot come from God. Likewise, the Mohammedans said that it was right to go and buy a man as if he were an animal. But with our intelligence, we understand that this Mohammedan law cannot come from the creator of man who made us equal, like brothers, so that we call our creator our father."

  o On so-called Holy Scriptures he said all religions claim theirs to be true, despite contradictions, but they can only be one truth. "My faith is right, and those who believe in another faith believe in falsehood and are the enemies of God.' … As my own faith appears true to me, so does another one find his own faith true; but truth is one".

  o On gender he criticised the law of Moses for excluding women because of menstruation, yet it is the basis of procreation and love. He said the law 'impedes marriage and the entire life of a woman, and it spoils the law of mutual help, prevents the bringing up of children and destroys love'. He gave Christianity, Islam, Judaism and Hinduism the same criticism.

- o He married Hirut, a servant woman or maid and treated her as a peer for 'husband and wife are equal in marriage'. He said Hirut 'was not beautiful, but she was good-natured, intelligent and patient'. 'Since she loved me so, I took the decision in my heart to please her as much as I could, and I do not think there is another marriage which is so full of love and blessed as ours.'

- Anton Amo (from about 1703-1755) who was an Akan from Axim, Guinea, now Ghana. He was enslaved and taken to Europe, German where he became a renowned philosopher.
  - o Enlightened perspective of reason, treating all humans alike.
  - o Challenged slavery in *On the Right of Moors in Europe* (1729).

- *Mwene* Njinga Mbande (1583 – 1663), sister and advisor of the Ngola (King) of Ambundu Kingdoms in present-day Angola. She had military training. The Kingdom had two nations, Ndongo and Matamba. In 1624 his brother died, potentially due to poisoning orchestrated by the by the Portuguese who were fighting the Kingdom for slaves. She was Queen for 37 years, defending the Kingdom from Europeans (the Portuguese and the Dutch) using her cultural, military, diplomatic and political skills. She defended her position as a *mwene*, queen or woman leader and appointed women to positions, including her sister successor. She fought many wars, won some and was defeated in some, driven from her nation and at one point only had 200 soldiers. The European Christians baptised her and changed her first name and surname to Dona Anna de Sousa hoping to neutralise her philosophy. The first name was taken from the Portuguese governor's wife and the surname was of the governor. However, due to her strategy, she created alliances and moves that helped her regain power and have the kingdoms under her rule again. Today, she is remembered as the mother of Angola, a protector and negotiator. She has a large statue in her owner and is largely in recognised for defending the self-determination, independence, and cultural identity of her people. Although she did not write her philosophy, she embodied it.

Picture 1: Mwene Njinga Mbande (Acknowledgement, Government of Angola)

This picture is in the public domain. We use it in this book ethically, and with respect to the memory of this person, their family, community and the person who created this image.

- *Mbuya* (Grandmother) Nehanda Nyakasikana (The Girl) (1862-1898) who originated from Manzou lands which is Mazowe in present day Zimbabwe. She led Shona people against colonists who were led by Cecil Rhodes but together with 13 others, she was hanged to death on a tree by the colonists with the help of Christian missionaries. Some of her last known messages were '*mapfupa angu achamuka*' – meaning my people will liberate themselves, decolonisation would happen. She also said '*tora gidi uzvitonga*' meaning Black people needed to take the gun to liberate themselves because no one was going to do it for them. She objected to political, economic, and spiritual colonialism. Among those who tortured her was a Christian Priest, Richartz who forced many of them to convert to Christianity, to be baptised and to adopt English Christian names. Mbuya Nehanda refused religious colonialism which was accepted by many of the men that were executed with her.
- Yaa Asantewa (1840-1921), the Queen Mother and Gate Keeper of the Golden Stool (Sika Dwa Kofi) of Ejisu, Ghana. When the

13

British defeated her brother who was King (Asantehene) and exiled him to Seychelles, she became leader. British Governor Frederick Mitchell Hodgson demanded to sit on the stool in 1900, and this was a demand the Queen could not accept. She said "If you the men of Ashanti will not go forward, then we will. We the women will. I shall call upon my fellow women. We will fight the white (British) men. We will fight till the last of us falls in the battlefields." The Ashanti was defeated, and the Queen and others were exiled to Seychelles where she died 20 years later. The Golden Stool has not been restored and is still a cherished symbol.

Njinga Mbande, Nehanda Nyakasikana and Yaa Asantewa were all women. Their story and prominence show that women had an important place and influence in Africa before colonisation.

Revolutionary, nationalist and other philosophers

Revolutionaries are interested in independence from colonialism while nationalists are interested in nation-building. They often express their philosophies in speeches and actions. Literary philosophers express themselves through writing novels, essays but also speeches. One person can both be a revolutionary or nationalist and a literary philosopher. There is usually no clear line separating them.

Table 1: Philosophy of Africa

Philosophers, country and names of philosophies	Philosophical ideas
John Samuel Mbiti (1931-2019), Kenya. *Africanism (Ubuntu) and the philosophy of African religion*	Africa has its own religion. Africa's religion was colonised by Christianity and Islam. Despite colonisation, Africa's religion exists and is also practised by the converted.
Kenneth Buchizya Kaunda (1921-2021), Zambia Pan-Africanist, freedom fighter, social worker and former President of Zambia *African humanism (Ubuntu)*	Africa has its own philosophy. Ubuntu solves many social problems including exploitation. Need to maintain an African identity.
Kwasi Wiredu (1931-2022), Kumasi, Ghana *Philosophy of African languages and the philosophy of African religion*	'Colonialism was not only a political imposition, but also a cultural one', (1998, p. 17). The language you learn can de-Africanise you. Challenges the belief that Africa has no philosophy and religion of its own (1980).
Lovemore Mbigi (1955-2023), Zimbabwe *Ubuntu management philosophy*	Africa has its own management philosophy grounded in Ubuntu.

15

Philosophers, country and names of philosophies	Philosophical ideas
Julius Nyerere, former president of Tanzania, Pan-Africanist, freedom fighter Books: Uhuru na Ujamaa: Freedom and Socialism (1964) and Ujamaa: The Basis of African Socialism (1968) *Ujamaa philosophy*	Need for a true African identity. *Uhuru* is the basis of identity. Ujamaa, being with no individualism. Family and community are at the centre of African philosophy.
Chinua Achebe, (1930-2013), Nigeria Novelist famous for Things Fall Apart (1958), No Longer at Ease (1960) and Arrow of God (1964) Regarded as the Father of African Literature *Decolonising philosophy*	Several western literatures had said African had no culture or religion and that western religion and culture were what African required. They said Africa was the dark continent or the heart of darkness. In 1958, Chinua wrote one of Africa's first novels to challenge this idea. In turn, he challenged spiritual, political, and economic colonisation led by missionaries and colonists.
Dedan Kimathi Waciuri (Kimathi wa Waciuri) (1920 – 1957)	'My blood will water the tree of Independence', Kimathi said to his wife Mukami just before he was executed by hanging. Kimathi led the fight against the British, who had taken Kenyan land. He led the Mau Mau Uprising as a senior military

Philosophers, country and names of philosophies	Philosophical ideas
Among those who tortured Kimati were Canon Webster and Marino, all Christian priests. *Liberation philosophy*	and spiritual leader and as leader of the Kenya Land and Freedom Army.
Cheikh Anta Diop (1923 – 1986), Senegal Historian, anthropologist, physicist, and politician Has a large university named after him in Senegal *One Africa philosophy and Diopian thought*	Cheikh Anta Diop is known for African origin of Ancient Egyptian civilization (Diop, 1974), The Cultural Unity of Black Africa: The Domains of Matriarchy and Patriarchy in-classical Antiquity (Diop, 1989). He was a proponent of the One Africa philosophy and African-centred thought. His ideas, known as Diopian thought, were centred on that Black African people have a common philosophy, they are one people who were capable of civilisation.
Léopold Sédar Senghor, Senegal Negritude et Humanisme (1964) and Negritude and the Germans (1967) *Negritude*	Opposed individualism and assimilation promoted by the Europeans. Importance of culture, language and communalism. Africa's identity was lost through colonisation and must be reclaimed. The Negritude movement expressed its decolonising thoughts not only through writings, in poems and books but also speeches. The movement was started by Black people in Paris to protest French colonial rule and the policies of assimilation, especially in West Africa.

Philosophers, country and names of philosophies	Philosophical ideas
Kwame Nkrumah, Ghana Books: Neo-colonialism: The Last Stage of Imperialism (1965), I Speak of Freedom: A Statement of African Ideology (1961), Africa Must Unite (1970), and Consciencism (1954). *Africanism and neo-colonialism*	Importance of African cultural system, moral values, communal ownership of land and a humanitarian social and political system, rediscovering her lost identity.
Aimé Césaire (1913 – 2008), Martinique Poet and politician *Negritude*	Co-founder of the Negritude movement with Léopold Sédar Senghor. Negritude is about restoring lost cultural identity.
Abbé Alexis Kagame, (1912 – 1981) Rwanda Linguist, historian, poet and Catholic priest Book title *The Bantu-Rwanda Philosophy* (1956)	Importance of indigenous philosophy and the philosophical similarity of Black people of Africa. Kagame used linguistics to show the similarity between Kinyarwanda and the rest of the Bantu people. He said African philosophy is only understood in African languages. According to Kagame, the categories of African philosophy are all centred around Ntu, and these are:

Philosophers, country and names of philosophies	Philosophical ideas
Bantu philosophy of being. *Four categories of Bantu philosophy*	• *Muntu – 'Human being' (Plural: Bantu)* – this includes living and deceased beings, spiritual beings and God. • *Kintu – 'Thing' (Plural: Bintu)* - plants, animals, minerals, and tools, among others. • *Hantu – 'Place/Space and Time.'* • *Kuntu – 'Modality',* not tangible but not metaphysical, e.g. beauty, laughing and laughter, among others. A key weakness of these categories is that they were based on similar systems of categorisation used by western philosophers, although Kagame used African languages and culture in-depth. 'All that there is must necessarily belong to one of the four categories and must be conceived not as a physical substance but as force. Man is a force; all things are forces including place and time, modalities. They are all also related to one another because they are forces and this relationship is vivid in their very names because if the determinative is removed, the stem *Ntu* remains and is constant in all of them.' 'Africans indeed have a thought system that is unique to them, which they use to appreciate themselves and understand reality'.
Amadou Hampate Ba (1901 – 1999), Mali. Writer, historian and ethnologist	A writer and promoter of oral knowledge. His greatest saying was 'Whenever an old man dies, it is as though a library were burning down'.

Philosophers, country and names of philosophies	Philosophical ideas
Frantz Omar Fanon (1925 – 1961), Martinique Psychiatrist and Physician Books: Black Skin, White Masks; The Wretched of the Earth (1961) *Double consciousness*	Psychopathology of colonisation. Black skin, white mind – postcolonialism. Family and community care instead of institutionalisation (mental health). Colonial languages subordinate Black people. Believed in radical action to end colonialism and neo-colonialism – joined Algeria's War of Independence from France as a member of the Algerian National Liberation Front.
Dani Nabudere (1932 – 2011), Uganda *Afrikology*	Scientific knowledge does not cover all knowledge. There is a need for holistic and integrated ways of knowledge production that make it possible to interface scientific knowledge with other forms of knowledge. Existing academic disciplines fragment knowledge and this creates a crisis. Afrikology allows for wholeness to understanding and knowledge production.

Other philosophers: Mogobe Ramose, Odera Oruka, Mnamdi Azikiwe, Amadou Hampate Ba, Obafemi Awolowo, Uzodinma Nwala, Emmanuel Edeh, Innocent Onyewuenyi and Henry Olela.

Philosophies of different people

Table 2: Philosophies of other people of the world

People and their philosophies	Who makes up this group?	What they value in their philosophies
Africans *Ubuntu philosophy or African philosophy*	Black Africans	Family Community Spirituality Environment Wholeness
Pacific people *Pacific philosophy*	Aboriginal and Torres Strait Islander people of Australia, Maori of Aotearoa (New Zealand), Papua Guineans, Fijians, Tongans and many others	Family Community Environment Spirituality
Asians *Eastern or oriental philosophy*	Chinese, Indians, Japanese, Koreans, Indonesians, Nepalese and many others	Collectivism Spirituality Virtue Philosophers: Lao Tzu, Tao, Gandhi, Mahayana Buddha and Confucius (Confucianism, Buddhism, and Taoism
Original people of America *Native American philosophy*	Indigenous people have different philosophies for example the Indians, Inuit and Métisin in Canada, Islanders in the Pacific region and the American Indians or Native Americans.	Varies but decoloniality is an important aspect

People of European ancestry *western or occidental philosophy*. The philosophy started in Rome and Greece and has its roots in Judaism and Christianity.	People of European origin including Europe, Americas USA, Canada and Mexico), white Australia, white Aotearoa and white Africa.	Individuality – the self is at the centre of everything. Choice and liberalism Supremacy Virtue Examples of philosophers: Immanuel Kant, Plato, Socrates, Hegel, Pythagoras, Locke, Descartes, Voltaire, Napoleon and Marx.
Middle Eastern *Islamic or Arab philosophy*	Original Arab speaking people.	
Mixed philosophies	Usually, people of a mixed race but also colonised people or those who assimilated.	Mixed but usually there is a dominant philosophy.

Often, African students are taught non-African philosophies and not their own philosophy. These non-African philosophies are contained in textbooks, journal articles, the internet, and other books. The process to undo this injustice is called decolonisation. Decolonisation in social work happens at several levels. Some of the levels are (1) undoing students, lecturers and librarians' personal internalised oppression and colonization (decolonising minds) (2) ensuring decolonised literature is used (3) having a decolonised syllabus (4) using indigenous teaching methods (5) researching and publishing in a decolonised way.

Ubuntu in simpler-practical terms and everyday usage

Familyhood (*Ukama*)

- In Ubuntu communities, we talk of families, not family. A person has family, not family. An adult married person has these families

(1) their children, husband or wife/wives (2) the husband or wife with their siblings, father and mother (4) grandparents and their children (5) clan – grandparents and their siblings and parents (6) tribe - grandparents and their grandparents (7) ancestors – all deceased members.

- Under Ubuntu, there are no aunties from the mother's side, there are mothers. There are no uncles from the father's side, there are fathers. An African has many mothers.
- There are no cousins, there are brothers and sisters.
- There is no stepmother or stepfather, they are fathers and mothers
- Father's sister, *Babekazi* or *Tete,* is an important person, she is a father.
- Adoption of children is only expected when there is a biological relationship. The adoption of African children by white people is viewed as colonisation and theft.
- Ubuntu does not allow, or promote wife or husband beating, domestic violence or abuse, it favours dialogue through other family members and community channels. If there is love, there is no violence. Wife beating is one of the strongest sources of devaluation for men.
- Having children is highly valued and actively promoted.
- Marriage (of a man and woman) is highly valued and actively promoted.
- Being a grandparent, holding and teaching your grandkids, is one of the highest honours in life.
- Exchange of gifts at marriage, between families is highly valued and promoted to cement relations started through marriage. The husband's family pays more because the children will have his surname and the wife will live with him and his family. The payment is made in several instalments of livestock or cash contributed by the family not just the person marrying. The total cost of gifts paid is a token, far less in value compared to a wedding ring or the cost of a western wedding. The priority is relations not economic gain. A human being can never be priced.
- Interracial marriages are devalued because of differences in values and the resultant negative impact this causes on couples, families, children, future generations and communities.
- Older people are not put in old people's homes or institutions - it is a shame. They are cared for at home.
- Parents and Elders – not to be disrespected.

Personhood (*munhu, muntu* or *kikuyu*)

- A long life is valued.
- Deep respect is valued.
- Generosity and sharing are valued.
- Giving, helping and volunteering are valued.
- Calling people by their first names is a taboo, rather use family names, clan names e.g. *Madiba* instead of Nelson for Mandela, tribal names, respect names e.g. Mzee, role names e.g. *Babekazi* which means aunt etc. For younger people first names can be used but respectable names are still preferable. The reason for doing this is to give prominence to families, roles, and histories. It is also an oral way to pass knowledge of genealogy, values and histories.
- Ubuntu names (or African names) are highly valued, even though colonial names were introduced by Europeans, Christians and Muslims. African names have meanings to families and communities and the nation. A name like Kofi means someone was born on a Friday; *Tichatonga* means we will liberate ourselves; *Achen* means a twin; *Kato* means second of twins; *Lutalo* means warrior; *Karabo* means answer.

Communityhood (*Ujamaa*)

- Under Ubuntu it is a taboo, and one of the highest offences in the community to beat your mother.
- Each person in the community looks after children – you keep them safe, teach them, reprimand, reward or punish them if there is need.
- Ubuntu gives peers the duty to mentor the age group behind them
- Incest is an unforgivable crime.
- There is no permanent migration under Ubuntu.
- Be good to your visitors. Visitors – be good with your hosts.
- There are no children's homes/institutions/residences under Ubuntu, because it is impossible to nurture children without parents and a community.
- In the community, some friends provide social and psychological support and counselling to others. These are usually older members of the community. This idea has motivated the globally

recognised and evidence-based Friendship Bench intervention in mental health.

Villagehood (*umisha* or *udunhu*)

- Under Ubuntu, childcare responsibilities are shared by the whole village; hence, it takes a village to raise a child
- The permanent home of an African is in a village, not an urban town unless your village was absorbed into a town or the land is still colonised

Societyhood (*ujamii*)

- Africa has its own philosophy.
- A person has no Ubuntu if they are corrupt, greedy, dishonest, disrespectful, irresponsible, individual (e.g. not sharing), not caring, abandon their relatives, abandon their permanent home etc.
- African welfare starts with the family, then the community and the state. For example, if a child's parents die, the first responsibility is with the family. If there is no family or they have abandoned their responsibility, then the community becomes responsible. If the community is not there or has abandoned their responsibility, then the state becomes responsible.
- Ceremonies – there are several Ubuntu ceremonies but most of them have been buried under colonisation and replaced with non-African ceremonies such as Easter ceremony, Christmas ceremony, Halloween ceremony, Valentine's etc.
- Patriarchy was an invention of colonial philosophy, modernisation and religion, not Ubuntu.
- Sex is done by mature adults out of purpose (procreation) and affection (love). Underage sex, which is rife among Abrahamic religion (Christian faith and Islamic faith) in Africa, is not a result of Ubuntu but the foreign beliefs in these faiths.
- Exhibition of sex and sexual organs is condemned under Ubuntu, and so is watching of pornography or sexual acts, including sex acts exhibited in films and movies.

Statehood (*unyika*)

- Good, respectful, and people-centred leadership is anticipated and promoted.
- A leader is a leader because of the people he/she leads.
- In Ubuntu society, women are leaders, fighters, and innovators just like men.
- African state structures that existed before colonisation, were disrupted but some survived.
- African Kings invented the King' granary e.g. one at Khami Ruins in Zimbabwe, where food was kept for the poor or for emergencies. Today, this initiative is known as *Zunde raMambo*, and is part of the welfare system in some African countries.

Environmenthood (*imvelo*)

- This encompasses land, water, sky, air, trees and animals.
- The highest form of injustice to Africans was to have African land taken by white people and the highest form of injustice to the ancestors was not to take that land back.
- Environmental identities – each African family has an animal or part of an animal or part of an environment that represents their identity. These identities are biological or genetic and they are crucial as DNA records.
- Land occupies an important position under Ubuntu. It connects all aspects of Ubuntu. It also provides permanency, for example, permanent home, community, and heritage.

Spiritualhood (*uroho*)

- Africa has its own beliefs and religion. Abrahamic religion that includes Christian and Islam beliefs came as a part of colonisation.
- Ubuntu sources of spiritual well-being include being on land, connection with family, being on the environment, certain parts of the environment, e.g. trees, dreams, funerals, ceremonies, rituals, rites, historical/heritage sites, helping, ancestors and God.
- Ancestors are to be respected for the role they played in creating, shaping or maintaining African spirituality for families and communities.

26

- Graves are to be respected for they are the homes of deceased members of the family.
- Social problems can have a spiritual origin and spiritual solution.
- Spiritualists can be consulted to diagnose and treat social problems. When diagnosing, they can use (1) observation (2) conversation or dialogue (3) spiritual power (4) a combination of these methods. When treating, they use conversation/dialogue, counselling, interpretation e.g. of dreams or occurrences, herbal healing, spiritual healing and other methods.
- Dreams have meaning and significance, and therefore are valued.
- Birth on one's land is valued since it connects the newborn to their land.
- Death and burial on one's land is valued as it provides connection to one's land and people.

Case studies

Case study 1: Institutionalisation

John Smith, a white man was transferred from London, United Kingdom to an African Kingdom by his congregation of the Church of England. His mission was to start a branch of the church to expand the influence of their doctrine. The doctrine of their church was guided by the white race's desire for supremacy in culture, religion, politics, education, law, and economics. This was a doctrine shared by their politicians, business, and academia, so they often worked together. When he arrived in the African Kingdom, there was a funeral and a big gathering in the first village he camped. An adult female had died and left behind a husband and five children aged between one and 14 years. When he went back to the city where he was staying, he arranged for the children to be put in an urban orphanage run by white nuns from his church. When he returned with the nuns, the children had been put in the custody of family members and the family and community were not willing to have them go. He went back and sought the support of the social welfare officers to take away the two youngest children, Upenyu and Thando. He succeeded.

Questions

1. What was the African Kingdom's philosophy?
2. How was it different from the United Kingdom's philosophy?

3. Are the two philosophies in this case study in competition? Provide examples.
4. The social welfare officers referred to in the case study were Black. Why is this surprising? What could have motivated their behaviour? What authority did they have?
5. In Africa, how important is it for children to grow up together, in a family of their culture and their community?
6. After several years of listening to Smith's philosophies, if the community thinks his philosophy is superior or is the only one, what one word could you use to describe this phenomenon?
7. How can this phenomenon be reversed?

Case study 2: Colonial philosophy in social work

Zenzele is a social welfare officer who was trained in 1956 in South Africa, his country of birth. His training took two years. He worked for two years after training before he was promoted to senior social welfare officer. He then got a scholarship to study advanced social science at Oxford University and graduated with a degree after three years. He came back to practice. He was exposed to about 11 philosophies in the social sciences, but none were African. He was also exposed to more than 30 textbooks of sociology, psychology, and anthropology and only one was about Africa. When he came back to practice, he realised that he was less effective than an untrained community or family worker. The skills he had gained only worked for the white clients he worked with. Many of his colleagues who had trained in western syllabi of social work were equally frustrated because the community did not appreciate the work they were doing.

Questions

1. If you were Zenzele, how could you have improved your professional standing?
2. How can the current education system ensure that there is no frustration?
3. What is the importance of relevant philosophy to learners?
4. Draw the table below in your notebook or computer. Write the names of philosophers in the empty boxes to correspond with their

contributions. It is ok to put more than one theorist per box. The choices are given at the bottom of the table.

Table 3: Philosophers and contributors (question)

Philosopher	Contribution
	African philosophy is a correction of historical misconceptions about the capacities and characteristics of Black African people.
	African life is community centred.
	Decolonisation and the fight for independence cannot be stopped.
	Africa has its own management philosophy and style.
	Africa has its own religion.
	Black Africa is one.
	Women have an equal role to play in African society.
	Language and the mind, once colonised, cultural genocide happens unless resisted.
	Cultural colonisation.
	Ubuntu solves many social problems including exploitation.

Choices of contributors for Table 3: Diop, Amo, Wiredu, Kaunda, Mbigi, Mbiti, Yacob, Asantewa, Nehanda, Mbande, Nyerere, Achebe

Guidance: Using Ubuntu philosophy in social services

Philosophy used in Africa's professions must be the society's foundation of knowledge. Trees have their roots in the soil down to rocks because that is where they are nourished. If they choose to have roots in the air, just because birds thrive in the air, then the trees will die. There are several ways to use philosophy, some are in the text box.

- Each provider of social services should have an organisational or service provider philosophy, sometimes called organisational culture - this should be grounded in Ubuntu philosophy.
- Ubuntu should guide the mission statement, objectives and aims of the service.
- Naturally, Ubuntu should shape values and ethics.

- Staff, workers and service receivers or users should be oriented to Ubuntu philosophy, and continuous professional development provided through training, short courses, publications, guest speakers and community visits so that they all remain grounded in the values of Ubuntu.

Summary

- Each group of people has their own philosophy.
- Ubuntu is the overarching philosophy of Africa.
- African philosophical ideas are largely not written, orature, they belong to the community.
- Individuals who have written African philosophy include Mbiti, Kaunda, Wiredu and Mbigi.
- Each group of people has their own philosophy which shapes their life and how social functioning is understood. Therefore, it naturally follows that social work cannot be the same. You cannot uproot it from one people to another.
- Philosophy shapes ideas about reality, existence, reason, knowledge, science, disciplines, religion, truth, race, values, mind, behaviour, justice, social problems, needs and even language.
- In social work, philosophy shapes values, ethics, theories, methods – in short, philosophy shapes all we do in social work
- There are a lot of misconceptions about Ubuntu, many are created to make it weaker and to facilitate colonisation.
- Ubuntu philosophy has lots of strengths and advantages but also some weaknesses.
- Africans value family, community, spirituality, environment, wholeness and decoloniality.

Further and advanced knowledge

- What have been the shortcomings of African philosophy and how can these be addressed.
- How is religion or culture related to philosophy? What came first? Is culture a result of philosophy or is philosophy a result of culture? Others have argued that to come up with culture, a people had to develop a philosophy first. What do you think?

- What were the philosophies of Thomas Sankara and Steve Biko?
- Who are the emerging African philosophers? What are their ideas?

Questions for in-class assessments and examinations

1. Summarise the philosophies of four African philosophers. Do further research.
2. What did Mbiti means by colonisation of the mind?
3. What is the purpose or importance of African philosophy?
4. What is your philosophy of life?
5. What is your lived experience of Ubuntu? If you do not have a lived experience, describe someone's lived experience of Ubuntu.
6. What do Africans value?
7. What is your lived experience of Ubuntu? If you do not have a lived experience, describe someone's lived experience of Ubuntu.
8. 'Colonialism was not only a political imposition, but also a cultural one', (Wiredu, 1998, p. 17). Discuss.

Potential questions for research

4. Find out the sources of oral philosophy in your culture? How can these be used in social work?
5. You have been asked to find out the usefulness of a family or community strengthening by your local government. What African philosophy could you use to guide this piece of research? Why?
6. Find out the philosophies of five founders of charitable organizations operating in your local area.
7. Jairos Jiri was a Zimbabwean philanthropist who founded the Jairos Jiri Association whose mission is to improve the conditions of persons with disability. Read his story from the African Journal of Social Work, Volume 10, Issue 1, 2020, pages 83-88. It can be said that although Baba Jiri (meaning Father Jiri) was later exposed to Christianity and rehabilitation, his philanthropy came primarily from his culture, family and community. Describe the research process that you could follow to prove that his background as a son from a royal family motivated him to become what he became?

8. Pick one of the authors listed at the end of this chapter and write their biography in 200 words. A biography is a written account of someone's life.
9. Design a research proposal using any of the research designs:
    a. African research methodology (ARM) (e.g. Khupe and Keane, 2017).
    b. Afrikology (Nabudere, 2011).
    c. Indigenous research methodology (IRM) (Chilisa et al, 2017).

Fieldwork ideas

1. Fieldwork is an important component of social work training. It involves a student practising to do social work under the guidance of supervisors, who are usually social workers. Usually, one supervisor is an academic, and the other is a practitioner. Fieldwork also involves families or communities where social work happens. We will collectively call these participants (not clients or service users). So, basically, fieldwork involves the student, two supervisors and the community although other people are involved as you will learn later. What do you think would happen if each of those people involved had a different philosophy of life? Can you truly practice social work when you share a different philosophy with the participants? Can you truly train a student social worker when your philosophies are different? On the side, how effective can social work be when those involved have a common philosophy?
2. Think about a person who helps others to achieve better social functioning in your family or community and visit or call them to answer these questions:
    a. What is their name?
    b. What do they do to help family or community members?
    c. Who gave them this role or authority?
    d. What motivates them to do what they do?
    e. What philosophies could be behind their work?

Key terms and their meanings

Africa philosophy – the foundation of African knowledge.

Conceptual decolonisation – 'is the elimination from our thought of modes of conceptualisation that came to us through colonisation and remain in our thinking owing to inertia rather than to our own reflective choices' (Wiredu, 2002, p. 5).

De-Africanisation – a process whereby an African's philosophy is changed to mimic that of another people.

Decolonisation of Africa philosophy – 'divesting African philosophical thinking of all undue influences emanating from a colonial past' (Wiredu, 1998, p. 17).

Indigenous – original, meaning original to a people or a geographical area.

Knowledge – the ideas that people have.

Onuma – frustration with non-African views, colonisation and neglect of African philosophy; results in an urge to decolonise African philosophy.

Philosopher – a thinker or person who has thought deeply about their people or society and made their ideas known, orally, practically or in writing.

Philosophy emptying – the process by which a people are emptied of their philosophy. It can also be referred to as philosophy genocide or philosophy assimilation.

Philosophy – the understanding, attitude of mind, logic and perception behind the way people think, act or speak in different situations of life (Mbiti, 1969, p. 2).

Ubuntu – a collection of values and practices that Black Africans origin view as making people authentic human beings. While the nuances of these values and practices vary across different ethnic groups, common among them is that an authentic individual human being is part of a larger and

33

more significant relational, communal, societal, environmental and spiritual world (AJSW, 2020).

References and recommended readings

Asante, M. K. (2024). *The history of Africa. The quest for eternal harmony.* New York. Routledge.

Asantewa Yaa (1840-1921). Life experience. (Asantewa did not write but her knowledge was shared orally and through writings done by colonists who executed her. In our work we decided to reference her and not the colonists).

Chilisa, B., Major, T. and Khudu-Petersen, K. (2017). Community engagement with a postcolonial, African-based relational paradigm. *Qualitative Research. 17.* (3), 326-339.

Diop, C. A. (1964). *The Cultural Unity of Black Africa: The Domains of Patriarchy and of Matriarchy in-classical Antiquity.* London, Karnak House

Diop, C. A. (1973). Parenté génétique de l'égyptien pharaonique et des langues négro-africaines modernes. Dakar, NEA.

Diop, C. A. (1974). *The African Origin of Civilisation: Myth and Reality.* Lawrence Hill Books, Chicago, Illinois.

Diop, C. A. (1989). *L'unité culturelle de l'Afrique noire: Domaines du patriarcat et du matriarcat dans l'antiquité classique.* Paris, Presence Africaine

Diop, C. A. (1990). *La grande confrontation: Religion, sciences exactes, sciences sociales.* Paris, Presence Africaine.

Diop, C. A. (1991). *Black Africa: The Economic and Cultural Basis for a Federated State.* Chicago, Lawrence Hill Books.

Diop, C. A. (2007). *Towards the African Renaissance: Essays in Culture and Development, 1946–1960.* (Revised Edition) Dakar, Codesria.

Jonathan O. Chimakonam. History of African philosophy. Internet Encyclopedia of Philosophy

Kaunda, K. (1966). *A Humanist in Africa.* London: Longman Greens

Kaunda, K. (1974). *Humanism in Zambia: A Guide to its implementation.* Lusaka. p. 131.

Kaunda, K. D. (1973). *The humanist outlook.* Longman Group Ltd., UK. p. 139.

Kaunda, K. D. (2007). Zambian humanism, 40 years later. The Sunday Post, October 28. 20-25.

Khupe, C. and Keane, M. (2017). Towards an African Education Research Methodology: Decolonising New Knowledge. *Educational Research for Social Change. 6.* 25-37.

Kurevakwesu, W. & Chizasa, S. 2020. Ubuntu and child welfare policy in Zimbabwe: A critical analysis of the National Orphan Care Policy's Six-Tier System. *African Journal of Social Work*, 10(1) (*Special Issue on Ubuntu Social Work)*, pp. 89-94

Maina, K. (2019). *History of Resistance in Kenya 1884-2002.* Nairobi: Mau Mau Research Centre.

Makinde, M. (2007). "The question of African philosophy"", in *African philosophy: The demise of A controversy.* Ile-Ife: Obafemi Awolowo University. 23-59.

Mbande Nzinga (1583 – 1663), (Mbande did not write but her knowledge was shared orally and through writings done by colonists who executed her. In our work we decided to reference her and not the colonists).

Mbeki, T. (2004). I am an African. Speech. 8 May 1996. Thabo Mbeki Foundation.

Mbigi, L. (1997). *The African Dream in Management.* Randburg: Knowledge Resources.

Mbigi, L. (2000), *In Search of the African Business Renaissance.* Randburg: Knowledge Resources.

Nabudere, D. W. (2005). Ubuntu philosophy: memory and reconciliation. Document. Kigali, Centre for Basic Research.

Nehanda (1862-1898) – Life experience. (Nehanda did not write but her knowledge was shared orally and through writings done by colonists who executed her. In our work we decided to reference her and not the colonists).

Wiredu, K. (1980). *Philosophy and an African Culture.* Cambridge: Cambridge University Press.

Wiredu, K. (1998). Toward Decolonizing African Philosophy and Religion. *African Studies Quarterly (1)(4),* 17-46.

Wiredu, K. (2002). Conceptual decolonization as an imperative in contemporary African philosophy: some personal reflections. *Rue Descartes, 36,* 53-64.

Wiredu, K. (2004). A Companion to African Philosophy

Yaqob, Zara (ዘርዐ ያዕቆብ) (1669). Hatata (There are no further reference details for this resource).

CHAPTER 2

Ubuntu values and ethics

Introduction

Values and ethics are derived from a group of people's ideas and beliefs, that is, philosophies. Each group of people have their own. Values are about what a group of people place importance on while ethics refer to good actions or character acceptable in each society. Values and ethics are different sides of an anthill. Values represent the side on an anthill that is facing the sun. The side facing the sun makes the other side have a shadow. That is, values shape ethics. Social workers work with people, hence, their own values and the values of the families and communities they work with are important. In this chapter, you will learn about African values and ethics that are derived from Ubuntu philosophy. You will also learn how values and ethics are used in social work and development.

Objectives of this chapter

After studying this chapter, readers will be expected to have acquired knowledge on:

- What the people of Africa value in their philosophy.
- What the people of Africa consider to be ethical actions.
- How to act ethically as a person and as a professional.
- How Africa's values have been undermined but thrived.
- Assessments that are suitable for the local context.
- Research questions and methods that are appropriate in Africa.
- Fieldwork, workplace-based and community-based learning.
- Guide on using Ubuntu values and ethics.

Skills and competencies addressed in this chapter

By the end of this chapter, readers will be expected to have acquired the following skills and competencies:

- Recognising values and ethics that come from African philosophy.
- Using African values and ethics.
- Decolonising social work values and ethics.
- Answer questions or assessments about the topic of this chapter.
- Create research questions and methods that are appropriate to the local context.
- Plan fieldwork, workplace-based and community-based learning that is contextual.

Understanding values

While a society usually has one philosophy, they have numerous values. Out of the numerous values, there are a few more common values, called core values. For Africa, the common values are:

1. Humanity – Africans value life, the human body and the spirit. This value extends to the environment.
2. Relations – Africans value family-hood that is, biological or blood relationships and mutual relationships with those not related by blood – socially, politically, economically, or otherwise.
3. Culture – Africans value the distinct ways that they have developed across generations to deal with social, political, environmental, economic, spiritual, and psychological issues and problems.
4. Wholism or holism – Africans value the interconnectedness of all things, social, political, environmental, economic, spiritual, and psychological.
5. Justice and freedom – Africans value self-determination, economic justice, social justice and all forms of justice.
6. Responsibility – Africans value being responsible to each other, for past and future generations and the environment. The rights of individuals are viewed through the individual's responsibilities to themselves, their family, community, society, environment and spirituality.

7. Community or collectivity and reciprocity – Africans value being a community or collective as opposed to being individuals. Africans value exchange of responsibility and respect as the basis for relationships. The exchange does not have to be immediate; it can take generations. Help is mostly provided in the hope that one day, help will also be received. Reciprocity, not competition, is valued.
8. Respect – Africans value respectful interaction and relationships, at individual, family, community, societal, environmental, and spiritual levels.
9. Spirituality – oneness of mind, body and spirit; connection between the dead, living and yet-to-be-born (Mbiti, 1970).
10. Indigeneity – Africans value being African, being the indigenous people of Africa, being Black, and being owners of Africa, the land and because of this value they resist assimilation into other races, domination by other races and dispossession of land.

The 10 broad values provided in the list provide a good summary of what Africans value. However, several secondary values derive from these 10. Some of these secondary values will be shared in the next section.

Understanding ethics

Ethics are more action oriented. When a value is put into action, the person taking the action must first ask themselves if what they plan to do is ethical or not. If they are sure, it is ethical, they will go ahead. If they are not sure, they will ask a friend, family member, community member, a leader or elder. If the action is judged to be unethical, it should not go ahead. When an unethical action is taken, it should not be repeated. Other unethical actions can result in punishment from the family, community, or society. Sanctions vary, but can include beating within expected norms, exclusion, professional sanction, imprisonment, or execution. The list below provides examples of values and ethics.

Table 4: Examples of values, ethics and their meanings

African value	Meaning	Ethic
Upenyu	Valuing life.	The ethic is not to harm or kill.
Umhuri	Familyhood, valuing family and lineages.	The ethic is protecting families and marriages.
Umuganda	Service to others.	The ethic is helping others in need or reciprocity.
Ururami, Ubulungiswa or Ubutabera	Justice.	The ethic is for people to be just.
Ukama or Harambee	Family-hood, valuing blood relations.	The ethic is protecting families and marriages.
Ujamaa	Family-hood or community-hood.	The ethic is promoting cooperation and collectivism.
Ubunyarwanda	Nationhood.	There are many ethics including promoting peace.
Uhuru	Liberty/independence/freedom.	The ethic is liberated and protects African liberation.
Umachobane	Sustainability.	The ethic is to do sustainable programs.
Itorero	Good members of society, and a strong sense of cultural values and leadership skills.	The ethic is to respect our cultures.
Umoja	Unity, peace and harmony.	The ethic is to promote oneness.
Kagisano	Good neighbourliness.	The ethic is to promote harmony.
Musha	A permanent home on ancestral lands.	The ethic is to protect and maintain permanent homes.

Simunye	Strengths in numbers, we are one.	The ethic is promoting cooperation and collectivism.
Shosholoza	Resilience.	The ethic is remaining strong despite adversity.
Kuumba	Creativity.	The ethic is not to imitate.
Ujima	Collective responsibility.	The ethic is to look after one another.
Utungamiri	Leadership.	The ethic is people-centred leadership.
Ushavi	Workmanship, enterprising.	The ethic is hardworking.
Urithi, Nhaka	Inheritance.	The ethic is to protect inheritance.
Uroho	Spiritual connectedness.	The ethic is to be holistic.
Unyanzvi	Professionalism.	The ethic is to act professionally.
Sankofa	Look back to inform the future.	The ethic is to respect history.

Ethics statements, proverbs or maxims

Ethics are usually presented as statements, proverbs or maxims. Maxims contain wisdom. They can include philosophy, values or ethics. Some examples of ethics statements, proverbs or maxims are:

- To possess virtue is better than gold, Akan ethic, Ghana.
- When virtue finds a town, the town thrives and abides, the Akan ethic, Ghana.
- *Onni suban* – lack of morals, ethics; Akan ethic, Ghana.
- *Onnye nipa* – lacks personhood; Akan ethic, Ghana.
- *Kushaya unhu* – lack of morals, ethics or character; Shona ethics, Zimbabwe.
- *Hapana munhu* – lacks personhood; Shona ethic, Zimbabwe.
- *Umhuka* – lacks personhood, acts like an animal; Shona ethic, Zimbabwe.

- *Nonomo mele si o* – lack of ethics, character or morals; Ewe ethic, Nigeria.
- *Onwe ghi ezi agwa* – lack of ethics, character or morals; Yoruba ethic, Nigeria.
- *Kushaya tsika* – lack of ethics, character or morals; Shona ethic, Zimbabwe.
- *Maemo a mabe* – lack of character or morals; Sotho ethic, South Africa.
- *Lokileng* or *boitswaro* – good character; Sotho ethic, South Africa.
- Good character is a person's guard; Yoruba ethic, Nigeria.
- *Kı̀ i se eniyan* – lacks personhood; Yoruba ethic, Nigeria.
- *Onipa ye fe sen sika*, the human being is more beautiful than gold; Akan ethic, Ghana.
- *Onipa ne asem: mefre sika a, sika nnye so, mefre ntama a, ntama nnye so; onipa ne asem*, I call upon gold, it answers not; I call upon cloth, it answers not; it is the human being that counts; Akan ethic, Ghana.
- *Onipa yieye firi onipa*, the well-being of man depends on his fellow man; Akan ethic, Ghana.
- *Wo nsa nifa hohorow benkum, na benkum nso hohorow nifa*, the right arm washes the left arm, and the left arm washes the right arm; Akan ethic, Ghana.
- *Obra ye nnoboa*, life is mutual aid; Akan ethic, Ghana.

Continuity of ethics

Children are born ethically neutral, they cannot make moral judgements. This is why children must be protected from making some decisions until they become human. Ethics and values are learned through socialization, observation, and practice. While learning ethics is a continuous process, at some stage a child becomes a human being. Their personality is accepted. The family and community play an important role in imparting good ethical conduct in their members. This is achieved through direct teaching of ethics, observation of ethics in practice, rewards and punishments. Ethics are not only applicable at the family and community level, but also at the societal level. In social work, as with other professions, ethics are part of the profession. They help regulate professional power. Enforcement of ethics for social workers is through self-regulation, meaning each person has a responsibility to be ethical. Ethics are stipulated in the code of ethics of the profession, of which every country has its own code. Laws of the community and nation are useful in enforcing the ethics of social workers.

Continuity of ethics means that ethics are part of life. They apply to all – individuals, family, community, leaders, student social workers, practising social workers or researching social workers. Good character is expected in society continually. Sources of responsibilities, rights and laws include:

- Families and tribes.
- Community's indigenous and oral laws.
- African leaders (village heads, chiefs and kings).
- Municipalities, for example, bye-laws.
- Parliament, for example, constitution.
- African Union.
- United Nations.
- Spiritual beings.
- Universe - natural rights and laws.

Morality and ethics

Morality is a measure or indicator of good (moral) or wrong (immoral). There is social morality and spiritual morality. They share a lot in common. There are many measures or indicators of morality for example:

- Moral good
- Moral failure
- Moral character
- Moral duty
- Moral value
- Moral deeds
- Moral sense
- Moral virtue
- Sense of moral guilt (*kamera* in Kinyarwanda or *tiboa* in Akan)

Ethics, religion and spirituality

Values and ethics are influenced by, and in turn influence religion and spirituality. Religion refers to an organised system upon which people use to show or share their beliefs or spirituality. Spirituality refers to a sense of connection to non-physical beings including a deity, deceased people and

42

objects. Religious people are spiritual but not all spiritual people are religious. In Africa however, ethics are (1) humanistic and (2) spiritual - they were created by people (living and deceased) to ensure good character in line with God's will.

Who creates and oversees ethics?

From the start of this chapter, we have shown that ethics are not created, maintained or overseen by one person. The roles and responsibilities are as follows:

Table 5: Creation and maintenance of ethics

Who?	What is their role?			
	Creating ethics	Applying ethics	Overseeing ethics	Sanctioning or rewarding
Individuals (me, us and you)				
Family				
Community				
Society				
Spiritual beings				
Others: leaders, elders				

Responsibilities, rights and laws

Values and ethics are directly linked to responsibilities, rights and laws. A responsibility is an expectation or duty to others (what you owe society) while a right is your expectation from others (what society owes you). Law is a collection of rules or guidelines about responsibilities and rights, and how sanctions are applied. Responsibilities, rights and laws exist in society in written and oral formats. African rights and laws are largely not written. The basic human rights are the right to life, food, shelter, health, security, culture, marriage, nationality, movement, equality, religion, social security, education, identity and freedom. At times rights and laws provided by parliament and the United Nations deviate from local values and ethics resulting in a dilemma. This is because, parliamentary laws were largely taken from Europe or America where they have a philosophy different from Africa. Laws that deviate from African values do not promote Africa but colonise it. Social workers should always be mindful of this, and work within African values and ethics.

Codes of values and ethics in social work

A code is an agreement between parties. Therefore, a code of values and ethics is a list of agreed values and ethics between social workers. The code usually applies to a specific geographical area, for example state or country. A code of ethics identifies the core values and mission of social work, sets standards, makes social work accountable and helps social workers decide when faced with conflict. A code sets professional standards, boundaries and sanctions. Each country has its code, and social workers in one country do not need to use a code from another country unnecessarily. African countries share one philosophy, so it is not surprising to see Togo using the code from Swaziland. However, if Namibia begins to use the code from England, America, Canada, Israel or China, that will be a misnomer.

Zimbabwe

The Social Workers (Code of Ethics) bye-law (Statutory Instrument, S.1.146/2012) to control and regulate social work professional behaviour and practice, hence putting in place a binding code of ethics for the profession. The by-law distinguishes social work as one of the very few professions with a legally binding, publicly published code of ethics in Zimbabwe, and indeed the world. The by-law sets out the core values on which the profession of social work is based and helps registered persons identify the ethical principles that inform the standards and core values of the social work profession and their day-to-day practice ethos. The Council of Social Workers (Zimbabwe) developed this by-law that binds social workers to professional behaviour with sanctions for offending social workers. This law was drafted in full participation and consultation with social workers. The code covers core values and principles of social work, responsibilities and obligations of social workers, misconduct, disciplinary procedure, penalties and appeal. A few of these are shown in the textbox.

The mission of social work includes -

a) enhancing the well-being and sustainable empowerment of individuals, especially the vulnerable, weak, powerless and oppressed members of the community; and
b) applying scientific and other validated knowledge for
c) the betterment of the individuals and the community; and promoting social justice, *unhu*/Ubuntu, human rights, positive change, problem solving and improvements in individual and community relationships and the development of society in general.

The core values of the profession of social work, which are shared by all social workers include -

a) service above self
b) social justice
c) *unhu*/Ubuntu
d) professional integrity
e) competence
f) importance of human relationships; respect of human rights
g) respect of diversity

The principles, based on the core values, and which facilitate the accomplishment of the mission of social work, and which set forth the ideas all social workers must aspire to, include the expectations that a social worker-

a) has, as a primary goal of helping people in need and addressing societal problems. This entails, service to others above personal interests, prioritizing the needs of service users, and occasionally offering service pro deo, especially in times of natural calamity and all the time drawing on all acquired skills, knowledge and values of the profession of social work.
b) promotes social justice. This includes being ready to challenge injustice in policies and practices discrimination, prejudice, promoting positive social change especially for the benefit of the vulnerable, weak and disadvantaged, encourage equity in opportunity and access to resources and full participation and empowerment of all.

c) recognises and promotes *unhu*/Ubuntu and appreciates that inherent in each person is dignity and values, and that each person deserves respect, and that person exists within a cultural setting and a community and that the individual and community shape, influence and benefit from each other.

d) exhibits the highest standards of professional integrity and will thus act in a manner that is trustworthy, dependable and responsible and engenders public confidence in the profession of social work.

e) practices within his or her area of expertise meaning that he or she will take necessary steps to enhance and develop his or her skills and use such skills and knowledge in the performance of his or her duties.

f) recognises the importance of human relationships and will thus purposefully strengthen and harness the relationships among people for positive social change and development, and in promoting the profession of social work.

A social worker shall be guilty of misconduct or improper or disgraceful conduct if he or she commits any of the following -

a) provision of grossly inadequate professional service.
b) serious criminal offence.
c) theft or fraud.
d) sexual impropriety.
e) practices without being registered, or being registered, without a valid practising certificate or a temporary dispensation granted by the Council.
f) disclosure without lawful authority or exercise, confidential information and/or records of a service user, to the potential or actual detriment of the service user.
g) making malicious false, wrong and harmful allegations against a colleague or a service under.
h) condoning or abetting any of the above misconduct.
i) bringing the profession into disrepute or otherwise

Information Box 1: Excerpt from Zimbabwe social work code of ethics

South Africa

Information Box 2: Excerpts from South Africa code of social work ethics

47

The South African Code of Ethics is comprehensive; however, it has some shortcomings. It is based on non-African literature, does not include African languages or local definitions of social work and does not cite other African codes. In creating the code, other codes from the United States of America, United Kingdom and laws from apartheid South Africa were used, so the code was created in a colonial frame even though the South Africa constitution was referenced. The committee and individuals consulted don't seem to be broad-based.

Nigeria

A code of conduct was adopted in 1982 by the Nigeria Association of Social Workers (NASoW). The 10 ethics statements in the code are:

1. I will hold as primary the welfare of the individual or group I serve. By this, I will give precedence to my professional responsibility to my client over my personal interest.
2. I will make distinction between my public work and private interests and would never allow the latter to becloud the former.
3. I will never discriminate negatively against my client on the basis of gender, age, ethnicity, belief, race, colour, social class and will prevent and protect my client against such negative discrimination in the work I do.
4. I will hold as strictly confidential and information with professional colleagues only in so far as to improve the quality of service render.
5. I will work to uphold the dignity of the human person and to respect the fundamental human rights of the clients I serve.
6. I will practice social work within the recognised knowledge and professional competence and will hold myself responsible for the quality of service I give to my client in relation to maximum utilization of available resources.
7. I will work to support the idea that social development work requires professional education and association.
8. I will take as my personal responsibility to contribute to the development of social work professional knowledge and practice and will treat with respect the findings, views and actions of other professional colleagues.
9. I accept responsibility to help, protect individuals or groups against unwholesome or unethical practices by any individual,

48

group or corporate organisation that is engaged in social development activities.

10. I will stand ready to provide professional service in times of public emergencies. I will act with integrity in the professional work and make myself accountable for the work I have done or would do.

Information Box 3: Excerpt from Nigeria social work code of ethics

Ghana

The code was put in place by the Ghana Association of Social Workers (GASOW). The code is intended to serve as a guide to the everyday conduct of members of the social work profession and as a basis for adjudication of issues in ethics when the conduct of social workers is alleged to deviate from the standards expressed in this code. The code serves six purposes:

1. To establish the core values upon which the social work profession is based.
2. To create specific ethical standards that should guide social work practice and reflect the core values.
3. To help social workers navigate professional considerations and obligations when ethical uncertainties arise.
4. To provide ethical standards to which the social work profession can be held accountable.
5. To initiate new social workers to the profession's mission, values, and ethical principles and standards.
6. To create standards by which the social work profession can assess if a social worker has engaged in unethical conduct. Social workers who pledge to abide by this code must cooperate with its implementation and disciplinary rulings based upon it.

Conduct/Comportment

Social workers must:

- Maintain high standards of personal conduct.
- Maintain a high degree of professionalism throughout their careers.

- Acknowledge service as the most important element of social work
- Maintain a high level of professional integrity.
- Engage in lifelong learning to maintain competence.
- Guide practice according to scholarly inquiry and use evidence to inform best practices.

Responsibility to clients

Social workers must:

- Make clients (individuals, groups and communities) their primary responsibility.
- Foster maximum self-determination in clients.
- Respect the privacy of clients and keep information that has been shared during the course of their duties confidential.
- Charge fees for services that are fair and considerate to clients.

Responsibility to colleagues and employers

Social workers should:

- Treat colleagues with respect, fairness, and courtesy.
- Respect confidences shared by colleagues in the course of their professional relationships and transactions.
- Extend to colleagues of other professions the same respect and cooperation that is extended to social work colleagues.
- Adhere to professional obligations as determined by their employers.
- Not exploit the problems of colleagues to gain personal enhancement in employment.

Responsibility to the Social Work Profession

Social workers should:

- Uphold, represent, and advance the values of the social work profession.

50

- Protect and enhance the dignity of the profession.
- Take action through appropriate channels to prevent the unauthorized and unqualified practice of social work.
- Help the profession make social services available to the public.
- Educate themselves to become culturally competent and understanding of diversity.

Responsibility to society

Social workers should

- Promote the general welfare of the society.
- Act to prevent and eliminate discrimination against any person on the basis of race, colour, gender, age, religion, origin, status, political belief, mental or physical handicap, or other preference.
- Advocate change in policy and legislation to improve social conditions and promote social justice.
- A high degree of professionalism throughout their careers.
- Acknowledge service as the most important element of social work.
- Maintain a high level of professional integrity.
- Engage in lifelong learning to maintain competence.
- Guide practice according to scholarly inquiry and use evidence to inform best practices.

Information Box 4: Excerpt from Ghana social work code of ethics

Significance of values and ethics in social work

Values shape the way we think about social work while ethics shape our actions. Therefore, values and ethics:

- Shape how we think and act as social workers.
- Together with philosophy, form the foundation of social work knowledge.
- They shape our religious beliefs.
- Shape how we teach and learn social work.

- Guide how we define social problems.
- Shape social work interventions and how we practice.
- Guide the behaviour of participants – individuals, families and communities.
- Help us distinguish indigenous from what is foreign or colonial.
- Increase creativity and innovation which is not possible when you use some people's values or ethics.
- Result in better decisions.
- Using African values and ethics will make social work more relevant to Africa.

Case studies

Case study 1: The colonial and local law – when values clash

Mago Mago's children were taken from him by a missionary, John Smith who was supported by the government social services department because 'they were at risk of being harmed' and therefore needed 'protection'. First, he consulted his family elders, who all did not understand why a person not related by blood could take care of children from another family. In short, they all denied. When John came back, Mago had gone to get spiritual counselling. Mago told John that the family and the spiritual advisor had rejected the idea of him taking custody of their children, but John said he was more interested in the children. Mago was advised to seek the Chief's counsel who asked both parties to appear at his court. But instead of John appearing at the Chief's court, he came with social welfare officers. The elders asked John "If the Chief has asked us to come to his court, we must respect the law of the land" to which he replied "I have in my hands the law of the land. This is the law of the land from the Crown - the Children's Act. And these people have a license from the Court of the Crown to take these children to their new home". The family went alone to the Chief, and the children went with John, the officers, and the nuns.

Questions for case studies

1. What actions show Mago's values? What actions show western values?

2. Families, communities, and kingdoms use unwritten laws. What are the advantages and disadvantages of unwritten laws?
3. What do you think happened to the children's socialization?

Case study 2: Unethical conduct

Violet was a white Anglican nun. When she received Upenyu Mago and Thandolwethu Mago, the two children from the village she had other children in care, about 30 more. She found it hard to pronounce the names Upenyu and Thando, and as she usually does with the other nuns, they gave the children new English names, John and Viola. The name John obviously came from John Smith who was a local missionary and Viola was from Violet. By changing the names, they were creating a connection between the children and them and this started a process of acculturation into white culture that was dominant at the home. A week later, the children were presented in church and given additional Christian names, Jacob and Debra, again, taking them further away from their religion and culture where they were known by their clan names of respect, that is, Mamoyo and Sinyoro respectively. Thando had a reed bracelet given to her by her aunt and Upenyu had had a knife, a well-respected tool in their tradition. Both were disposed. Two years passed without contact with their family and community and when their father and second mother (their biological mother's sister) managed to locate them, but they had lost sense of them, and more sadly, they were not able to communicate adequately in their language. The children were forced and trained to use a foreign called English in the institution and punished for using their own languages. To locate the children, one of the social welfare officers, who had helped John Smith, sympathised with them and shared the details of where the children had gone; as a result, he lost his job.

Questions for case studies

1. Make a photocopy of this case study. Use a green colour to highlight statements that show that ethics were broken. Use a red colour to show the people who broke these ethics?
2. Look at the list of ethics presented earlier and pick any four ethics that were broken in this case study.
3. Children deserve an identity of their family and race. What philosophy could have motivated Smith and Violet to act the way they did?

53

4. Mbiti (1970) asserted that African worldviews, religious beliefs and cultures were often neglected or dismissed as useless. Educational and social services were designed with this misconception in mind. However, this resulted in frustrations with the system. What are indications of that frustration in this case study?
5. What are the short-, medium- and long-term shortcomings of institutionalisation? Use examples from this case study.
6. African governments are dismantling institutions, but there are still some local and external people promoting them. What could be their motivation?
7. A child said 'I have many mothers and fathers, sisters and brothers, aunts and uncles, grandmothers and fathers. What does this mean and how useful is this concept of having many parents in the immediate and extended family useful for social work?
8. In the colonial period, some children were taken to....... where it was wrongly assumed they would have better spiritual, educational, economic, cultural and social opportunities but it turned out to be untrue. Most of the children became detached from their families and communities and failed to adjust after leaving these places A) orphanages B) children's homes C) institutions D) A-C.
9. Get a copy of the Code of Ethics of one social service profession of your country and answer the following questions (1) how it was created (2) the references (3) if it refers to African values (4) if it is inspired by African philosophy (5) what would you change.

Guidance: using Ubuntu values and ethics in social services

- Code of ethics for organisations, schools, colleges, companies and institutions must be based on Ubuntu values.
- Training manuals content must be grounded in Ubuntu values.
- Principles of casework and counselling should be grounded in Ubuntu values and ethics.
- Families, communities and society must be involved in making service provider values and ethics statements.
- Ubuntu's environmental values and ethics must be prioritised.
- Ubuntu spiritual values and ethics must be prioritised.

Summary

- Both values and ethics come from philosophy.
- Values are the things people place importance on.
- Each society has its core values (primary values) and secondary values.
- Ethics are the actions that people take that are acceptable. If unethical action is taken, it results in harm and sanctions .
- Africans value communality and collectivity as opposed to individualism.
- Responsibilities are more valued than rights.
- Values and ethics are not only for social workers, but they are also learned and practised at home and in the community from childhood.
- Each country has its own code of ethics for social workers (or other social service professions) and there is no reason social workers in another country should be using a code of ethics from another country.
- In the professions, a code of values and ethics sets standards and regulates professional work.

Further and advanced knowledge

- African religious beliefs
- African cultures and sub-cultures
- Code of ethics from other professions and countries
- Philosophy
- Decolonising values and ethics

Questions for in-class assessments and examinations

1. What are the core values of Africans?
2. Read case study 1 and 2. Discuss the impact of colonisation on African social services.
3. What is the purpose or importance of African values?
4. Pick any four African values and discuss them in detail.
5. Pick four ethics and show from which values they derive.
6. Speak with two or more people from your family and two or more from your community about African proverbs that promote

55

ethical conduct. Write a detailed statement about eight proverbs that you learned about. Add two that you already know.

7. Although westernisation is strong in urban areas, African values are still the basis of African societies today. Discuss.
8. Think about an incident when someone or you acted ethically. What happened/ Who witnessed it? Why was the action ethical?
9. Select one code of ethics of social work in Africa of your choice and analyse it.
10. Should social work students change their ethics to adopt those of richer countries?

Potential questions for research

1. Gaps in codes of values and ethics in Africa.
2. The history of institutionalisation and lessons.
3. The process to reverse institutionalisation – challenges and opportunities.
4. Children who grew up in institutions or children in institutions.
5. Values or ethics that social workers are using in practice and what their thoughts or reflections are.
6. Understanding codes of ethics in Africa.
7. Select two approaches from the list below and explain how they fit the philosophy of Africa.
   a) Ubuntu research approach
   b) Community-centred approach
   c) Sankofa methodology
   d) Collective research approach
   e) Cultural safety approach
   f) African-centred or Afrocentric research
   g) Empowerment or capability research approach
   h) Responsible research approach
   i) Developmental research
   j) Household, family or community-oriented research (HOFACOR)
   k) Participatory action research (PAR)
   l) Environmental approach
   m) Creative approaches

Fieldwork ideas

Make a one-hour appointment with a social worker and visit them at their workplace. Do an interview using the guide below, and record responses. Present the responses to a group of other students. This interview can be done by one student or a group. This fieldwork exercise could be an assessment or two hours can be obtained for fieldwork.

1. Ask a question to know each other.
2. Ask a question about what they do.
3. As a question about their personal social work philosophy.
4. Ask a question about values and ethics that they use in practice and ask for an example of where the practitioner applied the values and ethics.
5. Allow the practitioner to ask you one to three questions.
6. Do a short summary or transcription of the meeting and share with the practitioner to check.
7. Present a short report to a group of other students.

Key terms and their meanings

African-centred (Afro, Afrocentric or Afrocentricism) – focusing on Africa or people of Africa.

Ethical dilemma – a situation when an action can both be ethical and unethical.

Ethical principle – a guide for an ethic.

Ethical standard – an acceptable level of action.

Ethics – good actions or character acceptable in any given society.

Humanism – the act of putting human welfare, interests and needs at the front.

Humanistic – putting human welfare, interests and needs at the front.

Maxims – an expression of a value or ethic.

Morality – being right.

Religion – ways people express their spirituality.

Spirituality – connection between *Bantu* (living, deceased, spiritual and and the Supreme Being), *kintu, hantu* and *kuntu.*

Values – what a group of people place importance on.

References and recommended readings

Bewaji, J. A. I., 2(004). "Ethics and Morality in Yoruba Culture," in Kwasi Wiredu (ed.), *A Companion to African Philosophy*, Oxford: Blackwell Publishing, 396–403.

Busia, K. A., (1967). *Africa in Search of Democracy*, New York: Praeger.

Busia, K. A., (1954). *"The Ashanti of the Gold Coast,"* in Forde (ed.) 1954, 190–209.

Busia, K. A., (1962). *The Challenge of Africa*, New York: Frederic A. Praeger, Inc.

Chilisa, B., Major, T.E., Gaotlhobogwe, M. and Mokgolodi, H., (2016). *'Decolonizing and indigenizing evaluation practice in Africa*: Toward African relational evaluation approaches', *Canadian Journal of Program Evaluation 30(3)*. https://doi.org/10.3138/cjpe.30.3.05

Council of Social Workers Zimbabwe (CSWZ) (2012). *Social Work Code of Ethics*. Harare: CSWZ.

Ghana Association of Social Workers (GASOW) (no date) Code of Ethics of Social Workers. Ghana, GASOW.

Government of Namibia. (2004). Social Work and Psychology Act 6 of 2004.

Government of South Africa. (1978). Legislative mandate. http://www.dsd.gov.za/index.php/about/legislative-mandate https://laws.parliament.na/annotated-laws-regulations/law-regulation.php?id=56

Government of Zimbabwe. (2001). Social Workers Act. Harare, Government of Zimbabwe

Government of Zimbabwe. (2012). Social Work Code of Ethics. Harare, Government of Zimbabwe

Gyekye, K. (1997). Tradition and Modernity: *Philosophical Reflections on the African Experience*, New York, and Oxford: Oxford University Press.

Gyekye, K. (2004). Beyond Cultures: *Perceiving a Common Humanity* (Ghanaian Philosophical Studies 111), Washington, D.C.: The Council for Research in Values and Philosophy and Ghana Academy of Arts and Sciences.

Gyekye, K. (2011). "African Ethics", *The Stanford Encyclopedia of Philosophy* (Fall 2011 Edition), Edward N. Zalta (ed.), URL = <https://plato.stanford.edu/archives/fall2011/entries/african-ethics/>.

Gyekye, K. (1995). *An Essay on African Philosophical Thought: The Akan Conceptual Scheme*, Revised edition, Philadelphia: Temple University Press; original edition, Cambridge: Cambridge University Press, 1987.

Kaunda, K. (1966). *A Humanist in Africa*. London: Longman Greens

Kaunda, K. (1974). Humanism in Zambia: A Guide to its implementation. Lusaka. 131.

Kaunda, K. D. (1973). *The humanist outlook*. Longman Group Ltd., UK. 139.

Kaunda, K. D. (2007). Zambian humanism, 40 years later. Sunday Post, October 28. 20-25.

Makinde, M. (2007). "The question of African philosophy", in African philosophy: *The demise of A controversy Ile-Ife*: Obafemi Awolowo University. 23-59

Molema S. M., (1920). *The Bantu: Past and Present*, Edinburgh: W. Green and Son.

Ngugi wa Thiong'o (1986). *Decolonizing the Mind*: The Politics of Language in African Literature. London: J. Curry and Portsmouth, N. H: Heinemann, 1986.

Nigeria Association of Social Workers (NASoW) (1982) Code of Conduct for Social Work Practice in Nigeria. In the Constitution of the Nigeria Association of Social Workers, pages 21-22. Nigeria, NASOW.

Nyerere, J. K., (1968). *Ujamaa: Essays on Socialism*, Dar es Salaam, Tanzania: Oxford University Press.

South African Council for Social Service Professions (SACSSP). (2012). Policy Guidelines for Course of Conduct, Code of Ethics and the Rules for Social Workers. SACSSP, Pretoria

Wiredu, K. (1980). *Philosophy and an African Culture*. Cambridge: Cambridge University Press.

Wiredu, K. (1998). *Toward Decolonizing African Philosophy and Religion. African Studies Quarterly (1)(4)*, 17-46.

Wiredu, K. and Gyekye, K. (eds.), (1992). *Person and Community (Ghanaian Philosophical Studies 1)*, Washington, D.C.: The Council for Research in Values and Philosophy.

Wiredu, K. (1983). "Morality and Religion in Akan Thought," in H. Odera Oruka and D. A. Masolo (eds.), *Philosophy and Cultures*, Nairobi: Bookwise Limited.

Wiredu, K. (1992). *"Moral Foundations of an African Culture,"* in Wiredu and Gyekye (eds.) 1992, 193–206.

Wiredu, K. (1995). "Custom and Morality," in *Conceptual Decolonization in African Philosophy*, Ibadan, Nigeria: Hope Publications.

CHAPTER 3

Theories of social services

Introduction

We have already learned that each society developed its philosophy from where their values and ethics are derived. Philosophies, values and ethics form the foundation of knowledge used in all disciplines. This knowledge is not complete without theories. Theories are the interpretation of philosophy, values and ethics to make them 'applicable' to a learning, practice or research situation. Not all philosophical, value and ethical knowledge needs interpretation, most of the time they are applied as they are. Theories can be oral (proverb, maxim, poem, song, idiom or other) or written (statement, a list of points, a paragraph, a few paragraphs, a chapter or a book). They help us understand social problems and ways to prevent, reduce or eradicate them. In this chapter, you will learn about Africa's theories that apply to social work and development work. You will also learn how we use the theories in social work and development work.

Objectives of this chapter

After studying this chapter, readers will be expected to have acquired knowledge on:

- Giving African theories recognition and usage.
- Selecting appropriate theories.
- Applying theoretical knowledge in understanding social work knowledge, shaping skills and making interventions more relevant to Africa.
- Creating theories.
- Assessments that are suitable for the local context.
- Research questions and methods that are appropriate to the local context.

- Fieldwork, workplace-based and community-based learning is contextual.
- Guidance on using Ubuntu theories in social services.

Skills and competencies addressed in this chapter

By the end of this chapter, readers will be expected to have acquired the following skills and competencies:

- Valuing African theories.
- Using African theories.
- Developing theories.
- Answer questions or assessments about the topic of this chapter.
- Create research questions and methods that are appropriate to the local context.
- Plan fieldwork, workplace-based and community-based learning that is contextual.

What is a theory?

You often hear people say, 'That is theoretical'. Do they mean it is more valued or less valued? The answer is both yes and no. A theory in general use is a draft of an idea. However, in academia, a theory is the opposite – theory is an idea that has been clearly explained, used and accepted. At times it is tested, but others say the best test is time. A theory interprets the natural world or philosophies, values and ethics. A theory can provide an explanation of how and why things happen, what things mean and what is likely to occur next or in future. We can derive knowledge, facts, guidelines, models, laws, principles, and processes from theories.

Myths and truths about theories

It is a myth that theories should be developed in western countries or that useful theories are those developed in the West. Africans from several centuries ago have been developing theories, and we continue to do that. We have old but very useful theories that our ancestors developed. Most might not be written, they are orature (oral literature), but they are the old roots of our society. Most western theories are not useful to African communities; some are even dangerous to African society.

It is a myth that only professors can develop theories, anyone can develop a theory. A theory becomes important based on how much it is used. African theories are used less; therefore, they do not become important. Only when Africans use their theories can they become prominent. We have seen this with Ubuntu. It is a myth that when you write your essay, thesis, review, blog, presentation or report you need to rely on western theories. Strong writing uses appropriate, local and indigenous theories.

It is a myth that we only must use existing theories, no, you can develop your own. When you are writing an essay, report, thesis, book chapter or book or planning an intervention, you can start by presenting the data and information, and then propose a theory. Others call this a grounded theory approach or a bottom-up approach. The fact that you need to gather the information first often results in people avoiding the grounded theory approach in favour of established theories but it is important to develop theories. This theory is quite relevant to Africa, but it allows for more theories to be generated. This covers the current gap in the literature, and prevents us using theories, models and approaches that do not promote African values. It is a myth that theories only come from researchers. Most persuasive theories in western literature were not developed from research but by philosophers, thinkers or lay people.

When professional social work was introduced to Africa, as was the case in most developing countries of the Caribbean, Asia, the Pacific and South America, the foreigners who brought social work wrongly assumed that social work was new to these regions, and therefore chose to sideline, ignore and replace existing systems with theirs. In replacing existing systems, the foreign people depended on theories from outside. The local theories did not die, but thrived where western influence was not there, or alongside them. With time, most local theories found their way back into African social work.

Characteristics and strengths of African theories

Most African theories are not written, they exist as proverbs, maxims, poems, songs, idioms or others). The body of written theories is increasing. African theories are largely communal and collective, they are developed, used and reviewed by the community. The theories exist in African languages making them very easy to understand. African theories were developed from African philosophies, values and ethics and this makes them indigenous to the African situation.

List of African theories and models

Below is a list of theories, approaches, frameworks and models that are relevant and safe to use in social work and development in Africa. Some of these theories are discussed in the proceeding sections.

- Ubuntu Theories
    - Ujamaa Theory (African Community Theory)
    - Individual-in-Family Theory (IIF)
    - African Family Theory (*Ukama* Theory)
    - *Unhu* (Ubuntu) Education Theory
    - Ubuntu Psychology
    - Ubuntu Social Work, Welfare and Development Theory
    - Ubuntu Research Philosophy
    - Ubuntu Moral Philosophy (Ubuntu Morality)
    - Ubuntu Political Philosophy
    - Samkange's Theory of Ubuntu
    - Ubuntu Spirituality
    - Ubuntu Feminism
    - Ubuntu Engineering
    - Ubuntu Business Model
    - Ubuntu Management Theory
    - Ubuntu Social Justice, Criminal Justice and Jurisprudence Theory
    - Kaunda's Theory of African Humanism (Ubuntu)
- Africa Ageing Theory – Nyanguru model of ageing
- African Asset Theory
- African Environmental Theory
- African Feminism
- African Renaissance Theory
- African Research methodology (ARM)
- African Social Development (ASD) Model
- African Spiritual Theory
- African Strengths Theory
- African Theory of Education

- Afriture Theory
- Afrocentricity and Afrocentrism
- Ajayi's Model of Decolonising Higher Education
- Bottom-Up Approach
- Case Management Framework
- Colonial Theory
- Decolonisation/Decolonial Theory/Decoloniality
- Decolonised Research methodology/Design/Approach
- Decolonising the Mind Theory (Ngugi wa Thiongo)
- Developmental Social Work (DSW) Approach or Developmentalist Theory
- Diaspora Theory
- Disadvantage Expectations Theory (*Tarajio Hasara*)
- Double Consciousness Theory (Du Bois)
- Epistemic Decolonisation Theory
- Friendship Bench Approach
- Green Belt Movement (GBM) Model
- Holistic and Integrative Health Model
- Human Factor (HF) Approach to Development
- Ibrahim Index of African Governance (IIAG)
- Indigenisation Theory
- Indigenous Health Theory
- Indigenous Research Methodology/Approach
- Integrated Musha/Nyumba Theory
- Jairos Jiri Charity and Philanthropy Model
- Jairos Jiri Disability and Rehabilitation Model
- Kalinganire's Social Work Practice Model (2017)
- *Kudyiswa/Kurutsiswa* Theory of Decolonisation
- Kwanza Spirituality Theory
- Longwe's Empowerment Framework
- Longwe's Women Empowerment Tool
- Made in Africa Evaluation (MAE) approach.
- Mugabeism
- Neo-Colonial (Neo-Colonialism) Theory (Kwame Nkrumah)
- Nkrumaism
- Nziramasanga Educational Model
- One-Africa Theory
- Orature Theory (Zirimu's Orature Theory)

- Participatory Action Research (PAR)
- Paulo Freire's Theory of Education and Decolonisation
- Sankofa Theory
- Shaka Zulu Theory of Leadership and Management
- Six Tier System of Childcare, Welfare and Development
- Stages and Levels of Decolonisation
- Tesfaye's Developmental Social Work Curricula
- The *Zera* Model of children's growth and development in Zimbabwean culture
- Theories of Cheikh Anta Diop
- Theory of Dead Aid
- Theory of Grandparents
- Thiongo's Theory of African Languages
- Tree of Life model by Ncazelo Ncube
- Ubuntu Model of Migration and Refugees
- *Ukuru* Theory
- Women Empowerment Framework or Longwe Framework for Gender Analysis

List of theories or models that have colonised African theories or are not relevant or are dangerous to African work

- Assimilation theory.
- Biestek's principles of casework (too much focus on western individualistic and Christian values).
- Body mapping approach.
- Colonial and neo-colonial theory.
- Darwinism/theory of evolution by natural selection.
- Dependence theory (that Africa will do well by depending on the west).
- Individualism (as a philosophy it promotes smaller social networks, individualised (as opposed to family or community) identity, promotes autonomy which causes conflict, unnecessary competition, materialism and ultimately poor mental health).
- Maslow's hierarchy of needs (too maany individualistic ideals).
- Modernisation theory (too much focus on western market values for urban communities).
- Positivism (Auguste Comte).

66

- Psychoanalysis (Freud).
- Trauma theory (it magnifies 'trauma'; too much focus on deficits; views individual as weaker, the worker or organisation as experts; presents families and culture as sources of trauma; has been used to demonise African way of life and culture; neglects structural issues like colonialism, assimilation; advances western view of trauma and neglects the role of the individual in shaping their own present life).
- Western feminism (assumes western culture, values and aspirations are universal).

Ubuntu theories and models

Ubuntu as Africa's overarching philosophy gives rise to many theories directly and indirectly. Ubuntu is a collection of values and practices that black people of Africa view as making people and their communities authentic. While the nuances of these values and practices vary across different ethnic groups, they all point to one thing – an authentic individual human being is part of a larger and more significant relational, communal, societal, environmental and spiritual world. The term Ubuntu is expressed differently in several African communities and languages but all referring to the same thing. In Angola, it is known as *gimuntu,* Botswana *(botho),* Burkina Faso *(maaya),* Burundi (Ubuntu), Cameroon *(bato),* Congo *(bantu),* Congo Democratic Republic *(bomoto/bantu),* Cote d'Ivoire *(maaya),* Equatorial Guinea *(maaya),* Guinea *(maaya),* Gambia *(maaya),* Ghana *(biako ye),* Kenya *(utu/munto/mondo),* Liberia *(maaya),* Malawi *(umunthu),* Mali *(maaya/hadama de ya),* Mozambique *(vumuntu),* Namibia *(omundu),* Nigeria *(mutunchi/iwa/agwa),* Rwanda *(bantu),* Sierra Leonne *(maaya),* South Africa (Ubuntu/*botho*), Tanzania *(utu/obuntu/bumuntu),* Uganda *(obuntu),* Zambia *(umunthu/Ubuntu)* and Zimbabwe *(hunhu/unhu/botho/*Ubuntu). It is also found in other Bantu countries not mentioned here.

Unhu (Ubuntu) education theory

In education, Ubuntu has been used to guide and promote African ideas, and to decolonise it from western educational philosophies. Ubuntu education uses the family, community and environment as sources of knowledge but also as teaching and learning media. The essence of education is family, community, societal and environmental well-being. Interaction, liberation, participation, recognition, respect and inclusion are important aspects of Ubuntu education. Methods of teaching and learning include groups and community approaches. In short, Ubuntu shapes the objectives, content, methodology and outcomes of education.

Ubuntu psychology

This focuses on Ubuntu resilience, sensation, motivation, bereavement, mourning, memory, dreams, recovery, trauma and many others.

Ubuntu social work, welfare and development theory

This refers to Afrocentric ways of providing a social safety net to vulnerable members of society. Common elements include collectivity, *ukama* (relationality), ujamaa (collaboration) and looking at people holistically. These approaches are indigenous, and help to decolonise. Ubuntu is against materialism and individualism. The social interventions done by social workers, welfare workers and development workers should strengthen, not weaken families, communities, society, the environment and people's spirituality. These are the five pillars of Ubuntu intervention: family, community, society, environment and spirituality.

Ubuntu research theory

This is also known as the Ubuntu research paradigm, approach, or philosophy. Ubuntu guides research objectives, ethics and methodology, and decolonises research agenda and methodology. The objectives of Ubuntu research are to empower families, communities, and society at large. In doing Ubuntu research, the position of the researcher is important because it helps form relationships with the participants. The agenda of the research belongs to the community, and true participation is highly valued. *Ujamaa*, which means pulling together and is about collaboration, is highly valued. Oral literature (orature is valued because most of African thought is not written. Relational and collective approaches to research are valued. Human beings are seen as part of nature, not as separate from it. Data collection methods include *dare*, an approach that involves participants sitting together, often in a circle, and sharing respectively, in turn. Storytelling, narrations and dialogue are valued. In true Ubuntu research, written consent is of no significance, it is not valued because relationships are more important than contracts. Research is incomplete

68

without asking the participants to verify what you are going to publish, how you will gain from the research and how the community will gain. The research itself, together with feedback, must be provided in appropriate language and formats Ubuntu values good communication, that is, how you say what you have to say. How deep is what you say? Other participants and leaders, require opportunities to talk at length, orating using proverbs, idioms, folklores, maxims (short statements) and even songs. Ubuntu research values humane approaches and discourages cheating, deceit, harm and disrespect.

In summary, the major characteristics of Ubuntu research are:

- Relational – respectful relationships between participants and between researcher and participants are valued.
- Reciprocal – research is an exchange between the researcher and the community being researched, the benefits should accrue to all, including the financial benefits of the research.
- Decolonial – Ubuntu research seeks to overturn the centuries of colonisation on African ideas.
- Participatory – when individuals, families and communities are engaged in research, they are participants not research subjects or respondents.
- Collective – methods that involve the family and community are valued as opposed to individual methods.

Ubuntu moral philosophy or Ubuntu morality

'… actions are right roughly insofar as they are a matter of living harmoniously with others or honouring communal relationships' (Metz and Gaie, 2010, p. 273). 'One's goal should be to become a full person, a real self or a genuine human being (Metz and Gaie, 2010, p. 275). Relationships (ukama) are important. Among the Shona people for example, when a person dies, his or her property is shared amongst relatives and there are culturally approved ways of doing this. The practice is called *kugova*. Life is valued. As Samkange said, "If and when one is faced with a decisive choice between wealth and the preservation of the life of another human being, then one should opt for the preservation of life" (Samkange, 1980, p. 7).

Ubuntu political philosophy

Samkange (1980) said 'Is there a philosophy or ideology indigenous to (a) country that can serve its people just as well, if not better than, foreign ideologies?". Samkange's maxim for leadership is "The king owes his status, including all the powers associated with it, to the will of the people under him" (Samkange, 1980, p. 7). Here, a king refers to a leader of a home, family, school, workplace, village, community, organisation, country, nation or international. It also refers to a professional like a social worker because of the statutory authority they have when working with families, communities or clients.

Samkange's theory of Ubuntu

Whose fault is it if no one knows about the philosophy of your grandfather and mine? Is it not your fault and mine? We are the intellectuals of (Africa). It is our business to distil this philosophy and set it out for the world to see (Samkange, 1980). Samkange (1980) argued that Africans need to learn, write and practice Ubuntu. Just as westerners use philosophies of their ancestors, Africans should find pride in the philosophies of their ancestors like Ubuntu. There are several theories, frameworks and models built on Ubuntu. For a start, this article might be useful. More articles are available in the Special Issue published by the African Journal of Social Work in 2020. Samkange's theory has three maxims (short statements). These are:

- Human relations: "To be human is to affirm one's humanity by recognizing the humanity of others and, on that basis, establish respectful human relations with them" (Samkange and Samkange, 1980, p. 6 "The attention one human being gives to another: the kindness, courtesy, consideration and friendliness in the relationship between people; a code of behaviour, an attitude to other people and to life, is embodied in *hunhu* or Ubuntu" (Samkange and Samkange, 1980, p. 6).
- Sanctity of life: "If and when one is faced with a decisive choice between wealth and the preservation of the life of another human being, then one should opt for the preservation of life" (Samkange and Samkange, 1980, p. 7) This is an ethical principle.
- People-centred status: "The king owes his status, including all the powers associated with it, to the will of the people under him"

70

(Samkange and Samkange, 1980, p. 7)   Here, a king refers to a leader of a home, family, school, work place, village, community, organisation, country, nation or international. It also means a professional like a social worker because of the power they have when working with service users, community or clients.

Ubuntu spirituality

Ubuntu spirituality is communalised and values the family and environment.

Ubuntu engineering

Having designs, concepts, innovations, processes, and products that are inspired by Ubuntu values of the family, community, environment and spirituality.

Ubuntu social justice, criminal justice and jurisprudence

Ubuntu justice emphasises these elements:

- Deterrence which can be done socially, physically, economically, or spiritually.
- Returning and Replacement – meaning bringing back what has been stolen, replacing it or compensating. In Shona language this is called *kudzora* and *kuripa*.
- Apology, Forgiveness and Reconciliation (restoration of *ukama* or relations) after meeting the above.
- Warnings and Punishments (retribution) from community, leaders, and elders if the above has not been achieved or ignored.
- Warnings and Punishments from spiritual beings if the above has not been met. In Shona culture, these are called *jambwa* and *ngozi*.

Families, and communities are involved in the processes of justice.

African family (ukama) theory

Ukama means relations, it is about family-hood. Families look after each other. For an individual, the family includes immediate, extended, and

71

tribal relatives. The pillars of the African family theory are (1) the value of marriage (2) the value of child-bearing (3) value for blood-line and maintaining race-line (4) value for extended family (tribe or clan) (5) value for strengthening the bond between the families involved in the marriage e.g. exchange of gifts (6) value for a permanent home (7) value for sharing or dividing family roles (8) value for looking after one another and not putting individual needs first (9) value for community (10) maintaining African values.

Each member of the family has roles in the family, extended family, and community. If a member fails to play their role, the family, extended family or community will not function effectively. Some of the roles include:

1. Mothers (includes mother's sisters)
2. Fathers (includes fathers' brothers)
3. Brothers and sisters
4. Aunts
5. Grandparents

Ukama is an asset, it is social capital. From the family and extended relationships an individual gets (1) resource or economic support when needed (2) moral and psychological support, for example during sickness, disasters or death (3) social support, for example, mentoring (4) information, for example, family history (5) care (6) alternative family (7) dispute resolution (8) inheritance, for example of a home or land, livestock (9) identity and belonging.

Integrated musha/nyumba theory

Musha means homestead Shona language and *nyumba* in Swahili. Musha is the permanent home for Africans and it is in the village. Musha is the first and smallest geographical unit of African society. It is a place to live, enjoy culture and a resting place for deceased ones. This socio-economic development theory promotes *nyumba* as a place for farming activities throughout the whole year while incorporating science and technology to make *musha* an economic enterprise that generates income for each family to sustain its livelihood and benefit the community and the nation. The theory combines culture, community, technology and enterprise. An integral *musha/nyumba* promotes household trade to enhance family livelihoods and helps in creating an active and vibrant village and regional economy (Taranhike, 2021)'.

Characteristics of an integrated *musha/nyumba* are:

- It maintains the communal way of life – doesn't disrupt the African cultural social fabric because people do not move out of their community in search of employment.
- Promotes family unity and community cohesion – people earn a living while they are in their family homestead setting which is grounded in nature.
- People live in harmony with nature – harvesting sunshine to produce solar energy and harvesting both rainwater and underground water to ensure that farming is carried out throughout the whole year using drip irrigation, keeping bees for honey and pollination, soil conservation.
- Growing traditional crops that are drought resistant.
- Growing high value crops such as garlic, ginger, turmeric, etc, thereby even enabling the rural folk to earn foreign currency as these crops can be exported.
- Rural tourism – draws on African values of hospitality and respect
- Reversing colonisation and urbanisation – making African rural communities proud of who they are, their culture and their history
- Combines indigenous and exogenous knowledge.
- Processing and value addition – instead of selling raw produce.

'As a whole, the integral *kumusha* provides a holistic and integrated approach in rural development and enhancing livelihoods, starting with the traditional homestead within the community, living in harmony with nature while promoting our culture and improving knowledge co-creation through science and technology and using the integral *kumusha* as an enterprise to generate income for the home, the community and the nation at large', (Taranhike, 2021).

Ubuntu models in social work, human services and development

- Samkange's theory of Ubuntu (Samkange and Samkange, 1980)
- Ubuntu social justice framework (Rankopo, Osei-Hwedie and Modie-Moroka, 2007)

- *Unhu* ethical model (Council of Social Workers Zimbabwe (CSW), 2012)
- Ubuntu as a philosophical framework for African social work (Mugumbate and Nyanguru, 2013)
- Ubuntu as a pan-African philosophical framework for social work in Africa (Mupedziswa, Rankopo and Mwansa, 2019)
- The Tswana Kagisano framework (2016)
- Anti-poverty and social protection model of Ubuntu (Metz, 2016)
- Ubuntu ecological and eco-spiritual perspective (van Breda, 2019)
- The decolonial framework of Ubuntu (several authors)
- An integrated framework of Ubuntu (Mugumbate and Chereni, 2019)
- Nyanguru model of ageing (Nyanguru, various years)

Decolonisation theories

Decolonisation theory

The starting point to understanding decolonisation is to understand colonisation, which is:

- People leaving their country/land to occupy another by force and deception (this is what the Berlin Conference achieved).
- Monarchies taking over another monarchy or its land by force or deception (as was done by the British Monarchy and other European monarchies.
- Imposing culture, and displacing local culture.
- Colonising countries creating companies to exploit local resources for the benefit of the colonial country. This includes taking away minerals, forestry resources etc.
- Colonists replacing local rulers, armies, police and prisons with their own.
- Colonists bringing in their laws and judges.
- Colonists bringing in their administrative system.
- Implanting foreign languages e.g. English, French, Portuguese and Arabic.
- Implanting foreign religions e.g. Christianity or Islam.

74

- Replacing or attempts to replace another race through killings/genocide or assimilation through rape and killing of males (for example, in areas like Sydney in Australia, black Aboriginal people have become extinct, and they have been replaced by white Aboriginal people, descendants of the Black Aboriginal people because of a planned process to wipe-out the Black race in those areas).
- Replacing names of people and surnames and names of places and things with foreign – replacing identities.

In the colonist's mind, they want to dominate, increase their wealth, and influence, and see themselves as the 'chosen race', the other races are sub-human. Colonisation is not only physical, but cultural, psychological, social, economic and if not controlled, it can be perpetual affecting generations. Ngugi wa Thiongo (1986, p. 16) "The real aim of colonialism was to control the people's wealth: what they produced, how they produced it, and how it was distributed; to control, in other words, the entire realm of the language of real life. Colonialism imposed its control of the social production of wealth through military conquest and subsequent political dictatorship. But its most important area of domination was the mental universe of the colonised, the control, through culture, of how people perceived themselves and their relationship to the world. Economic and political control can never be complete or effective without mental control. To control a people's culture is to control their tools of self-definition in relation to others. For colonialism this involved two aspects of the same process: the destruction or the deliberate undervaluing of a people's culture, their art, dances, religions, history, geography, education, orature, and literature, and the conscious elevation of the language of the coloniser. The domination of a people's language by the language of the colonizing nations was crucial to the domination of the mental universe of the colonised. The seven dimensions of colonisation are:

1. Pre-colonisation – this period was characterised by uprooting people from their lands and enslaving them in America, Europe or other lands.
2. Colonisation of the mind – the weapons of this form of colonisation are the Abrahamic religion (Christianity and Islam); European languages (English, French, Portuguese etc.) Arabic language and European and Arabic education. This form of colonisation continues today.

3. Land colonisation – the major weapons were guns, horses, dogs, fire and European laws. This form of colonisation was largely defeated but impacts millions of people today in Africa as white people refuse to give back stolen land using European laws and so-called international laws.
4. Political colonisation – achieved by taking power from local leaders and replacing them with European Kings (e.g. the British Monarchy), administrators, laws, police and army. A major weapon was dividing the local population, coercion, taxation and bribery.
5. Extended colonialism –several colonial practices were maintained, most of them in disguise. Examples include:

   - Maintenance of the French currency in former colonies.
   - Former French colonies were forced to bank 85% (later reduced to 60%) of their currency reserves with the French government in France which invested them for the benefit of the French.
   - White people not giving up colonised land in South Africa, Zimbabwe, Namibia etc.
   - Western education, literature (books, journals, laws, guidelines etc), syllabus etc still being used. This results in miseducation.
   - Continued dominance of non-African religious and cultural institutions, particularly the Abrahamic religion.

6. Aid – aid is assistance, gift or relief provided by a family, community, organisation (donor, giver or aider) or country to another family, community, organisation or country (receiver) in the form of money (e.g. cash or grant), food, clothing, water, houses, energy, medicines, body organs (e.g. kidneys or sperms) equipment, books, toiletries, jobs (allowing people from another country to work in another), labour (e.g. experts like researchers, doctors and engineers or general like drivers), security personnel, arms, jobs, scholarships, adoption home, foster home and subsidies (e.g. cheap loans or reduced tax). Aid can be driven by humanitarian or voluntary altruism or aimed at some economic, social, cultural, diplomatic and political benefits in return.

7. Neo-colonialism – this includes all new forms of colonisation and does not include extensions of colonisation. Examples include:

- Intellectual colonialism – mass recruitment of professionals from former colonised nations that are meeting all costs of education and training but end up with no doctors, nurses, social workers, engineers etc. All this leads to loss of intellectual capital and intellectual poverty.
- New economic colonisers, for example, China.
- Threat of sanctions and actual sanctions.
- Funding of the African Union budget by foreigners, more than 50% of the budget is foreign funded.
- Structural adjustment programs.

Decolonists refuse colonial theorists' racist assumption that for Africa to develop, we need to embrace colonial thinking (philosophies, values and literature), artefacts, institutions, economies and religions. Decolonization starts at the family and community and moves onto the school through to all other institutions of society. Examples of decolonisation include:

- Fighting for independence, freedom, and liberation by whatever means, guns, pens, boycotts, terror, tongues, resistance etc. The liberation movement in Africa achieved this.
- Giving African monarchies their role and land back.
- Using African languages, orature and literature (read *Ngugi*).
- Stopping migration to former colonies for study, work, or other reasons.
- Taking back stolen resources, for example land (Robert Mugabe of Zimbabwe achieved this for his people).
- Using African philosophies, values, ethics, and methods (read *Mbigi* among others).
- Using and valuing African religions (read *Mbiti*).
- Use local laws.
- Using and valuing own culture.
- Restitution or former colonies paying so that the cost of decolonisation is met.
- Decolonising the mind.

Decolonisation is a process that involves the coloniser and the colonised. It can be measured as follows:

Stages of decolonisation	What does this mean?
Stage 0-1 (colonial)	Still at the level of colonisation.
Stage 2 (tokenistic)	There is no genuineness to decolonise. Colonial practices are maintained in disguise.
Stage 3 (transitional)	There is potential to decolonise, in between.
Stage 4 (original, indigenous)	Decolonisation has happened. Indigenous or original does not mean going back to what things were before colonisation, but where they could have been now had colonisation not been there.
Stage 5 (permanent)	Full decolonisation has been achieved.

Framework 1: A framework to measure decolonisation

This framework can be used to measure decolonisation at any level: continental, country, institutional, community or individual. It can also be used to measure decolonisation by sector – economic, political, social, cultural, religious and other. In social work, it is used to measure how these have been decolonised – syllabi, library, examinations, teaching staff, methods, fieldwork, international work, recruitment of students (do you prefer students who have passed foreign languages), language (how much do you value local languages in teaching or literature) and research. The strengths of decolonisation vary, it exists on a continuum, and it can be measured as follows:

Stage 1: Doing nothing to decolonise, maintaining the status quo.
Stage 2: Colonist led decolonisation, focuses on the interests of the coloniser.
Stage 3: Hesitation. Slow negotiation means used to decolonise.
Stage 4: Radical means used to decolonise.
Stage 5: Forceful means used to decolonise.

New colonialism (neo-colonialism)

It is also important to understand neo-colonialism, the new methods of colonisation that followed liberation wars. Neo-colonial theory is credited to Kwame Nkrumah who described it as the continuation of colonisation through several means, hidden or open. The elements of neo-colonialism are:

- Colonial monarchies still find ways to maintain dominance (e.g. forming Commonwealth institutions).
- Land and artefacts that were stolen during colonialism were not returned and claimed by colonists.
- Brain drains and migration.
- Aid.
- International organisations.
- Literature.
- Language.
- New foreign countries replacing the former colonisers e.g. China's influence in Africa.
- The United Nations, its organisations, laws, policies and conventions are used as tools to continue with colonisation.
- Whiteness, white superiority, or white supremacy continues in all industries and facets of life.
- Media and internet.
- Colonising the mind.

African social development theory

This theory is credited to (Association of Schools of Social Work, ASWEA, 1974, 1974, 1976, 1977, 1981, 1985; Gebre, 1976; Yimam, 1990). Social development is about dealing with social problems at the macro level – social policies, social structures and social institutions. Social work is often practised at the micro to mezz levels, that is the individual, family and community levels. The macro level, involving social work with the whole of society (the social), is often ignored, especially in Africa. Social development addresses this gap by working to address social policies, social structures and social institutions - it deals with social problems from a structural and holistic angle (Association of Schools of Social Work, ASWEA, 1974, 1974, 1976, 1977, 1981, 1985; Gebre, 1976; Yimam, 1990). Kaseke (2001) said social development seeks to ensure that individuals have access to resources necessary for meeting basic needs and in conditions that do not undermine their self-esteem. The pursuit of social justice and egalitarian ideals is at the core of the social development model.

"Social development emerged because of dissatisfaction with a development model that puts undue emphasis on economic growth at the neglect of social factors. Economic growth did not necessarily result in an improvement in the welfare of the people. Thus, social development emerged as an attempt to draw attention to the importance of social factors in the development process. The starting point for the social development model is that the modernisation approach has failed to transform developing countries. The benefits of economic development have not trickled down to most of the people. Instead, the wealth is concentrated in the hands of few people while the majority live in absolute poverty. Thus, the social development model represents a shift from the residual (welfaristic) model. A social development model sees the role of social work as that of facilitating social change and ultimately enabling individuals to realise their potential" (Kaseke, 2001). He concluded by saying social workers have been dealing with symptoms rather than the root causes of the problems. To change the material welfare of the poor, there is need for intervention at both the macro and micro levels.

Developmentalist theory or developmental social work theory

Unlike social development, developmental social work involves both social and economic development. Developmental strategies can be applied when doing work with individuals, groups, families, communities, and society at large. In short, the developmental approach cuts across all methods of social work. At times, is referred to as socio-economic development. Characteristics and intentions of the developmental approach are:

1. Improving poor people's productive capacity to address poverty.
2. Ensures access to means of production, particularly land, including introducing land reforms.
3. Focuses on maximising people's form of production e.g. farming, mining, fishing, trading, processing and others.
4. Creates and supports policies that support people to realise their full potential.

80

5. Focuses at both micro or local (families, villages and communities) and macro or large-scale (district, provincial and national) levels.
6. Community-level framework or plan locks into national framework or plan.
7. The social work curriculum is designed from a social development perspective.
8. Economically viable social assistance programs e.g. start-up capital, support, public assistance or others.
9. Infrastructure development.
10. Adequate funding for rural programs and rural workers.
11. Does not look at public assistance as an end, but to ensure that people become socially and economically active.
12. Casework and groupwork are not prioritised because they are remedial and palliative, they perpetuate and maintain social exclusion.
13. Economic and social strategies are meant to address poverty and underdevelopment.
14. Disagrees with western modernisation's view that poverty and underdevelopment result from the setup of African communities, lifestyles, cultures and methods.
15. Disagrees with the view that economic growth is the answer to poverty, in fact, economic growth with no human face is the facilitator of inequality.

Some roles of development and social workers are:

- Creating opportunities for economic productivity (e.g. farming, irrigation, mining, fishing, off-farm income-generating projects, self-employment, and enterprises).
- Lobbying and advocacy for social justice.
- Mobilising local savings.
- Improving people's economic productivity skills.
- Community workers mobilise the rural communities to improve infrastructure such as roads, bridges, clinics and schools.
- Assisting communities to develop development projects (proposals, plans, funding and feasibility).
- Ensuring that the community's contribution is valued, pursued and recognised.

Afriture theory

The thesis of this theory is that African orature and literature (Afriture) must not be seen as inferior to others. The major proponents are Ngugi wa Thiongo and Pio Zirimu but there are many others. Their theory says:

- African languages must be the basis of African communication, learning, memory and writing – not French, Portuguese, English, Arabic or other foreign languages.
- Language and literature carry people's culture and memories and by replacing our languages we are replacing our cultures and memories. Linguicide is when African languages are displaced and resultantly disappear because of favour of foreign languages.
- Literature is a silent colonial tool – the pen is a colonial tool in the same manner the gun was.
- Literature is a neo-colonial strategy.
- Oral literature is rich, relevant, and powerful.
- Syllabi in universities, colleges and schools must focus on African literature, and it is the role of teaching departments and academics to decolonise the syllabi.

How theories are developed?

Theories can be divided into:

- Theories that are derived directly from philosophy. These theories are part of a philosophy.
- Theories that are an interpretation of philosophy and how it is applied. These theories are developed by the community, thinkers, researchers or practitioners. The process for theory development is usually as follows:
  - Germination – a need for a theory is identified and clearly defined. This process can happen unconsciously or can be planned.
  - Seeding – a theory is grown.
  - Growth – the theory grows or sleeps.
  - Maturity – the theory is widely used.
  - Multiply – the theory can develop branches, including opposing views.

- o   Aging – the theory is used less but still influential.
- o   Spirit age – theories never sleep forever or die, they keep coming back to enhance knowledge.

Other sources of knowledge

We have so far learnt that the knowledge that we use in social work comes from philosophies, values, ethics and theories but these are not the only sources of knowledge. The other sources are:

1. Personal experience of workers, including the mistakes they make.
2. Experiences and sentiments of individuals, families and communities that we work with.
3. Research reports and journal articles.
4. Opinions of writers and thinkers in books, websites, newspapers and social media.
5. Laws and policies.
6. Models created by workers, researchers or community.
7. Cultural knowledge.
8. Spiritual knowledge contained in religious stories, books or laws.

The African Journal of Social Work (AJSW) (2019) framework of sources of knowledge.

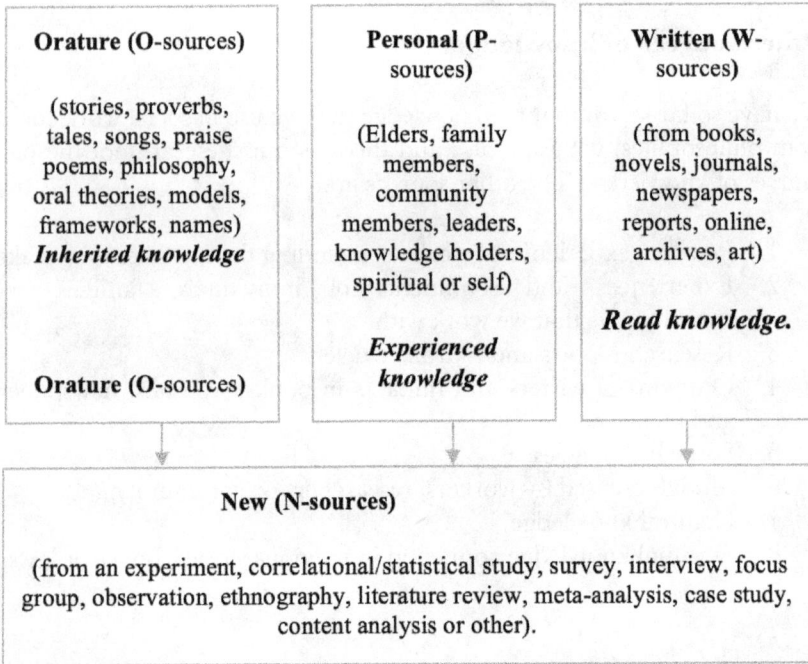

Orature (O-sources)	Personal (P-sources)	Written (W-sources)
(stories, proverbs, tales, songs, praise poems, philosophy, oral theories, models, frameworks, names) *Inherited knowledge*	(Elders, family members, community members, leaders, knowledge holders, spiritual or self)	(from books, novels, journals, newspapers, reports, online, archives, art) *Read knowledge.*
Orature (O-sources)	*Experienced knowledge*	

New (N-sources)

(from an experiment, correlational/statistical study, survey, interview, focus group, observation, ethnography, literature review, meta-analysis, case study, content analysis or other).

Framework 2: Classification of sources of knowledge

All the sources are useful for social work, including oral sources.

Guidance: using Ubuntu theories and models social services

The theories used must be relevant to the situation. When you are farming, you do not need kitchen tools, you need farming tools. There are several ways to use theories, some are listed below.

- Use Ubuntu theories to interpret philosophy, values and ethics.
- Use Ubuntu theories to identify and understand social problems.
- Use Ubuntu theories to inform methods of solving social problems.
- Using Ubuntu theories to inform research methods.

- Use Ubuntu theories to predict what is likely to happen.
- Use Ubuntu theories to understand the past.
- Use Ubuntu theories to design appropriate, culturally relevant and decolonial approaches to social work.

Summary

- Theories are, by definition, the interpretation of philosophy, values and ethics to make them 'appliable' to a practice situation.
- Theories can be oral or written.
- African theoretical ideas are largely not written, or orature, they belong to the community.

Further and advanced knowledge

- What have been the shortcomings of African theories and how can these be addressed?
- If you were to contribute a new philosophical idea, what would that be? How will it have its foundation in existing philosophical ideas?

Questions for in-class assessments and examinations

1. What are the characteristics and strengths of African theories?
2. Discuss Samkange's theory of Ubuntu.
3. Identify five theories contained in the orature and describe how you think the theory started and how it can be used in social work.
4. In some cases, workers in Africa do not use theories or use non-African theories. Identify one area of social or development work where theories are lacking. Propose a theory.
5. Use Yes or No to answer the following questions (answers are at the end of this chapter):
   a. Indigenous theories exist.
   b. Africa has its theories.
   c. I can develop a theory.
   d. Theories of Africa reduce the quality of my writing.
   e. In the hierarchy of knowledge, theories are higher than philosophy.
   f. Theories are colonisable.
   g. Theories are always written.

h. Theories are found in stories, art and symbols.
i. There are many theorists in Africa.
j. Theories from outside that can be harmful to Africa.

Potential questions for research

1. Design research proposal to identify oral theories that could be used in social work.
2. Find two workers working in human services and do a discussion about the theories that they use and why they use those theories.
3. Do a document analysis of 10 of your subject or course outlines. Identify the theories in each of the outlines and make conclusions about their relevance to Africa.
4. In some cases, workers in Africa do not use theories or use non-African theories. Do research to identify areas of social or development work where theories are lacking.
5. Select two research methods from the list below and explain how they fit the philosophy of Africa.

   a. Stories approach
   b. Orature review
   c. Experiential method
   d. Auto-ethnographic method
   e. Diaries
   f. Notes
   g. Art
   h. *Dare* or *indaba* method.
   i. *Baliano* (plural is *mabaliano*) method.
   j. Decolonised interviewing
   k. Insider research method
   l. Side-by-side approach or collaborative research
   m. Narrative approach
   n. Self-praise or self-poetry or praise poetry
   o. Griot approach
   p. Community projects
   q. Stories research approach (SRA)
   r. Tree of life approach
   s. Dialogue approach.
   t. Action research

u. Visual methods
v. Social media reactions (sentiments) approach
w. Work party research
x. Task method
y. Walks method
z. Prayer method
aa. Experimental approaches
bb. *Kuumba* (creativity) method
cc. Mixed methods

Fieldwork ideas

1. Identify 10 fieldwork reports that were written by students on placement. Identify the theories in each of the outlines and make conclusions about their relevance to Africa.
2. Using social media analysis, identify five emerging theories in Africa that are relevant to social work practice and elaborate how each could contribute to social and developmental work.

Key terms and their meanings

African theory – a theory founded on African knowledge (including philosophy, values and ethics).

Emerging theory – a theory that is new, at infancy or development stage.

Inherited knowledge – knowledge passed on to present generations by previous generations which will also be passed on to future generations.

Myths of theories – the wrong belief that African people cannot develop theories but should use theories developed from outside. Everyone can develop a theory.

Oral theory – a theory that is not written but exists in stories, proverbs, actions and songs.

Research – is a process of investigation that results in new or improved knowledge.

Theory – an oral or written statement or proposition about how knowledge (including philosophy, values and ethics) can be applied to a learning, practice or research situation.

References and recommended readings

Africa Social Work and Development Network (2023). African Theories of Social Work and Development. Accessed from https://africasocialwork.net/african-theories-of-social-work/ on 12 December 2023

Association of Schools of Social Work in Africa (ASWEA). (1973). Case Studies of Social Development in Africa, Vol. 1. Addis Ababa: ASWEA publication. https://africasocialwork.net/association-of-social-work-education-in-africa-aswea-1965-to-1989/

Association of Schools of Social Work in Africa (ASWEA). (1974). Relationship between Social Work Education and National Social Development Planning, Doc. 6. Addis Ababa: ASWEA publication.

Association of Schools of Social Work in Africa (ASWEA). (1974). Case Studies of Social Development in Africa, vol. 2. Addis Ababa: ASWEA publication

Association of Schools of Social Work in Africa (ASWEA). (1976). Realities and aspirations of social work education in Africa, Doc. 11. Addis Ababa: ASWEA publication.

Association of Schools of Social Work in Africa (ASWEA). (1977). The Role of Social Development Education in Africa's Struggle for Political and Economic Independence, Doc. 12. Addis Ababa: ASWEA publication.

Association of Schools of Social Work in Africa (ASWEA). (1981). Social Development Training in Africa: Experiences of the 1970s and Emerging Trends of the 1980s, Doc. 17. Addis Ababa: ASWEA publication.

Association of Schools of Social Work in Africa (ASWEA). (1982). Survey of Curricula of Social Development Training Institutions in Africa, Doc. 18. Addis Ababa: ASWEA publication.

Association of Schools of Social Work in Africa (ASWEA). (1982). Seminar on the organization and delivery of social services to rural areas in Africa, Doc. 19. Addis Ababa: ASWEA publication.

Association of Schools of Social Work in Africa (ASWEA). (1985). Training for Social Development: Methods of Intervention to Improve People's Participation in Rural Transformation in Africa with Special Emphasis on Women, Doc. 20. Addis Ababa: ASWEA publication.

Kaseke, E. (2001). *Social development as a model of social work practice*: the experience of Zimbabwe. School of Social Work Staff Papers. Harare, School of Social Work.

Kaunda, K. D. (2007). *Zambian humanism, 40 years later*. Sunday Post, October 28. 20-25.

Khupe, C. and Keane, M. (2017). Towards an African Education Research Methodology: *Decolonising New Knowledge*. *Educational Research for Social Change*. 6. 25-37.

Council of Social Workers Zimbabwe (CSW) (2012). Social workers code of ethics. Statutory Instrument 146 of 2012.

Bangura, A. K. (2005). 'Ubuntugogy': An African educational paradigm that transcends pedagogy, andragogy, ergonagy and heutagogy. *Journal of Third World Studies, XXII (2): 13-53.*

Chilisa, B. (2012). *Indigenous research methodologies.* Los Angeles: Sage.

Dziro, C. and Rufurwokuda, A. (2013). Post-institutional integration challenges faced by children who were raised in children's homes in Zimbabwe: The Case of "Ex-girl" Programme for one children's home in Harare, Zimbabwe. *Greener Journal of Social Sciences, 3, 268-277.*

Gade, C. B. N. (2011). The historical development of the written discourses on Ubuntu. *South African Journal of Philosophy, 30, 303-329.*

Gade, C. B. N. (2012). What is Ubuntu? Different interpretations among South Africans of African descent. *South African Journal of Philosophy, 31, 484-503.*

Gebre, S. S. (1976). Government and the promotion of social equality – a comparative analysis of selected developing countries. Thesis. University of Michigan.

Metz, T. (2016). Recent philosophical approaches to social protection: From capability to Ubuntu. Global Social Policy, 16(2), 132–150

Mugumbate, J. (2020). Samkange's theory of Ubuntu and its contribution to a decolonised social work pedagogy. In Morley, C. (Ed.), Ablett, P. (Ed.), Noble, C. (Ed.), Cowden, S. (Ed.). Routledge Handbook of Critical Pedagogies. London: Routledge.

Mugumbate, J. R. and Chereni, A. (2019). Using African Ubuntu theory in social work with children in Zimbabwe. *African Journal of Social Work, 9(1), 27-35.*

Mugumbate, J., and Nyanguru, A. (2013). Exploring African philosophy: The value of Ubuntu in social work. *African Journal of Social Work, 3(1), 82-100.*

Mupedziswa, R., Rankopo, M. and Mwansa, L. (2019). Ubuntu as a Pan-African Philosophical Framework for Social Work in Africa. *Social Work Practice in Africa Indigenous and Innovative Approaches.* Eds J. M. Twikirize and H. Spitzer. Kampala: Fountain.

Ngugi wa Thiongo (1986). *Decolonising the Mind. The politics of language in African literature.* Nairobi, Heinemann Kenya/Harare, Zimbabwe Publishing House.

Rankopo, M. J., and Osei-Hwedie, K. (2011). Globalization and Culturally Relevant Social Work: African Perspectives on Indigenization. International Social Work, 1, 137-157.

Samkange, S. and Samkange, T. M. (1980). Hunhu or Ubuntu: A Zimbabwean indigenous political philosophy. Harare: Graham Publishing.

Taranhike, D. S. (2021). Integral Kumusha: A Case of Buhera – Towards Self-Sufficiency in Zimbabwe via Nhakanomics. PhD Thesis. Da Vinci University and TRANS4M Academy for Integral Transformation.

Tshoose, C. (2009). The emerging role of the constitutional value of Ubuntu for informal social security in South Africa. *African Journal of Legal Studies, 3, 12–19.*

van Breda, A. D. (2019). Developing the notion of Ubuntu as African theory for social work practice. Social Work, 55(4), 439-450.

Whitworth, A. and Wilkinson, K. (2013). Tackling child poverty in South Africa: Implications of Ubuntu for the system of social grants. Development Southern Africa, 30, 121–134.

Yimam, A. (1990). *Social Development in Africa, 1950-1985: Methodological Perspectives and Future Prospects.* Aldershot: Gower.

Zirimu, P. (1973). An approach to Black Aesthetics, in Pio Zirimu and Andrew Gurr, eds. (1973). *Black Aesthetics: Papers from a Colloquium Held at the University of Nairobi, June, 1971.* East African Literature Bureau.

Zirimu, P. (1973). Oracy as a tool of development, in Pio Zirimu and Andrew Gurr, eds. *Black Aesthetics: Papers from a Colloquium Held at the University of Nairobi, June, 1971.* East African Literature Bureau. with Austin Bukenya

Answers to Yes or No Questions

a. Yes
b. Yes
c. Yes
d. No
e. No
f. Yes
g. No
h. Yes
i. Yes
j. Yes

CHAPTER 4

History of social services and social work in Africa

Introduction

Now that we have covered philosophy, values, ethics, and theories, we now turn to the history of social services and social work in Africa. The development of social work in Africa has taken several but related phases. These include the customary indigenous phase, missionary phase, colonial-missionary phase, African philanthropists' phase, independence phase and indigenized-developmental phase. This chapter traces the five phases in the development of the profession. After the phases, we will provide information about social work institutions and publications across Africa.

Objectives of this chapter

By writing this chapter, we hope to achieve the following:

- Share the stages that led to present-day social services and social work.
- Showcase the founders of professional social services in Africa and social work.
- Describe the work of early and present-day institutions of social work in Africa.
- Provide ideas for research and fieldwork.
- Help students of social work to see the value of history in understanding, planning, and evaluating social services.
- Assessments that are suitable for the local context.

- Research questions and methods that are appropriate to the local context.
- Fieldwork, workplace-based and community-based learning is contextual.
- Guide on using Ubuntu to understand the history of social services in Africa.

Skills and competencies addressed in this chapter

By the end of this chapter, readers will be expected to have acquired the following skills and competencies:

- Applying historical knowledge in understanding social work, shaping skills and making interventions more relevant to Africa.
- Valuing the work of our predecessors.
- Using Africa's aspirations as passed from previous generations.
- Decolonising social services and social work.
- Answer questions or assessments about the topic of this chapter.
- Create research questions and methods that are appropriate to the local context.
- Plan fieldwork, workplace-based and community-based learning that is contextual.

Overview

From time immemorial, social problems for Africans were handled using local cultural indigenous methods. Africans have several ways of preventing social ills and ensuring the social functioning of their families, villages and societies. Before colonization, systems that grew naturally were in place to provide welfare to the vulnerable. Some of these systems were merged with or submerged in foreign ways of welfare with the coming of missionaries, traders and colonialists. Colonisation brought with it numerous upheavals including colonial wars against imperialists. Other challenges created include landlessness due to the dislocation of people caused by colonial settlers, and industrialization which eventually created urban centres. The creation of urban centres resulted in another social problem, the migration of people in search of jobs. This led to the urban centres growing rapidly, resulting in several social problems: unemployment, homelessness and overcrowding for black people. For the white population, problems of vagrancy, delinquency, and destitution increased among their children and youths. In response, the white settlers introduced a model of social welfare based on western values. To support this model, they hired probation officers from Europe and started training social welfare staff based on a western curriculum. Initially, the social services were directed at white settlers but later included blacks as urban social challenges multiplied. The increasing urban plight resulted in the emergence of philanthropists.

History of the handling of social problems

- From the beginning – Africans developed ways and means to prevent and address social problems that were shaped by their philosophy – religion, values, knowledge, and aspirations.
- 332BC – North Africa was invaded by the Greeks and Romans of Europe.
- 1100 – North Africa was invaded by Arabs, and they spread southwards.
- 15000 – Christian missionaries colonised Africa, focusing on colonizing religion and minds. They provided social services that were meant to steal Africa's religion and thinking capacity. They provided health, education, vocational training and charity.
- 1500 – Europeans colonised and enslaved Africa south of the Sahara. They provided social services which were focused on exploiting African resources and Africans.
- 1884 – Europeans divided Africa's land among themselves at a conference initially called the Congo Conference held in Berlin, Germany, and now most known as the Berlin Conference.
- 1931 – the first training program for white people in Africa related to social work was started at the Transvaal University College leading to the creation of the Department of Sociology and Applied Sociology at the University of Pretoria. This was followed by the University of Stellenbosch (1931), University of Cape Town (1933).
- 1934 – Alexandria School in Egypt (for the French) in, the Cairo School of Social Work (1937) by the Egyptian Association for Social Studies (EASS) (renamed Higher Institute of Social Work

in Cairo in 1972); 1939 - Egypt formed the Ministry of Social Affairs.

- Jan H. Hofmeyr School of Social Work, South Africa (for the training of Black people) (1941-1960).
- Ghana (1945) – (The list of early schools is provided later)
- 1950 – Decolonisation escalated; several countries liberated themselves.
- 1963 – Organisation of African Unity (OAU) was formed.
- 1970 – Mali closed two schools of social work that were using a French curriculum and created the National Training Centre for Social Work and Community Development/Centre National de Développement which was a rural-focused 4-year.
- 1971 – Association of Social Work Education in Africa (ASWEA) was formed in Addis Ababa, Ethiopia because of dissatisfaction with western models of social services and curricula with funding from the African Union, IASSW, United Nations and other international organisations.
- 1977 – African Centre for Applied Research and Training in Social Development.
- 1990s – Structural Adjustment Programs (SAPs) instigated by the (World Bank (WB), International Monetary Fund (IMF) and the World Trade Organization (WTO). These were plans for economic development that focused on reducing social spending. The results were dismal.
- 1989 – ASWEA stopped operation due to lack of funding, the death of the Secretary General and political unrest in Ethiopia where it was headquartered.
- 1990s – The Human Immuno-Deficiency Virus (HIV), which causes AIDS, spread rapidly resulting in deaths and orphanhood. Urban areas were the hardest hit and were the major source of the virus.
- 1994 – South Africa became the final African country to gain political independence.
- 1994 – EASS was formed.
- 2005 – ASSWA was formed.
- 2019 – Africa Social Work and Development was formed (ASWDNet) (started as ASWNet).

Five phases in the development of social services and social work in Africa

Customary indigenous phase

In Africa, since time immemorial, there have been people interested in preventing death, disability, sickness, and suffering or making life easier and enjoyable for others. This has continued even up to this day.

The first phase is customary because social services were provided according to custom and they were indigenous because they did not have foreign influence. This phase was made up of customary, indigenous or indigenous social support systems. Social problems were seen because of individual shortcomings, evil spells or family failure. Ubuntu was the guiding principle. Ubuntu values the family and community and theorises that an individual person becomes human only through working with and contributing to their family and community. Other Ubuntu values include hospitality, care for others, being willing to go the extra mile for the sake of another (Samkange and Samkange, 1980).

Theories that best describe the application of 'social work' during this phase include *Unhu/Ubuntu*, communal theory, family theory, African systems theory, African religion theory and others (Mugumbate and Nyanguru, 2013, Mugumbate and Chereni, 2019). Using these theories, the target populations for 'social work' included the poor, prisoners, refugees, the distressed, family members, the sick, orphans and others. During this phase, social work roles were diffused in the community, no individual had this ultimate responsibility, but the community was the centre for problem solving.

This phase has not ended and continues even when professional social work is now present in Africa. Most social problems are solved in the family and community without social workers.

Missionary phase (from 1500 to 1900)

This phase is termed so because missionaries arrived from western and eastern countries to spread their religious beliefs and values (Bar-On, 1999). In spreading their values, they intended to change Africa's religion or replace it with the Abrahamic religion, mainly through the Christian faith and the Islamic faith. These Christian and some Islamic faith missionaries started arriving around 1500. Their teachings were resisted because they despised local forms of worship and beliefs, and made their religious books, symbols, institutions, histories and figures superior. They competed amongst themselves and were colonists themselves. They made it easier for other colonisers to come and provided them with maps and information about the local situation. The most horrible crime of the missionaries was to make people submissive with messages like 'god wants people who will struggle on earth so that they inherit his kingdom', 'if someone slaps you, give him the other side to slap', and 'you shall forgive countless times'. They spoke of a god of white people, who 'opened up his kingdom for heathens.' The heathens were us, Black people. Besides teaching submissiveness using their holy books, they also enticed people using charitable gifts and services like education and health. They started new institutions to advance their vision including mission centres that had clinics and schools. The cadre at these institutions was the church leader, mainly a European or Arabian missionary. The London Missionary Society was one of such institutions. Sadly, the work of these missionaries was inherited by other Africans who today preach the same message of doom and cause mass psychological fear of the unknown.

Colonial-missionary phase

This phase is called colonial because it started with the colonization of Africa by Europeans. During this period, national and urban social services became more centralised by the colonists with the help of missionaries who had already planted western religious values in most communities. The Europeans introduced Departments of Native Affairs to deal with Black people and helped move colonised communities from their productive land into overcrowded unproductive reserves (Fisher, 2010). In new towns, the administrators were assisted by the church and volunteers to address emerging social challenges.

This period, saw the arrival of probation workers from Europe who were imported to work in African social welfare systems. The main role of these probation workers was to deal with juvenile delinquency, mainly for children of White settlers. Social problems were largely seen because of urbanisation and industrialization, so, professional services were relegated to Europeans who were living in urban areas. Later, these services expanded to African townships to contain social problems that affected the lives of White people.

During this period, social services were funded by colonial governments, municipalities, corporates, and donors. Methods utilized were mainly curative, characterized by casework and social welfare. In most if not all

97

rural communities, professional social work did not reach-out, but remained on stage one, the customary phase.

This phase relied on theories of colonialism, apartheid and residualism. Using these theories, the target populations for social work included delinquent White children and youths but also Black workers and so-called African vagrants. Practice settings included the Department of Social Welfare, municipalities, and industries. Methods of social work that applied at this stage included casework and community work. Social work during this phase was marked by segregating practice, in which delivery of service was on black and white separatist basis, starting at first with no services for blacks, because blacks were expected to reside in the rural areas with only a few employed males being allowed into the urban areas without their families. In colonial Zimbabwe, indigenous populations relied on their families, extended families, clans, and communities for support since social welfare provisions were discriminatory in nature (Moyo, 2007). Urban areas became dormitory corridors for men who came to work for the white populace and retired in their rural areas, without any employment social security. The separation of families for employment purposes in the urban dormitory corridors created many social problems such as breakdown of marriages, juvenile delinquencies and prostitution.

Liberation phase (from 1930 to 1994)

This is phase dates to the start of Black social service providers in the 1930s until the last colonised country in Africa, South Africa, was politically liberated in 1994. During the colonial period, the first black do-gooders and philanthropists emerged to challenge discriminatory social services and to provide services to the Black population in the 1930s. It is also the same phase Black social workers emerged. Some of these people are discussed later.

Indigenous-post-colonial-developmental phase (from 1994 to present day)

This phase has two outstanding but interdependent approaches, developmental and indigenous social work but also increased social work training and internationalization. During this phase, there has been a louder call for the decolonisation of social work to come up with indigenised and authentic methods (Kaseke, 1991, 2001; Mupedziswa and

98

Sinkamba, 2014; Hall 1990; Mabvurira, 2018). Developmental social work is seen as the most appropriate method for Zimbabwe's situation because it builds individual income through improving skills, production, infrastructure, markets, savings, insurance, and ecology. This is because imported social work failed to expand to all communities due to factors including western values and a lack of fiscal resources. The problems that colonial social work had come to address had multiplied several times, and populations in need of social work services expanded rapidly especially soon after independence (Osei-Hwedie, 1993). Poverty became clearer in both rural and urban areas, with more people moving to urban areas to escape rural poverty. Social workers then proposed developmental social work that seeks to build individual income through improving skills, production, infrastructure, markets, savings, insurance, and ecology.

Theories for this phase include social development, indigenization, Ubuntu, decolonization, liberation, action research, independence, asset-based, developmentalism, human rights, empowerment, social justice, sustainability, people-centred development and many others.

African social work is going back where it started, and where it should be. In the beginning, social services were governed by indigenous customs and they were offered in the community. This ensured that everyone had access to forms of help. This changed with the coming of missionaries and colonialists, who brought western systems. Later, they merged western with local systems, but they were only able to reach communities in towns, and these were mainly White communities. There is a move towards expanding social work and making it more developmental and relevant. By making it more relevant, it returned to phase one, the phase of indigenous social work. The most recent definition was provided in the AJSW. The definition says:

> *Social work is an academic discipline and profession that embraces and enhances long-held methods of addressing life challenges in order to achieve social functioning, development, cohesion and liberation using diverse African indigenous knowledges and values enshrined in the family, community, society, environment and spirituality (AJSW, 2020, p.1).*

While this definition still favours professional social work at the expense of indigenous social work, it is strong in that it recognises the importance of long-held methods of addressing life challenges. It also acknowledges five important elements of African society: family, community, society, environment and spirituality.

99

Biography of African social services (1870-1950)

There are many Africans who contributed to the founding and development of social services in Africa. However, the work of these people was not fully recognised for a very long time, and their contribution has been marginalised. The history of social services in Africa has been written from a colonial perspective which sidelines African actors and stories, something this book address by sharing the biographies of Charlotte Makgomo-Mannya Maxeke (1871-1939), Zahia Marzouk (1906 – 1988), Mai Musodzi Chibhaga Ayema (1885-1952), Jairos Jiri (1921 – 1982), Wangari Maathai (1940 –2011), Kenneth Kaunda (1924 – 2021), Regina Gelana Twala (1908-1968), Nnoseng Ellen Kate Kuzwayo (1914-2006), Winnie Madikizela-Mandela (1936–2016), Joshua Mqabuko Nyongolo Nkomo (1917 – 1999), Priscilla Ingasiani Abwao (1924 – 2009), Aïcha Chenna (1941 –2022), Jember Teferra (1943 –2021), Mitri Widad (1927-2007), Victoria Fikile Chitepo (1928 –2016), Mame Seck Mbacké (1947 – 2018), Arega Yimam (not known – about 1989) and Selassie Seyoum Gebre (1936 – not known).

Charlotte Makgomo-Mannya Maxeke (1871-1939)

Picture 2: Charlotte Makgomo-Mannya Maxeke (1871-1939), South Africa

This picture is in the public domain. We use it in this book ethically, and with respect to the memory of this person, their family, community and the person who created this image.

Mama Maxeke was born in 1871 (other sources say 1874) in Ramokgopa, Polokwane District (then Pietersburg District), Limpopo Province, South Africa. At this point there was no formal social work training globally. Those who practised 'social work' at this time were either educated in other disciplines or had skills in welfare, management, church or political work. She was the first welfare worker or 'social worker' in South Africa, was 'a campaigner for women's and workers' rights and was a 'native welfare officer' or parole officer for juvenile delinquents at the Johannesburg Magistrate's Courts (Smith, 2021, p. 165). She obtained a degree in 1901 (others say 1902 or 3) from the University of Wilberforce in the USA, becoming the first black South African to do so. She organised women to protest segregation laws, including the infamous pass laws. She wrote about social injustices in isiXhosa.

Zahia Marzouk (1906 – 1988)

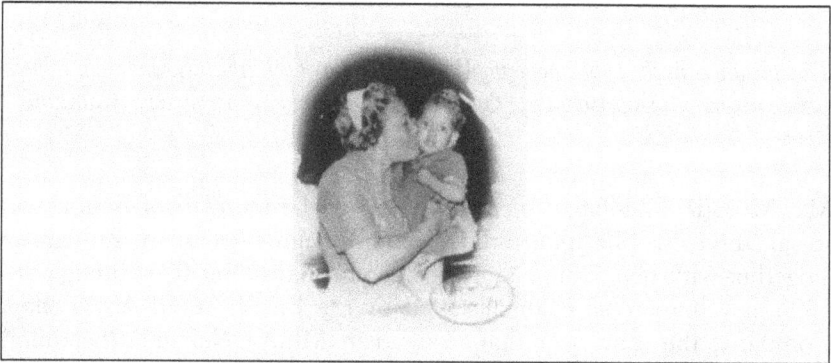

Picture 3: Zahia Mazuk (1906-1988), Egypt

This picture is in the public domain. We use it in this book ethically, and with respect to the memory of this person, their family, community and the person who created this image.

Zahia Marzouk was a teacher, psychiatric social worker and an activist. She was trained in teaching and medical social work. She was from Egypt. She is most known as an advocate of family planning. With others, she started Egypt's first school of social work in Alexandria and another one in Cairo and this work led to the establishment of Egypt's Ministry of Social Affairs. She formed disability and rehabilitation organisations and also the

Regional Federation of Social Services, the Happy Childhood Association, the Institute for Training and Research in Family Planning and the Alexandria Family Planning Association.

Mai Musodzi Chibhaga Ayema (1885-1952)

Picture 4: Mai (Mother) Musodzi Chibhaga Ayema (1885-1952), Zimbabwe. Mai Musodzi and Musodzi Hall in Mbare, Harare, Zimbabwe

This picture is in the public domain. We use it in this book ethically, and with respect to the memory of this person, their family, community and the person who created this image.

Mai Musodzi Chibhaga Ayema was one of the founders of Zimbabwe's social services. She pioneered women's rights work in Zimbabwe. Together with her siblings, they became orphans after Chimurenga 1 of 1896, a war to repel colonialists led by the British South Africa (BSA) Company, the same war that resulted in Mbuya Nehanda (her aunt), Sekuru Kaguvi and other leaders being hanged by white colonialists. Mai founded Harare African Women's Club in 1938. She served on the Native Advisory Board and the National Welfare Society's African committee where she advocated for rights of black people. Mbare, Zimbabwe's oldest suburb for Black people, has a Recreation Hall renamed Mai Musodzi Hall in her honour (pictured above). Like Jairosi Jiri, she became a social reformer, do-gooder and philanthropist of good standing in her era.

Jairos Jiri (1921 – 1982)

Born in 1921, Baba Jairosi Jiri was not a trained in social services but is one of the early people who provided social services at a national scale

102

using the values of *unhu* that form the bedrock of Zimbabwe's social functioning.

Picture 5: Baba (Father) Jairos Jiri (1921-1982), Zimbabwe

This picture is in the public domain. We use it in this book ethically, and with respect to the memory of this person, their family, community and the person who created this image.

The legend learned about indigenous forms of social assistance from his parents and community. He perfected these values with work that he did as a general hand at a rehabilitation facility in Bulawayo. The facility catered for former African 'world war' fighters. He founded the Jairos Jiri Association for Disabled People in 1940 initially using his own labour and resources. In 1982 when he died, he was honoured with National Hero of Zimbabwe status but his family opted to be buried in his rural home village of Bikita instead of at the National Heroes Acre in Harare. Later, the government of Zimbabwe honoured him by awarding him the Jairosi Jiri Humanitarian Award given to people who contribute significantly to helping others. In recognition, he received numerous other awards nationally, regionally, and nationally.

By 1982, the association he founded, had grown from one centre in 1950 to 16 centres. These include schools, special schools for the deaf and blind, hostels and homes, vocational training centres, agriculture skills training centres, clinics, orthopaedic workshops and satellite units, a community-based rehabilitation programme, craft shops and gender empowerment programs (Mugumbate, 2020). His work has been analysed and two models have been created (Models 1 and 2).

Baba Jiri charity or philanthropy model (The HOPESS model)

H	Have natural values of *hunhu*
O	Observe the environment for opportunities to help.
P	Provide help using your own physical, financial and other resources.
E	Encourage and treat people you want to help as your friends and family.
S	Seek outside help.
S	Start and sustain a charity organisation.

Model 1: Jiri charity and philanthropy model (The HOPESS model)

Baba Jiri rehabilitation model (TO PARENT model)

T	Take people you want to help as your friends or family (*ukama*)
O	Only use existing facilities like friends, hospitals and homes (*ujamaa*).
P	Provide resources like transport people to facilities because they may not be able to go on their own.
A	Adequate care, education and support. Provide practical ideas about how rehabilitation could be done.
R	Reduce stigma and cost of care by providing housing (institutionalization).
E	Enterprises (*ushavi*) for income.
N	Need for supporting carers like his wife and friends.
T	Training opportunities for self-reliance.

Model 2: Jiri rehabilitation model (TO PARENT model)

Wangari Maathai (1940 –2011)

This picture used in this section is in the public domain. We use it in this book ethically, and with respect to the memory of this person, their family, community and the person who created this image.

Picture 6: Wangari Maathai (1940-2011), Kenya

Wangari Maathai was born in Ihithe village, Tetu division, Nyeri District, Kenya. Her work transformed families, communities and society in several ways. Wangarĩ Muta Maathai, Kenya formed the Green Belt Movement to champion the planting of trees, environmental conservation, and women's rights. Only when communities recapture the positive aspects of their culture will people relearn how to love themselves and what is theirs.

Kenneth Kaunda (1924 – 2021)

Picture 7: Kenneth Kaunda (1924-2021), Zambia

This picture is in the public domain. We use it in this book ethically, and with respect to the memory of this person, their family, community and the person who created this image.

Kenneth Kaunda was a pan-Africanist, teacher, welfare officer, farmer, politician, theorist, thinker, philosopher and philanthropist. In social work, we will remember not only for his pan-African ideals but for being the founder of the theory and philosophy of African humanism. He was born at Lubwa Mission in Chinsali, then part of Northern Rhodesia, now

105

Zambia, on 28th April 1924. He together with his compatriots led a struggle against African colonisation, and later became Zambia's founding president from 1962 to 1991, 27 years. In Zambia he is remembered for advancing education, health, uniting over 73 tribes (using the "one Zambia one Nation" motto which he coined) and being a selfless people-centred leader. In Africa, he is remembered for supporting African liberation. As a young professional he worked as a teacher at the Upper Primary School and Boarding Master at Lubwa and then Headmaster at Lubwa from 1943 to 1945 in the then Northern Rhodesia. He then worked as a teacher in Tanzania before trying work opportunities in Salisbury and Bindura Mine. In Tanzania he was influenced by the work President Mwalimu Julius Nyerere was spearheading, particularly pan-Africanism and ujamaa. This led him to think about African liberation and African ways of thinking and doing things. The result was him becoming a nationalist and pan-Africanist. He wrote a book about African humanism, Ubuntu. This is an important piece of literature for African social work. After leaving politics, Kaunda focused on philanthropy. He founded the Kenneth Kaunda Children of Africa Foundation, focusing on the effects of HIV/AIDS on children but also the military. Like Thabo Mbeki, his guiding principle was 'you can't defeat AIDS without defeating poverty'. The major themes and features of Kaunda's pan-African model are:

1. Need for maintaining an African overarching philosophy in all spheres of life – political, economic and social.
2. Doing away with colonial mentality, breaking with the colonial past.
3. Appreciation of African values, heritage, and worldviews.
4. Socialism – ensuring that the means production, distribution, and exchange is community-owned and controlled.
5. Authentic African identity.
6. African spirituality.

Regina Gelana Twala (1908-1968)

Picture 8: Regina Gelana Twala (1908-1968) (Image from The Wall of Great Africans)

This picture is in the public domain. We use it in this book ethically, and with respect to the memory of this person, their family, community and the person who created this image.

In 1948, Regina Twala became one of two women to get a social science degree from University of the Witwatersrand. She was also one of the first to start writing about social issues in her country. Under colonial apartheid, many of her several manuscripts were deemed unfit for publication. In 1913, the white repressive rulers of South Africa passed the Native Land Act, shared most of the land of black people among themselves and moved black people to crowded urban villages. This is what Gelana, her family and community experienced when she was 30 years old – they were moved from rural Natal to Johannesburg. She later studied social work at the Jan Hofmeyr School of Social Work where Minnie Mandela and Joshua Nkomo also studied. After finishing the program, she could not find a job and ended up as a domestic worker at a home of white people. This shows the inappropriateness of western styled social work education in Africa. As an activist, she was jailed in 1952 after taking part in the popular Defiance Campaign against colonisation. She did more activism in Eswatini where his husband came from. Her research work on women and African society was remarkable but was not recognised but the white researchers she worked with got awards because

107

of her work. A key pillar of her research was her refusal that researcher and anthropologist Hilda Kuper, who was white, owned 'research sites and research subjects.' For her, this was absurd. Another white researcher, an anthropologist from Sweden, had Twala do research without credit. Kuper is known in the western world for that research, but Regina is not known at home and abroad.

Nnoseng Ellen Kate Kuzwayo (1914-2006)

Picture 9: Nnoseng Ellen Kate Kuzwayo (1914-2006), Lesotho and South Africa

This picture is in the public domain. We use it in this book ethically, and with respect to the memory of this person, their family, community and the person who created this image.

Nnoseng Ellen Kate Kuzwayo was a born in Lesotho and lived in South Africa. She was a teacher, social worker and politician. At the age of 39, she enrolled to do a social work degree at the Jan Hofmeyr School of Social Work on top of a higher diploma in social work from the University of Witwatersrand. She worked for the Johannesburg City Council, later the South African Association of Youth Clubs and for the YWCA-Dube Center. She became President of the Black Consumers' Union, member of the executive committee of the Urban Foundation. She published two books: Call me Woman (1985) and Sit and Listen: Stories from South Africa (1996). The *Star* publication awarded Ellen the Woman of the Year award in 1979. She got an honorary doctorate from the then-University of Natal, University of Port Elizabeth and University of Witwatersrand. Appointed ANC Member of Parliament in 1994.

Winnie Madikizela-Mandela (1936–2016)

Picture 10: Winnie Madikizela-Mandela (1936-2016), South Africa

This picture is in the public domain. We use it in this book ethically, and with respect to the memory of this person, their family, community and the person who created this image.

She married Madiba Nelson Mandela in 1958. Mrs Winnie Madikizela-Mandela trained at the Jan Hofmeyr School of Social Work beginning in 1953 and finishing in 1955. This was the same college attended by Joshua Nkomo in Johannesburg. She worked at Baragwanath Hospital after refusing a scholarship to go to the USA. She became more interested in social justice activism and research on infant mortality and other topics among Black people (Allucia and Masoga, 2019). One of her major research findings was that high infant mortality rate among township dwellers, it was 10 deaths in every 1,000 births. She was also interested in HIV/AIDS and land repossession. In 1990, Winnie was appointed African National Congress's the head of social welfare. In 2019, the University of South Africa posthumously honoured her with a doctorate in social work for contributing to social work with individuals, groups and communities

109

in South Africa. After marrying, she continued her political activism, resulting in her being restricted and monitored, her home being raided and her being jailed.

Joshua Mqabuko Nyongolo Nkomo (1917 – 1999)

Picture 11: Joshua Mkabuko Nyongolo Nkomo (1917-1999), Zimbabwe

This picture is in the public domain. We use it in this book ethically, and with respect to the memory of this person, their family, community and the person who created this image.

The first trained black social worker in Zimbabwe, Joshua Nkomo, is known more for liberation and nationalism than social work. Joshua Nkomo was born in Bukalanga or Bulilima, now known as Semokwe Reserve, Matabeleland South and was one of eight children. After primary school, he did a carpentry course at the Tsholotsho Government Industrial School and then attended Adams College and the Jan H. Hofmeyr School of Social Work in South Africa where he met Nelson Mandela and other future nationalist leaders. It was at the Jan Hofmeyr School of Social Work that he was awarded a Bachelor of Arts Degree in Social Science in 1952. He became a highly influential Zimbabwean, revolutionary leader who led in landmark trade unionism and the first political movement against the oppressive minority government of Southern Rhodesia. He was jailed for ten years by Rhodesia's white minority government. He joined the trade union movement for black rail workers and rose to the leadership of the

110

Railway Workers Union and then to the leadership of the Southern Rhodesian chapter of the African National Congress in 1952 (later the Southern Rhodesia African National Congress). He served as the president of the National Democratic Party (NDP), Zimbabwe African Peoples Union (ZAPU) and various government portfolios including Vice President of Zimbabwe and ZANU PF under the Unity Accord with Robert Mugabe from 1987 until he died in 1999.

Selassie Seyoum Gebre (1936 – not known)

Seyoum Gebreselassie born in 1936 in Ethiopia. He had a BA from University College Addis Ababa in 1959. An MA in Social Service Administration from the Tata Institute in India in 1961 and another MA in Sociology led to a PhD in Sociology and Social Work at the University of Michigan in 1976. He worked for the Awassa Community Development Training and Demonstration Center in Ethiopia, becoming its director between 1961 and 1964. He taught social work at Haile Selassie University between 1967 and 1968 and was Dean. He was a founder of the first effort to establish an African Association of Schools of Social Work (ASWEA) and served as a member of the executive and vice president of the International Association of Schools of Social Work (IASSW) representing the Africa region. He served as a member of the executive of the International Council of Social Welfare between 1968 and 1972. He was one of the leaders in the re-establishment of social work education in Ethiopia in the 21st century and achieved the highest academic rank, full professor, in 1995. His thesis was titled Government and the promotion of social equality – a comparative analysis of selected developing countries.

Yimam (not known – about 1989)

Yimam's date of birth is not known but probably died in 1989. He was a passionate advocate of social develop-ment with a deep concern for the future of Africa. He argued for a holistic concept of development. Arega Yimam was closely involved with the Association for Social Work Education in Africa (ASWEA). He was born in Ethiopia. He died before the publication of his Doctor of Philosophy (PhD) thesis and the responsibility for continuing with publication was undertaken by Phyllida Parsloe, Professor of Social Work at Bristol University who was his supervisor. From his thesis was published the book Yimam, A. (1990). *Social Development in Africa, 1950-1985: Methodological Perspectives and Future Prospects.* Aldershot: Gower. In his book, Yiman reviewed the range of external and

111

internal factors contributing to Africa's underdevelopment before providing a useful, but brief, history of social welfare and social development from the colonial period to the 1980s. He wrote about the emergence of concepts of social development and the problems of reaching an agreed definition which could provide the basis for a unified African policy and practice. Much of the material on conceptualising social development is drawn from documents produced by organisations like ICSW (International Council on Social Welfare), IASSW (International Association of Schools of Social Work) and ASWEA and reflects their historical isolation from mainstream thinking on development. He examined problems, policies and programmes related to education, health, housing, urbanisation, population, income distribution and social security and finally looked at training in social development. The chapter on training, benefitting from the author's long involvement with ASWEA, provides new material on the development of training institutions, curriculum content and efforts by ASWEA to achieve general agreement on training. Yimam stressed the role of ASWEA and other pan--African agencies in guiding curriculum development. Yimam emphasised the need for self-reliance, redistributive policies, popular participation, cooperatives, a focus on rural development and greater public expenditure on social development. He looked to China as a model. He was critical of aid and structural adjustment. He described social welfare and health provision as 'heavily depended on voluntary input' (p. 111). The relationship between NGOs and government includes the dilemma between co-ordination and autonomy. He worried about the underfunding of services in Africa, except for education. He emphasised more science and technology in education. He criticised African governmental health services for urban bias, wastage and insufficient resources.

Priscilla Ingasiani Abwao (1924 – 2009)

Priscilla Ingasiani Abwao was a Kenyan social worker and advocate for women's rights, a freedom fighter, and the first African woman to serve on the Legislative Council in 1961 in Kenya. Even before independence, Priscilla Abwao was instrumental in the fight for equal rights between women and men. At a women's conference she organised in 1962, she said "It is not time to sit and gossip. We have to work and build," she said. A

112

suffragette is a woman seeking the right to vote through organised protest. Abwao died on November 13, 2009, at the age of 85.

Aïcha Chenna (1941 –2022)

Aïcha Chenna was a Morocco social worker, nurse, women's rights advocate, and activist who worked with disadvantaged women and founded the Association Solidarité Féminine (ASF) in 1985 in Casablanca. Before then, she volunteered in child welfare, assisting single mothers. Chenna received various humanitarian awards for her work, including the 2009 Opus Prize (worth US$1 million). In 1996, Chenna published Miséria: témoignage (Misery: Testimonies), in which she narrated twenty stories of women she had worked with. Chenna self-described as having "a Muslim heart with a secular mind". During her time as an employee of the Ministry of Health, she became known for her work in areas subject to social and religious taboos, including family planning, single mothers' status, illegitimate children and abandoned children, and the status of incest victims. She regularly received criticism from social conservatives, who said that her work legitimised immoral behaviour.

Jember Teferra (1943 –2021)

Jember Teferra was an Ethiopian nurse, development worker, and anti-poverty campaigner. She devoted to efforts to combat poverty and poor health in Addis Ababa. In 1969, she became health education and social services coordinator for the Red Cross in Ethiopia. In 1976 Jember herself was jailed as a result of her social activism. When she was released in 1981, Jember continued to work to alleviate poverty, initially with Save the Children, then setting up and running the Integrated Holistic Approach-Urban Development Project, a scheme that eventually improved housing, health, education and employment opportunities for more than 50,000 people in the slums of Addis Ababa. Her work received international recognition and funding, and the project still operates today.

Mitri Widad (1927-2007)

Mitri Widad was a nationalist from Egypt, leftist, social worker, teacher, and activist for women's rights. She became a prominent figure in the nationalist leftist movement and the women's peace movement to end the British occupation. In her later years she continued to be a member of the

113

Women's Committee of the Arab Lawyers Federation, the Afro-Asian Solidarity Organisation, and the Association of Cairo University Women Graduates. She represented Egyptian women during the 1986 Nairobi Conference on Women and visited Palestinian camps under siege in solidarity with the Palestinian people.

Victoria Fikile Chitepo (1928 –2016)

Victoria Fikile Chitepo was born as Victoria Mahamba-Sithole in the South African coal-mining town of Dundee in KwaZulu-Natal. She was educated in South Africa and attended the University of Natal, where she was awarded a Bachelor of Arts degree, and took a postgraduate degree in education at the University of Birmingham in the UK. She met her future husband, Herbert, at Adams College near Durban in South Africa. In Zimbabwe, she campaigned for women's rights and the rights of Africans in general. She went with her husband to Tanganyika (now Tanzania) and worked as a social worker aiding black Rhodesian refugees in Dar es Salaam for three years, between 1966 and 1968. In 1975. Herbert Chitepo, her husband was a leader of the liberation movement in Zimbabwe but was later assassinated in Lusaka, Zambia by agents of the Rhodesian government. She later worked in government until her death on April 8, 2016.

Mame Seck Mbacké (1947 – 2018)

Mame Seck Mbacké was a writer from Senegal and founder of publishing house Éditions Sembene. She wrote in French and Wolof. She was born in Gossas. Mbacké studied Social and Economic Development at the Institute of Higher International Studies in Paris. She worked as a diplomat in France and Morocco, then as a social worker at the Senegalese consulate in Paris. In Paris, she completed an International Relations degree at the Sorbonne and post-graduate studies in public health and nutrition at the Pantheon-Sorbonne University. She later worked for the Ministry of Foreign Affairs in Dakar. Her short story "Mame Touba" was included in the anthology Anthologie de la Nouvelle Sénégalaise (1970–1977). In 1999, she received the Premier Prix de Poésie from the Ministry of Culture of the Republic of Senegal. Mbacké established the publishing house Éditions Sembene in 2006.

114

Many other contributors

In Egypt, Fatima Al-Harouni, Ahmed Al-Sanhouri, and Saleh Al-Shobokshi wrote and published on social services and casework in the 1930s (Saleh, 2023). Many other people contributed to the work of ASWEA, including Dr Chibogu, Nigeria; Dr Ibo, Cote d' Ivoire; Dr Onyango, Kenya; Dr Tesfaye, Ethiopia; Dr Muzaale, Uganda; Mr Allouane, Tunisie; and Professor Twagiramutara, Rwanda.

Social work educational institutions (SWEIs)

The first training program for white people in Africa related to social work was started at the Transvaal University College leading to the creation of the Department of Sociology and Applied Sociology at the University of Pretoria in 1931.

- This was followed by the University of Stellenbosch (1931).
- The University of Cape Town (1933).
- Alexandria School in Egypt (for the French) in 1934.
- The Cairo School of Social Work (1937) by the Egyptian Association for Social Studies (EASS) (renamed Higher Institute of Social Work in Cairo in 1972).
- The Jan H. Hofmeyr School of Social Work, South Africa (for the training of Black people) (1941-1960).
- Ghana (1945).
- Uganda (1954).
- Tanzania (1958).
- Burkina Faso (1960).
- Tunisia (1964); School of Social Work, College of Social Sciences.
- Addis Ababa University (1959-1974, reopened 2004).
- Zambia one-year certificate in community development at Oppenheimer College of Social Service (now Ridgeway Campus) (1962).
- Four-year Bachelor of Social Work, University of Zambia (1964).
- School of Social Welfare (Zimbabwe) (1964).

- the Higher Institute of Social Work for Girls (Egypt) now under Helwan University (1975).
- Fayoum University, Egypt (1983) (Saleh, 2023).

Associations, networks, regulators and global collaborations

National associations

Almost all African countries have a professional association of social work. Some associations are independent of the government, yet others are formed by the government as public or semi-public bodies. Other countries have both an independent association and a government body for social workers. An independent association has a constitution and is run by members themselves or by their employees. Joining is usually voluntary. Independent associations provide self-regulation of their members. Government or semi-government bodies are established through public law, public funding and joining them is usually mandatory. Their role roles are:

- Creating a code of ethics relevant to Africa: To create a code of ethics guided by African values that have been used to provide social services since time immemorial.
- Societal recognition: make social work known in families and communities including what social work is in the local language, the roles of social workers and how the complement does not replace or compete with the roles of families and communities. Presently, in most African communities, social work is not understood and at times it is hated because of its focus on western ideas, knowledge, philosophy, theories, methods and literature.
- Creating a local definition of social work: to help social work be understood and appreciated. Definitions in local languages will be more useful.
- Creating relevance: making social work in Africa more developmental to enable it to respond to the social issues, challenges, and problems on the continent. Social work must respond to mass poverty in a developmental not remedial way.

116

- Professional recognition: To raise social work to the level of other professions, and to give social workers respect and recognition for their service.
- Professional regulation: Ensure that social workers follow ethical principles that make them accountable for any professional misconduct, breach of ethics or confidentiality.
- Professional standards: To oversee social workers' performance, attitude towards families, communities, peers, profession, and the society, to build trust and ensure the credibility of social work.
- Training monitoring: To monitor social work training and fieldwork.
- Produce literature: To research, write and publish relevant literature for social work training and fieldwork.
- Advocacy: To advocate for social justice and social services.
- Continuous training: To lead continuous professional development (CPD) of social workers and all people providing social services. This is important especially for social workers trained in the colonial period, those trained using colonial syllabus or those trained outside Africa.
- Supporting and empowering indigenous services: To support families and communities in their roles of providing social services and not disempower them.
- Trade unionism: Act as the trade union of social workers to represent their interests and labour rights as workers, entrepreneurs, volunteers, and social innovators.
- Consumerism: protect families, communities and employers from poor services from social workers, receiving complaints and dealing with them.
- Collaboration with other associations: Work and collaborate with other professional bodies in the country, in the region, in Africa and globally.
- Policy work: Creating policies or alternative policies to advance social development and to scrutinise existing policies of the government.
- Recognising social workers: Celebrate social workers through National Social Work Day, the Global Social Work Day and provide awards to social workers, students, academics, and social work organisations.
- Networking: providing opportunities for social workers to network, share experiences and listen to others through Indaba,

conferences, webinars, newsletters, journals, websites, and social media e.g. groups on Facebook or WhatsApp, dinners etc.

- To decolonise social work to make it relevant to African communities.

Examples:

- Angola: Association of Social Workers in Angola, Associação dos Assistentes Sociais de Angola.
- Benin: Benin National Union of Social Technicians, Syndicat National des Techniciens Sociaux du Benin.
- Botswana: Botswana Association of Social Workers, Mokgatlho wa Badiri ba Tsa Selegae mo Botswana.
- Burundi: National Social Worker's Association in Burundi.
- Cameroon: Cameroon Association of Social Workers, Association Nationale des Travailleurs Sociaux du Cameroun.
- Congo (DRC): National Coordinating Body – Democratic Republic of Congo.
- Congo: National Association of Social Workers of the Republic of Congo.
- Djibouti: Djibouti Association of Social Workers, Association des Assistants Sociaux du Djibouti.
- Egypt: General Syndicate of Social Professions in Egypt النقابة العامة للمهن الاجتماعية في مصر
- Eswatini: Eswatini National Social Workers' Association.
- Gambia: Gambia Association of Social Workers.
- Ghana: Ghana Association of Social Workers, 1971.
- Guinea-Bissau: Guinea-Bissau Association of Social Workers.
- Guinea: Guinean Association of Social Worker, Association Guinéenne des Travailleurs Sociaux.
- Kenya: Kenya National Association of Social Workers.
- Lesotho: Lesotho Social Workers' Association.
- Liberia: National Association of Social Workers of Liberia.
- Libya: Public Syndicate of Libyan Social and Psychological Specialists.

118

- Madagascar: Madagascar Association of Social Workers.
- Malawi: Association of Social Workers in Malawi, Bungwe la Ogwira Ntchito Zosamalira Anthu m'Malawi.
- Mauritius: Mauritius Association of Professional Social Workers
- Morocco: Moroccan Association of Social Workers, Association Marocaine des Assistants Sociaux, الجمعية المغربية للمساعدين الاجتماعيين
- Niger: Niger Association of Social Workers.
- Nigeria: Nigeria Association of Social Workers, Association. Nigerienne es Travailleurs Sociaux.
- Rwanda: Rwanda National Organization of Social Workers, Umuryango Nyarwanda w'Abavugururamiberho.
- Senegal: Senegal Association of Social Workers, Association Nationale des Assistantes Sociales du Sénégal.
- Sierra Leone: Sierra Leona Association of Social Worker.
- South Africa: National Association of Social Workers in South Africa.
- South Africa: South African Association for Social Workers in Private Practice (SAASWIPP).
- South Africa: South African Council for Social Service Professions (SACSSP).
- Sudan: Sudan National Social Workers' Association.
- Tanzania: Tanzania Association of Social Workers, Chama Cha Wataalamu wa Ustawi wa Jamii Tanzania.
- Togo: National Association of Social Workers of Togo – Association des Professionnels du Développement Social.
- Uganda: National Association of Social Workers of Uganda
- Zambia: Social Workers Association of Zambia.
- Zimbabwe: The National Association of Social Workers Zimbabwe, 1988.

Association of schools at national level

An example is the Association of South African Social Work Educational Institutions (ASASWEI). According to ASASWEI (2023), the organisation is an association of schools of social work, other tertiary-level social work educational programs, and social work educators. The ASASWEI

119

promotes the development of social work education throughout South Africa, develops standards to enhance the quality of social work education, encourages international exchange, provides forums for sharing social work research and scholarship, and promotes human rights and social development through policy and advocacy activities (ASASWEI, 2023). Its mission is to:

- To maintain and support a community of social work educators who are committed to the continuing development of social work education, training, research and practice in South Africa". In pursuing its mission and vision the association aims to:
    - Facilitate collaboration and exchange of information on social work education, training research and practice with relevant networks (governmental and non-governmental) on national, regional and international levels.
    - Develop strategies that enhance the recognition of social work as a profession.
    - Promote recognition of the contribution of social work to social and economic development and to the transformation of South African society.
    - Support the development of appropriate and locally specific research, theory and practice Contribute to the development and implementation of social welfare and education policies in the South African context.

Regulators

Most countries have regulators for social work. A regulator is a public or semi-public institution tasked with implementing the law of social work laws of the country. Examples include:

- South Africa: South African Council for Social Services Professions which administers the Social Service Professions Act.
- Zimbabwe: Council of Social Workers which administers the Social Workers Act.

- Namibia: Social Work and Psychology Council of Namibia (SWPCNA) which administers the Social Work and Psychology Act.

There is currently no Africa-wide regulator of social work.

Regional associations and networks

African Centre for Applied Research and Training in Social Development (ACARTSD)

It was founded in 1977 in Tripoli, Libya to promote and coordinate applied research and training in social development; and assist African countries in formulating national development strategies. It was founded at a Conference of African Ministers of Social Affairs of the Organization of African Unity (OAU) with support from organisations including the United Nations Economic Commission for Africa (ECA). The structure was as follows: Conference of African Ministers of Social Affairs, Governing Board, comprising of Executive Secretary of ECA as ex officio Chairman, a representative of General Secretariat of OAU, and 2 representatives of each of the 4 sub-regions of Africa, designated by Conference of Ministers. Technical Advisory Committee. Executive Director. Research Coordinator; Training Coordinator; Librarian; Computer Programmer; Finance and Administration; General Service.

Association of Social Work Education in Africa (ASWEA)

The pan-African, Association of Social Work Education in Africa (ASWEA), was formed in Alexandria, Egypt, in 1965 and operated from 1971-1989. It was a non-profit organisation dedicated to social work education in Africa. Its members included schools of social work and individuals working in community, agricultural and rural development workers training. By 1978, ASWEA had OAU observer status, 50 social work and development training institutions and 100 individual academics from 50 countries. The objectives of ASWEA were to address issues related to social work education, including the dominance of western social work curricula and provide opportunities for member schools to meet regularly to discuss social work's role in national development planning.

121

Shortcomings of social work in Africa	Solutions
The dominance of western social work curricula.	Change the curricula.
Inadequacy of western models of social services.	Change the services.
Dissatisfaction with the Christian approaches to services.	Centre social work on Africa's religion.
Western centred teaching and education focused on lectures and examinations.	Develop and promote African-cantred pedagogy, content and approaches, for example, more oral and participatory approaches or using African case studies, role plays and groupwork. Another example is making education interdisciplinary or integrated.
Eurocentric knowledge.	Develop, through research, a body of social work knowledge that would meet the needs of Africans.
Focused on remedial, curative or maintenance approaches.	Move to a social developmental or developmental social work approaches that is preventative.
Focused on individual problems.	Redefine social work to focus more on national development planning and policy.
Culturally opposing social work.	Develop culturally relevant social work.
Lack of professional identity and defined area of competence.	Redefine social work to make it more suitable for African. problems and solutions and form professional associations
Urban-focused and elitist.	Focus on most of the people who are poor and residing in rural areas e.g. having rural

	research unit, a rural fieldwork unit, rural placements and rural case studies.
Focused on social issues without economic issues.	Focus on income, self-sufficiency, and growth.

Model 3: ASWEA model of social work and development.

Recommendations from ASWEA archives (summary from Gray, Kreitzer and Mupedziswa, 2014):

(1) Develop teaching material for African social work in the classroom, based on local and regional case studies, to develop African curriculum content.
(2) Engage in the development of social development policies to confront contemporary challenges facing social work in Africa.
(3) Formulate an African code of ethics for social work in Africa, involving multiple stakeholders across the African continent.
(4) Strengthen national professional associations to speak out on national issues from a social work perspective.
(5) Hold regular pan-African conferences, workshops, and symposia.
(6) Publish 'indigenous' teaching models and materials, with reflections on evolving practice approaches in different contexts engaging with the specific challenges of the social work profession in Africa.

ASWEA had a good model, however, several reasons impacted progress, until today. According to Kreitzer (2013) these problems are (i) the colonial legacy; (ii) the gap between educated Africans and the majority of Africans; (iii) social work's absence from national development planning; (iv) the need for trained human resources for national development; (v) institutional changes following structural adjustment; (vi) the lack of Indigenous teaching materials; (vii) inappropriate teaching styles; (viii) better use of social research; (ix) the reorientation from social services to development and aid; (x) the establishment of a strong professional identity and powerful professional associations; and (xi) the tensions between social development and social welfare practice. There is an archive created by Kreitzer (2013) with 3500 pages of documents from ASWEA meetings, reports, case studies and conference presentations.

ASWEA was closed in 1989 due to a shortage of finances but also other reasons that followed. The leaders of ASWEA never intended to close it forever, they were hoping to open when conditions improved. The organisation did well by encouraging grassroots membership, expanding African social work to include development and taking a pan-African approach that supported liberation and decolonisation. However, it seems, they relied more on funding from outside, although they also had funding from AU.

Journal for Social Work Education in Africa

There are no articles available for this journal which was published by ASWEA. ASWEA ceased operations in 1989. It has ceased operations. An option could be for an Africa-wide institution to revive this journal with a focus on social development which ASWEA started and promoted in Africa.

East and Southern Association of Schools of Social Work (ESASS)

The East and Southern Association of Schools of Social Work (ESASS) was formed in 1994, to succeed ASWEA but it was ineffective from the start and folded immediately. One reason EASS did not live long was that it could not attract members from all parts of the continent. As the name suggested, it started with East and Southern Africa.

Association of Schools of Social Work in Africa (ASSWA)

In 2005, the Association of Schools of Social Work in Africa (ASSWA) was formed. The ASSWA promotes the interests of social work education in the African region. The objectives of the association include providing opportunities for consultation and exchange of ideas, educational resources, faculty, and students, serving as a body for channelling resources to social work educational institutions in the region, and promoting inter-regional, regional and international cooperation in social work education. The association strives to uphold the social work values, principles and human rights of all people and social justice. The composition of ASSWA includes schools of social work, other tertiary-level social work educational programs, and social work educators. By 2022, the ASSWA had 22 school members out of a possible 300 schools on the continent. This low membership could be a result of their failure to take a pan-African focus,

124

probably because of dominance by members from the South, notably South Africa but also an overreliance on the IASSW.

Africa Social Work and Development Network (ASWDNet)

The Africa Social Work and Development Network (ASWDNet) creates, aggregates and disseminates information and resources to facilitate Social Work and Development on the African continent. Membership of the Network includes academics, practitioners, and students of social work and development. It was formed in 2022. In its work, the ASWDNet has adopted a pan-African focus and utilizes technology to achieve its goals. Technology makes it cheaper, and more people are reached. By 2022, the network had 100 members from all regions of the continent. Programs included collecting information about African social work and putting it on a website, publishing, blogging, mentoring, promoting indigenous ethics, managing three journals, Annual Ubuntu Lecture, Africa Day Indaba and Ubuntu Research Group.

International Federation of Social Workers (IFSW) Africa Region

This is a region of the IFSW, and not an independent African association. They promote the work of the IFSW in Africa by organising a conference once in two years, membership recruitment and promoting IFSW programs and policies. By 2022, they had 22 members. Reasons for not attracting more members could include that being under IFSW, they cannot truly pursue an African agenda.

International collaborations

The global social work organisations have regional representatives in Africa. These global organisations include the International Federation of Social Workers (IFSW), the International Council on Social Welfare (ICSW), the International Association of Schools of Social Work (IASSW) and the Consortium for Social Work and Social Development (CSWSD).

Missing links in African social work

- Literature - It is important to have at least 75% of local literature used by students, lecturers, practitioners, clients and researchers.
- Publishing is not enough and is not constant.

125

- Continuous Professional Development (CPD) for qualified social workers to ensure that they update their skills and knowledge and contribute to the production and dissemination of literature.
- Brain and energy drain continues to make Africa a training ground while other continents benefit from the people it trains.
- On the other side, we need stronger and sustainable institutions, including professional associations, schools and regulating bodies.
- Today, African social work is concerned with making indigenous methods work and using developmental approaches to address mass poverty.
- Most countries in Africa with more than one SWEI do not have an umbrella association.
- Africa does not have an independent continental trade union or federation of social workers.

Guidance: Using Ubuntu to understand the history of social services and to shape current and future social services

Africa's history has been colonised and neglected but this has changed. In Ghana, in the Twi language of the Akan people, they have one word that sufficiently describes the positive contribution of history in the present and future, Sankofa which means, to always look back to inform the future, go back and get it or *se wo were fi na wosan kofa a yenkyiri*, which means it is not taboo to look or go back to what may have been forgotten, neglected or left behind.

The Sankofa symbols are in the public domain. They are part of more than 120 symbols that make up the Adinkra alphabet.

- Use knowledge of Ubuntu to decolonise understanding of the history of social services.
- Use Ubuntu as a motivation to do philanthropic work just as Ubuntu inspired early philanthropists.
- Use Ubuntu to drive social services just as Ubuntu inspired early social service providers.
- Look back to strategies and methods used in the past to inform current and future strategies.
- Use Ubuntu to address Africa's social challenges to overturn colonising philosophies.
- Use Ubuntu to address global social challenges to overturn the dominance of other philosophies.

Summary

- Each part of the world developed social services in line with their environment and culture.
- Africa developed its social services based on its environment, resources, philosophy, values and culture.
- Africa's social services are centred on the family and community.
- When missionaries of the Abrahamic religion came, they focused on individualistic social services, provided by people outside families and communities.
- When social services were imported to Africa from outside the continent, mainly Europe and America, they followed the Abrahamic tradition with new values coming from western philosophy The major western values were apartheid and colonisation, where local resources were used for the social services of the white population in Africa, Europe, or America.

127

- Both Abrahamic and western values largely differed in African values, resulting in conflict and ineffective social services.
- Later, western social services evolved into a study discipline and professional called Social Work, in about 1900.
- Social work spread to Africa, again, with Abrahamic and western values.
- The first Black social worker in Africa was in 1903.
- Many people, among them, offered social services to the black populations, using meagre resources, without training.
- Later, black social workers were trained.
- In the 1950s, there was a realisation that western social work was selective, and discriminatory and was not designed for the black people, so the organisation ASWEA was formed to create a profession suitable to the African situation. Many other organisations were formed afterwards.
- The continents now has many training institutions for social services, social work and social development, as well as many professional associations at the country level.

Further and advanced knowledge

- What have been the shortcomings of the discipline and profession of social work and how can these be addressed.
- How does philosophy shape training for social services, social work and development work?
- What are the similarities and differences between social services, social work and development work?
- Select 4 founders of social services and social work in Africa and provide their biographies and the work they did. What ley lessons have you derived from studying them? If they were alive today, what would you tell them has improved or has remained the same?
- Visit or read about one of the places or institutions founded by one of the founders of social work in Africa. What were the original objectives, and what are the current objectives? What has changed and what has remained the same? If you were to start your own organisation or a community-based foundation, what would it be named and what would be its aim, objectives and activities?

- What inspiration do we derive from the work of ASWEA? Looking back, what do you think ASWEA could have done to survive? What are the lessons for social work institutions?
- Search 4 publications for social work and development in Africa. For each state, the name, where it is published, summary of editorial policy and author guidelines.
- Choose one journal article published in Africa that has used African philosophy, values, ethics or theories and provide a 500 summary of the article.
- Visit one social work association (or your lecturer will invite them) and learn about their history, code of ethics, activities or services, roles, and duties of members. Write a formal application letter to the association indicating what you will learn and bring to the association.

Questions for in-class assessments and examinations

- What have been the shortcomings of the discipline and profession of social work and how can these be addressed.
- How does philosophy shape training for social services, social work and development work?
- What are the similarities and differences between social services, social work and development work?
- Select 4 founders of social services and social work in Africa and provide their biography and the work they did. What key lessons have you derived from studying them? If they were alive today, what would you tell them has improved or has remained the same?
- Visit or read about one of the places or institutions founded by one of the founders of social work in Africa. What were the original objectives, what are the current objectives? What has changed and what has remained the same? If you were to start your own organisation, community-based organisation or foundation, what would it be named, what would be its aim, objectives and activities?
- What inspiration do we derive from the work of ASWEA? Looking back, what do you think ASWEA could have done to survive? What are the lessons for social work institutions?
- Search 4 publications for social work and development in Africa. For each state, the name, where it is published, summary of editorial policy and author guidelines.

129

- Choose one journal article published in Africa that has used Africa philosophy, values, ethics or theories and provide a 500 summary of the article.
- Visit one social work association (or your lecturer will invite them) and learn about their history, code of ethics, activities or services, roles and duties of members. Write a formal application letter to the association indicating what you will learn and bring to the association.

Potential questions for research

- A biography is a written account of someone's life. Research 4 people who have contributed to social work and social services in your country and create a 500 biography of each of them. Ensure gender balance, if possible.
- A literature review is a method of research where a researcher gathers literature on a topic and analyses it to come up with new understandings. Look for social services or social work publications published in Africa at least 50 years ago. These can include letters, books, papers, poems, speeches, newspaper articles, journal articles, subject outlines, and event programs. You should have between 10 and 20 articles. Read each of them and summarise in a table with the following details: author/creator, date, where you found it/source, key messages, or themes.
- Orature review is research method that d analyses oral sources of knowledge to come up with a new understanding of social problems and solutions. Orature sources include poems, stories, proverbs and songs. Identify four different sources of orature and draw a table that indicates the source of the orature, a summary of the orature and themes that inform social work and development work. Sources include your own experience, family members, elders, cultural experts, and books.

Fieldwork ideas

- Visit a person over the age of 80 years (or your lecturer may invite them to class) and sit down with them to learn about their names and what the names mean; where they were born; family and community social service during their time and their view of social problems of the past and now Use all local and ethical protocols in your engagement with them. Write 1000-word research report about the visit.

- Visit two places that are geographically different, one being urban and one being rural. Make observations of social issues in the two areas focusing on housing, economic production, transport, health, social welfare, and infrastructure.
- During a placement, have a conversation with the leader of the agency or organisation about their history. Illustrate to the leader how the work they are doing links with social problems of the past, and how it will connect with the future.

Key terms and their meanings

Abrahamic religion – beliefs that were founded on the life, culture, and history of Abraham, including beliefs of Jews, Christians, and Muslims.

Africa religion – beliefs of people of Africa based on their cultures, religions, and histories.

Africa-centred – based on the philosophy of Africa.

Colonisation – the act of imposing the philosophy, religion, education and culture on other people through preaching, deception, coercion, colonisation, manipulation, incentives, and force. Colonists included politicians, missionaries, educators, social workers and development workers.

Customary – in line with a people's customs.

Decolonisation – the act of reversing colonisation, which includes refusing, war, demonstrating, renaming, returning, speaking against it and revaluing.

Europe-centred – based on the philosophy of Europe.

Indigenous – the original status of things or what things could be at present if the original route had been followed.

Liberation from colonisation – a situation where freedom from economic, social, political, environmental, spiritual, educational, and philosophical colonisation is achieved. Political independence is part of liberation.

Missionary – a person whose duty (mission) is to preach the values of another religion to convert people. Missionaries use different other techniques besides preaching, including deception, coercion, colonisation, manipulation and incentives.

Social problem – an issue that causes a person, family, community or society to fail to provide for their needs.

Social services – the different strategies to prevent or address social services such as development, welfare, security, production, health, education, housing, and others.

Social welfare – services provided by families, communities, and society to those members of society unable to meet their needs temporarily or in the long term.

Social Work – is a discipline and profession whose mission is to prevent or address problems that individuals, families, communities, and society face after studying the causes and solutions.

Social work – the act of preventing or addressing problems that individuals, families, communities and society face after studying the causes and solutions.

Uhuru archives – historical literature (documents) that was created by the ASWEA.

References and recommended readings

Africa Social Work and Development Network (ASWDNet) (2023). Africa Social Work and Development Network. Accessed from https://africasocialwork.net on 12 December 2023.

Allucia, L.S. and Masoga, M. A. (2019). "Social work as protest: conversations with selected first black social work women in

South Africa", *Critical and Radical Social Work*, vol. 7, no. 3, pp. 435-445.

Association of Social Work Education in Africa (ASWEA) (1972a). Community Services, Lakota Project Methodology, Doc. 2. Addis Ababa: ASWEA publication.

Association of Social Work Education in Africa (ASWEA) (1972b). *The Important Role of Supervision in Social Welfare Organisations*, Doc. 3. Addis Ababa: ASWEA publication.

Association of Social Work Education in Africa (ASWEA) (1972c). The Use of Films in Social Development Education, Doc. 4. Addis Ababa: ASWEA publication.

Association of Social Work Education in Africa (ASWEA) (1973a). *Case Studies of Social Development in Africa*, Vol. 1. Addis Ababa: ASWEA publication.

Association of Social Work Education in Africa (ASWEA) (1973b). *Guidelines for Contacting Young People in Informal Groups in Urban Areas*, Doc. 5. Addis Ababa: ASWEA publication.

Association of Social Work Education in Africa (ASWEA) (1974a). *Relationship between Social Work Education and National Social Development Planning*, Doc. 6. Addis Ababa: ASWEA publication.

Association of Social Work Education in Africa (ASWEA) (1974b). *Curricula of Schools of Social Work and Community Development Training Centres in Africa*, Doc. 7. Addis Ababa: ASWEA publication.

Association of Social Work Education in Africa (ASWEA) (1974c). *Case Studies of Social Development in Africa*, vol. 2. Addis Ababa: ASWEA publication.

Association of Social Work Education in Africa (ASWEA) (1975a). *Directory of Social Welfare Activities in Africa* (3rd edn). Doc. 8. Addis Ababa, ASWEA publication.

Association of Social Work Education in Africa (ASWEA) (1975b). *Report of ASWEA's Workshop on Techniques of Teaching and Methods of Field Work Evaluations*, Doc. 9. Addis Ababa: ASWEA publication.

Association of Social Work Education in Africa (ASWEA) (1976a). *Techniques d' Enseignement et methodes d'Evaluation des Travaux Pratiques*, Doc. 10. Addis Ababa: ASWEA publication.

Association of Social Work Education in Africa (ASWEA) (1976b). *Realities and aspirations of social work education in Africa*, Doc. 11. Addis Ababa: ASWEA publication.

Association of Social Work Education in Africa (ASWEA) (1977). *The Role of Social Development Education in Africa's Struggle for Political and*

Economic Independence, Doc. 12. Addis Ababa: ASWEA publication.

Association of Social Work Education in Africa (ASWEA) (1978a). *The Development of a Training Curriculum in Family Welfare*, Doc. 13. Addis Ababa: ASWEA publication.

Association of Social Work Education in Africa (ASWEA) (1978b). *L'Elaboration d' un programme de formation en benêtre familial*, Doc. 14. Addis Ababa: ASWEA publication.

Association of Social Work Education in Africa (ASWEA) (1979a).*Guidelines for the Development of a Training Curriculum in Family Welfare*, Doc. 15.Addis Ababa: ASWEA publication.

Association of Social Work Education in Africa (ASWEA) (1979b). *Principes directeurs pour l'establissement d'un programme d'etude destine a la formation aux disciplines de la protection de la famille*, Doc. 16. Addis Ababa: ASWEA publication.

Association of Social Work Education in Africa (ASWEA) (1981). *Social Development Training in Africa: Experiences of the 1970s and Emerging Trends of the 1980s*, Doc. 17. Addis Ababa: ASWEA publication.

Association of Social Work Education in Africa (ASWEA) (1982a). *Survey of Curricula of Social Development Training Institutions in Africa*, Doc. 18. Addis Ababa: ASWEA publication.

Association of Social Work Education in Africa (ASWEA) (1982b). Seminar on the organization and delivery of social services to rural areas in Africa, Doc. 19. Addis Ababa: ASWEA publication.

Association of Social Work Education in Africa (ASWEA) (1985). Training for Social Development: Methods of Intervention to Improve People's Participation in Rural Transformation in Africa with Special Emphasis on Women, Doc. 20. Addis Ababa: ASWEA publication.

Association of Social Work Education in Africa (ASWEA) (1986). Association for Social Work Education in Africa. Addis Ababa: ASWEA publication

Association of Social Work Education in Africa (ASWEA) (n.d.). An Effort in Community Development in the Lakota Sub-prefecture, Doc. 1. Addis Ababa: ASWEA publication.

Association of South African Social Work Educational Institutions (ASASWEI) (2023) About us. https://www.asaswei.org.za

Bar-On, A. (1999). Social Work and the 'Missionary Zeal to Whip the Heathen Along the Path of Righteousness', *The British Journal of*

134

Social Work, 29, (1): 5–26, https://doi.org/10.1093/oxfordjournals.bjsw.a011440

Gray, M., Kreitzer, L., Mupedziswa, R. (2014) 'The Enduring Relevance of Indigenization in African Social Work: A Critical Reflection on ASWEA's Legacy', *Ethics and Social Welfare 8(2)*: 101–16.

Kaseke, E. (1991) 'Social Work Practice in Zimbabwe', *Journal of Social Development in Africa 6(1): 33–45.*

Kaseke, E. (2001a). Social development as a model of social work practice: the experience of Zimbabwe. School of Social Work Staff Papers. Harare, School of Social Work.

Kaseke, E. (2001b). Social work education in Zimbabwe: strengths and weaknesses, issues and challenges. *Social Work Education, 20(1),* 101–109.

Kreitzer, L. (2023). Decolonizing Social Work Education in Africa: A Historical Perspective Gray, M., Coates, J., Hetherington, T., and Yellow Bird, M. (2013). *Decolonizing social work.* Burlington: Ashgate.

Lengwe-Katembula Mwansa (2011) Social Work Education in Africa: Whence and Whither? Social Work Education,30:1, 4-16, DOI: 10.1080/02615471003753148

Mugumbate J. R. (2020). Baba Jairos Jiri's Ubuntu models of charity, disability and rehabilitation. *African Journal of Social Work, 10(1), p. 83-88.*

Mwansa, L.-K. (2011). Social Work Education in Africa: Whence and Whither? Social Work Education, 30(1), 4–16. https://doi.org/10.1080/02615471003753148

Osei-Hwedie, K. (1993) 'The challenges of social work in Africa: Starting the indigenization process', *Journal of Social Development in Africa 8(1): 19–30.*

Saleh, E. (2023). Private Practice Social Work in the Arab World: Sultanate of Oman as a Model. IntechOpen. doi: 10.5772/intechopen.106284

South Africa History Online, Charlotte (née Manye) Maxeke, https://www.sahistory.org.za/people/ charlotte-nee-manye-maxeke

CHAPTER 5

Social services at different levels of society

Introduction

This chapter summarises the different levels of social work and development work. The first level of social work is the family, and this level includes the individual. After the family, we have the village level, and this is followed by the community. The other levels are 'country'/district/county, national, continental, and global.

Objectives of this chapter

After studying this chapter, readers will acquire knowledge on:

- Services that already exist in families, villages and communities without the intervention of professions.
- Services that professionals provide to families, villages and communities.
- Services that professionals provide at national, continental, and global levels.
- Assessments that are suitable for the local context.
- Research questions and methods that are appropriate to the local context.
- Fieldwork, workplace-based and community-based learning is contextual.
- Using Ubuntu to provide social services at each level of society.

136

Skills and competencies addressed in this chapter

By the end of this chapter, readers will be expected to have acquired the following skills and competencies:

- Distinguish services that already exist in families, villages, and community with those provided by professionals.
- Select suitable services for each level.
- Identify providers of services at each level.
- Answer questions or assessments about the different levels of social work and development work.
- Create research questions and methods that are appropriate to the local context.
- Plan fieldwork, workplace-based and community-based learning that is contextual.

The levels and types of social services

The seven levels of social work and development work are:

1. Family level
2. Village level
3. Community level
4. County or district level
5. National level
6. Continental level
7. Global level

Each level has its needs, interventions and people who intervene. These levels can be divided into micro or primary (family and village levels), meso or secondary (community/ward and county/district levels), and macro or tertiary and quaternary (national and continental levels) and global macro or quinary (global level). The different types of social services are:

- Agriculture services
- Production and resource extraction services
- Development services
- Marketing and exporting services
- Manufacturing and value addition services

- Infrastructure services
- Health services
- Cultural services
- Social assistance, social welfare, and social security services
- National cultural, psychological, and spiritual services
- Voting services
- Environmental services
- Food and nutrition services
- Spiritual services
- Housing services
- Health, public health, and vaccination services
- Security, crime, law, and order services
- Justice services
- Research services

Work at the family level

A family is a social, biological, cultural and economic unit made up of a male and female parent and their offspring. Offspring include children and grandchildren. At times, there is one parent or no offspring. As a social unit, they have shared roles and responsibilities. Biologically, a family can expand and is connected genetically. A family has language, norms, values and aspirations that come from their culture. Ordinarily, a family has resources including a home, consumables, assets, and savings but at times some or all of these resources may not be available.

Geographically, the centre of a family is a homestead. Usually, a family has one permanent homestead but can have other temporary homesteads. In Africa, most permanent homesteads are in the rural areas. A permanent homestead is not easily disposable or sold, it is connected to family land and a permanent village or community. On a permanent homestead, several houses can be erected, each serving a purpose: parent's bedroom, children's bedrooms, cooking and eating room, food storage room and shelters for livestock. A family can have multiple homes including one permanent and several temporary homes. Temporary homesteads usually have a higher commercial value but can be easily disposed of and do not have cultural ties. A temporary homestead usually has one house, which could be rented, that is it belongs to someone else, mortgaged means it was bought on credit or titled meaning it has title deeds from a local authority.

138

The user or owner does not have full rights to the land on which the house is built, and there are limits in terms of what they can develop on the property. At a temporary home or house, there can be multiple unrelated families. A household is tied to a family and refers to all families or people residing at a homestead.

Families can be described as immediate, larger, extended, tribal and extended tribal. An immediate family usually consists of parents and children while a larger family is intergenerational, consisting of parents, their own parents, children and grandchildren. An extended family includes siblings of parents and grandparents. A tribe consists of members of the family tree while an extended tribal family is much larger, and it includes all people who share the same totem. If they are composed adequately and function very well, families can prevent and solve most social issues, problems or challenges. However, at times, some reasons cause families not to be able to meet their roles, such as:

- Lack of one or more parents.
- Lack of a larger family.
- Lack of a home.
- Lack of resources.
- Lack of extended or tribal family support.
- Lack of community support.

Each family has ways to address social challenges to ensure the social functioning of its members. As a worker, the first question to ask when working with families and individuals is, "What functions and solutions do you already have in the family". As social workers, we build on top of what is already there in the family, we do not impose. However, families usually struggle with newer social issues, especially those that arose from processes of colonisation, urbanisation, globalisation and 'modernisation'. These include unemployment, family poverty, urban poverty, urban homelessness, drug abuse and delinquency.

Role players and roles at this level

- Parents – being role models, producing, providing rewards, discipline, and necessities.
- Older siblings – mentoring, production, discipline, and necessities.
- Children – listening to adults with respect and carrying responsibilities.

139

- Members of the larger family (family mothers, family fathers, siblings, aunts and uncles) – mentoring, production, discipline and necessities.
- Members of the community – mentoring, production, discipline, and necessities.
- Cultural teachers and experts – teaching and mentoring at the rite of passage schools or ceremonies.
- Older members of the family and community – teaching, mentoring, guidance counselling and advice on production, in the family and community.

Specific roles of social workers and development workers

Social work's role is not to replace the social functioning of the family but to support them where they are facing shortcomings. Specific roles include:

- Listening to the family and understanding the solutions that they have tried and those they prefer.
- Income building and maintenance.
- Identifying and challenging colonial practices that could be impacting the social functioning of the family.
- Connecting families with work and what is happening at village level.

Work at the village level

A village is a collection of homesteads. Other terms for the village are commune, villa, vile or vale. It can also be referred to as a small settlement. While the noun is used more in rural communities, every town or urban area is made up of villages, but they can be called streets or lines. In a rural village, most people know each other, and they may be related. In an urban village they may know each other but are almost always not related. In rural villages, they have leaders who inherit the position from their families while in urban areas, leaders are elected. In rural villages, they have more sense of belonging, compared to urban villages. This is because families in urban villages people are usually living there temporarily, as described above while those in rural areas are permanent.

Role players and roles at this level

- Village head – ensure unity and cooperation, resolve disputes, enforce laws, represent the village, and lead the creation and implementation of development plans. Chairs the development committee.
- Families – mentoring, production, discipline, and cooperation.
- Village police – security and enforcement of laws.
- Members of the community – mentoring, production, discipline, and necessities.
- Cultural teachers and experts – teaching and mentoring.
- Older members of the village – teaching, mentoring, guidance counselling and advice on production.
- Village development committee – leads development planning and implementation.

Specific roles of social workers and development workers

- Consulting with the village leaders and members.
- Provide feedback on village development plans.
- Identifying social challenges and working with the village to develop solutions.
- Village infrastructure improvement.
- Income building and maintenance.
- Identifying and challenging colonial practices that could be impacting the social functioning of the village.
- Connecting the village with work that is happening at the family and community level.

Work at the community level

A community is made up of villages or households. Therefore, a community is much larger than a village, and it can consist of two or several villages. A community usually does not have a clearly defined leadership. It can consist of a cultural or elected leader. There are shared responsibilities, infrastructure, and resources. Communities have a shared history and past.

Role players and roles at this level

- Community leader – ensures unity and cooperation, resolves disputes, enforces laws, represents the village and leads the creation and implementation of development plans. The leader chairs the development committee.
- Village heads – ensure their village's contribution to unity and cooperation, represent the village and lead the creation and implementation of development plans.
- Community police – security and enforcement of laws.
- Members of the community – contribution to unity and cooperation, participate in community development planning and activities.
- Cultural leaders – monitoring, advising, and advocating for cultural values.
- Older members of the community – teaching, mentoring, guidance counselling and advice on production.
- Volunteers – mobilize for development.
- Community-based organisations (formed by members of the community) – provide monitoring of service providers and initiate programs for welfare and development.
- Community development committee (may be ward or area development committee) – leads development planning and implementation.

Specific roles of social workers and development workers

Professional workers have multiple roles, and they can have different titles such as community worker or community development worker. Their roles include:

- Community infrastructure improvement.
- Feedback on community development plans.
- Income building and maintenance.
- Identifying and challenging colonial practices that could be impacting social functioning.
- Connecting the community with work that is happening at lower and higher levels.

142

Work at the 'country', district or county level

Communities form a 'country', district or county. Before colonisation, Africa was divided into culturally defined boundaries called countries. When colonisers came, they combined these cultures into one 'country'. Some were changed to counties or districts while some maintained countries but had to work side by side with districts or counties. A country has a governing leader, who can be a Chief or King. The people in a country are often bound together by culture, history, migration and a common colonial history of displacement and resistance. Each country has its laws and ways to administer them. Districts and counties are run by elected or appointed officials of government. Other associated terms include a ward, which usually means area superintendent by an elected official. The partition of countries into districts, counties and wards was a way of taking away power from Chiefs and Kings to put it into colonial systems of administration and government.

Role players and roles at this level

- District/county leader – ensures their county's contribution to unity and cooperation, represents the community and leads the creation and implementation of development plans.
- Chief or King – ensures unity and cooperation, welfare, resolves disputes, enforces laws, represents the village, and leads creation and implementation of development plans at the country level.
- Country police – security and enforcement of laws working with national police.
- District development office – provides development services.
- District social development office – provides social development services.
- District social services – provides social services.
- Members of the country – contribution to unity and cooperation, participate in community development planning and activities.
- Cultural leaders – monitoring, advising and advocating for cultural values.
- Influential members of the community – teaching, mentoring, guidance counselling and advice on production.
- District-based organisations (formed by members of the district) – provide monitoring of service providers and initiate programs for welfare and development.

- Volunteers – mobilize for development.
- District development committee – leads development planning and implementation.

Specific roles of social workers and development workers

- Identifying or assessing individuals in need of social assistance.
- Identifying communities in need of welfare and development.
- Infrastructure improvement.
- Analysis of development plans.
- Income building and maintenance.
- Identifying and challenging colonial practices that could be impacting social functioning.
- Cultural development.
- Connecting this level with work that is happening at lower and higher levels.

Work at the national level

A nation is a collection of countries. It can be divided into provinces, states or regions or can have several sub-divisions. A nation has one leader, who can be a cultural leader (King or Queen) or elected leader (e.g. President). Colonists wanted European cultural leaders (and at one time succeeded in doing so) as heads of countries in Africa but the idea was defeated during political decolonisation.

Role players and roles at this level

- Head of nation or state – ensures unity and cooperation, ensures social services, leads creation and implementation of development plans at the national level and represents the nation at regional, continental, and global levels. The head of the nation gets support from deputies, governors (provincial or state leaders), and advisors.
- Chiefs or Kings – represent their country at the national level.
- Cultural leaders – monitoring, advising, and advocating for cultural values.

- Government ministers – provide leadership for ministries.
- Government workers – administer social services and development.
- Citizens of the nation – defend their nation, voting for leaders and participating in development.
- Members of parliament – creating laws and policies that ensures support social services and development.
- The military and police – maintain security, law and order.
- Judiciary – interpret the law, resolve disputes, and protect.
- Non-government organisations (operating at national level) – provide monitoring of service providers and initiates programs for welfare and development.
- Provincial or state office – lead services at the state or province levels.

Specific roles of social workers and development workers

- Administer social services.
- Infrastructure creation and improvement.
- Analysis or creation of development plans.
- Income building and maintenance.
- Identifying and challenging colonial practices that could be impacting social functioning.
- Cultural development.
- Connecting this level with work that is happening at lower and higher levels.
- Training and mentoring other workers.
- Research.
- Development and review of socio-economic policies.

Work at the continental level

A continent represents any of the six large land blocks of the world – Africa, Asia, Europe, the Pacific (including Australia) and the two Americas. Africa is a continent with 55 countries. It has continental organisations, both public and private. The most important of these is the African Union (AU), which started as the Organisation of African Unity (OAU) in 1963 (AU, 2023). The AU started in 2002 and has social programs and therefore employs or uses the services of social workers. A social worker working with the AU is basically doing continental social work. The continent is divided into regions, with regional institutions where social workers are also employed. A region includes a collection of countries that are geographically connected. The secretary generals of the OAU and chairpersons of the AU were:

- Kifle Wodajo, 1963–1964.
- Diallo Telli, 1964–1972.
- Nzo Ekangaki, 1972–1974.
- William Eteki, 1974–1978.
- Edem Kodjo, 1978–1983.
- Peter Onu, 1983–1985.
- Ide Oumarou, 1985–1989.
- Salim Ahmed Salim, 1989–2001.
- Amara Essy, 2001–2002.
- Alpha Oumar Konaré, Mali (2003–2008).
- Jean Ping, Gabon (2008–2012).
- Nkosazana Dlamini-Zuma, South Africa (2012–2017).
- Moussa Faki, Chad (2017–current).

The regions of Africa

Africa is divided into five regions: East, South, West, Central and North. The regional organisation for all these regions is the African Union (AU) with 55 countries.

East Africa	
Tanzania, Kenya, Uganda, Rwanda, Burundi, South Sudan, Djibouti, Eritrea, Ethiopia, and Somalia.	
Southern Africa	
Angola, Botswana, Lesotho, Mozambique, Namibia, South Africa, Eswatini (which decolonised its name from Swaziland in 2018), Zambia, Zimbabwe.	
West Africa	
Benin, Burkina Faso, Cape Verde, Côte D'Ivoire, Gambia, Ghana, Guinea, Guinea-Bissau, Liberia, Mali, Mauritania, Niger, Nigeria, Senegal, Sierra Leone, and Togo.	
Central Africa	
Angola, Cameroon, Central African Republic, Chad, Congo Republic - Brazzaville, Democratic Republic of Congo, Equatorial Guinea, Gabon, and São Tomé and Principe.	
North Africa	
Algeria, Egypt, Libya, Morocco, Sudan and Tunisia.	

Figure 2 Regions and countries of Africa

There are regional economic communities (RECs) and regional mechanisms (RMs) which are the pillars of AU, although they were formed independently and have differing roles. According to the AU, RECs facilitate regional economic integration. All RECs work through the African Economic Community (AEC), which was established under the Abuja Treaty (1991) and has been operating since 1994 to create an African Common Market. The eight RECs are:

- Arab Maghreb Union (UMA).
- Common Market for Eastern and Southern Africa (COMESA).
- Community of Sahel–Saharan States (CEN–SAD).
- East African Community (EAC).
- Economic Community of Central African States (ECCAS).
- Economic Community of West African States (ECOWAS).
- Intergovernmental Authority on Development (IGAD).
- Southern African Development Community (SADC).

Purpose of the AU

- To promote the unity and solidarity of the African States.
- To coordinate and intensify their cooperation and efforts to achieve a better life for the peoples of Africa.
- To defend their sovereignty, their territorial integrity and independence.
- To eradicate all forms of colonialism from Africa.
- To promote international cooperation, having due regard to the Charter of the United Nations and the Universal Declaration of Human Rights.

Divisions

- Agriculture, Rural Development, Blue Economy, and Sustainable Environment (ARBE)
  - The Department of Agriculture and Food Security
  - Rural Economy
  - Rural Development
  - Sustainable Environment and Blue Economy (SEBE) Directorate
- Economic Development, Tourism, Trade, Industry, Mining (ETTIM)
- Education, Science, Technology and Innovation (ESTI)
- Infrastructure and Energy
- Political Affairs, Peace and Security (PAPS)
- Health, Humanitarian Affairs and Social Development (HHS)
  - The Department of Health, Humanitarian Affairs and Social Development (HHS) works to promote the
  - Humanitarian Affairs Division
  - The AIDS Watch Africa (AWA) Secretariat
  - Directorate of Social Development, Culture and Sports
  - Labour Employment and Migration Division
  - Social Welfare, Drug Control and Crime Prevention Division
  - Culture and Sport Division
- Women, Gender and Youth
- Civil Society and Diaspora
- Legal Affairs

148

Regional agreements

1. Agenda 2063 implemented by the New Partnership for Africa's Development (NEPAD).
2. Common Market for Eastern and Southern Africa.
3. African Continental Free Trade Area (AfCFTA).

Principal decision-making organs.

- The Assembly of Heads of State and Government
- The Executive Council
- The Permanent Representatives Committee (PRC)
- Specialised Technical Committees (STCs)
- the Peace and Security Council
- The African Union Commission
- Pan-African Parliament
- Economic, Social and Cultural Council (ECOSOCC)

Organs on judicial, legal matters and human rights issues

- African Commission on Human and Peoples' Rights (ACHPR)
- African Court on Human and Peoples' Rights (AfCHPR)
- AU Commission on International Law (AUCIL)
- AU Advisory Board on Corruption (AUABC)
- African Committee of Experts on the Rights and Welfare of the Child
- The AU is also working towards the establishment of continental financial institutions.
  - The African Central Bank
  - The African Investment Bank
  - African Monetary Fund

The Regional Economic Communities (RECs) and the African Peer Review Mechanism are also key bodies that constitute the structure of the African Union.

149

Africa's social, economic, cultural and political background

Africa is a continent endowed with land for agriculture, mining, and water for fishing. Most of Africa's population lives in rural communities and most of the people living in urban areas have a permanent rural home or connection. This makes it important for community workers and community development workers to plan from a non-elitist urban approach. The elitist approach has its roots in colonisation, where white people developed services for urban communities using western modernisation approaches founded on their culture and values. The elitist approach resulted in segregation, apartheid and the creation of reserves where black people were forced into small pieces of unproductive land. Colonization took many forms – spiritual, religious, political, environmental, cultural, psychological, and educational.

Seventy-five percent or more of African people with very low income, with most living in temporary but also permanent poverty. For income and livelihoods, most Africans work on the land – farming, mining, fishing and doing other economic activities.

African culture is centred around the family, village and surrounding community. Families are much larger in size, they include the extended family, that is members of the clan or tribe. Africa has a rich cultural heritage of family life, dance, music, food, marriage, childcare, Ubuntu, *ujamaa* and others. Africa's spiritual heritage is also rich.

Politically and administratively, Africa has dual systems because of colonisation. The first is the indigenous system of governance. In Zimbabwe, they include *Samusha* (Village Head), *Sadunhu* (Sub-Chief), *Ishe* (Chief) and *Mambo* (King). Different systems and different names are used in other countries. The second is the western form of politics and governance, and in some countries, the Arabic form. The indigenous system works together with western systems of ward, sub-county, county or district, province and state. Western democracy, as a system of politics and governance, has produced mixed results. It has promoted stability and cohesion in some communities, but it has also resulted in disharmony, violence, death and loss of sovereignty.

It is also important to state the role of the African Union (AU), and regional bodies for South, East, Central and West Africa. The AU and these bodies set policy direction at their levels and these policies influence state policies. Examples include the African Charter on Human and Peoples' Rights, the African Charter on the Rights and Welfare of the

Child and the African Union Convention on Preventing and Combating Corruption.

Roles of members at this level

- Chairperson of the AU – ensures unity and cooperation, leads the debating, creation and implementation of policies and represents Africa at global levels. The Chairperson gets support from a deputy, eight commissioners and directors.
- Heads of state or nations – represent their states or nations.
- Parliamentarians/Chiefs or Kings – represent their states or nations at the Pan-African Parliament.
- Government ministers – represents their states or nations at ministerial meetings.
- AU organs – develop plans in line with AU policies – protocols and procedures.
- AU workers – administer social services and development plans.
- RECs – they are the building blocks of the AU, working to achieve economic and social integration at the national, regional and continental levels.
- Regional or continental NGOs - represent their interests.

Specific roles of social workers and development workers

- AU workers – administer social services and development plans of the AU.
- Analysis or creation of development plans.
- Identifying and challenging colonial practices that could be impacting social functioning.
- Cultural development.
- Connecting this level with work that is happening at lower and higher levels.
- Research.
- Supporting, observing, and monitoring elections.

Work at the global level

The global includes all continents and countries of the world. A key question in global social work and development work is whether they are the same throughout the world. The answer is no because:

- Philosophies are not universal.
- Knowledge is not universal.
- Values, ethics and theories are not universal.
- Social problems are not universal.
- Environments both ecological, social, economic, cultural and spiritual are not universal.
- Languages are not universal.
- Histories are not universal.

Those who support universalism of social work and development work are promoting professional imperialism or colonisation. Global social work and development work is full of colonial and new-colonial practices that can be transmitted to Africa by expatriate social workers, development workers, foreign social workers, international social work students, literature, conferences, social media and international social work organisations. Colonial ideas are often transmitted as human rights, knowingly and unknowingly. There are many global organisations, but the major one is the United Nations (UN), founded in 1945 and now has 193 member states (UN, 2023). The UN (2023, paragraph 1) describes themselves as 'One place where the world's nations can gather to discuss common problems and find shared solutions. The UN has multiple institutions covering several social, economic, political, and cultural areas. It is led by a Secretary General (SG). The SG list is as follows:

- Trygve Lie, from Norway, 1946-1952.
- Dag Hammarskjöld, from Sweden, 1953-1961.
- U Thant, from Burma (now Myanmar), 1961-1971.
- Kurt Waldheim, from Austria, 1972-1981.
- Javier Perez de Cuellar, from Peru, 1982-1991.
- Boutros Boutros-Ghali, from Egypt, 1992-1996.
- Kofi A. Annan, from Ghana, 1997-2006.
- Ban Ki-moon, from Republic of Korea, 2007-2016.

- António Guterres, from Portugal, 2017-present.

Some UN laws and programs where social work and development work are prominent include:

- Universal Declaration of Human Rights (UDHR)
- International Covenant on Economic, Social and Cultural Rights (ICESCR)
- International Convention on the Protection of the Rights of All Migrant Workers and Members of Their Families (ICRMW)
- International Covenant on Civil and Political Rights (ICCPR)
- Millennium Development Goals (2000-2015) and Sustainable Development Goals (2015-2030)
- Convention on the Rights of the Child
- Convention on the Elimination of All Forms of Discrimination against Women
- Convention on the Rights of Persons with Disabilities
- Paris Agreement on Climate Change
- United Nations Convention Relating to the Status of Refugees
- United Nations Declaration on the Rights of Indigenous Peoples
- Sendai Framework for Disaster Risk Reduction

Some organs, institutions, funds and programs of the UN

- Principal organs
  - General Assembly
  - Security Council
  - Economic and Social Council
  - Trusteeship Council
  - International Court of Justice
  - UN Secretariat (led by the Secretary General)
- Some specialised agencies
  - World Health Organisation (WHO)
  - High Commissioner for Refugees (UNHCR)
  - Food and Agriculture Organisation (FAO)
  - UN Scientific and Cultural Organisation (UNESCO)
  - UN Children's Fund (United Nations International Children's Emergency Fund, UNICEF)

- o   International Monetary Fund (IMF)
- o   World Bank (WB)
    - ▪ International Bank for Reconstruction and Development (IBRD)
    - ▪ International Development Association (IDA)
    - ▪ International Finance Corporation (IFC)
- o   International Labour Organisation (ILO)
- o   Joint United Nations Programme on HIV/AIDS (UNAIDS) (UNAIDS)
- o   UN Women
- o   International Organization for Migration (IOM)
- o   International Trade Centre (ITC) (supporting the internationalization of small and medium-sized enterprises (SMEs))
- Some funds and programs
    - o   United Nations Population Fund (UNFPA)
    - o   United Nations Human Settlements Programme (UN-HABITAT)
    - o   United Nations Environment Program (UNEP)
    - o   UN Development Program (UNDP)
- Research
    - o   United Nations University (UNU)
    - o   United Nations Research Institute for Social Development (UNRISD)
    - o   United Nations Institute for Disarmament Research (UNIDIR)
    - o   United Nations Institute for Training and Research (UNITAR)
    - o   United Nations System Staff College (UNSSC)
- Regional commissions
    - o   Economic Commission for Africa (ECA)
    - o   Economic Commission for Europe (ECE)
    - o   Economic Commission for Latin America and the Caribbean (ECLAC)
    - o   Economic and Social Commission for Asia and the Pacific (ESCAP)
    - o   Economic and Social Commission for Western Asia (ESCWA)
- Some Departments and Offices

154

- o Development Coordination Office (DCO)
- o United Nations Youth Office (UN Youth)
- o Office of the United Nations High Commissioner for Human Rights (UNHHR)
- o Department of Economic and Social Affairs (DESA)
- o Office for the Coordination of Humanitarian Affairs (OCHA)

International NGOs

International NGOs (INGOs) have a presence at the global level and are recognised in more than one continent and have recognition of the UN. Some examples are:

- Red Cross
- World Vision
- Save the Children
- Oxfam
- International Bureau for Epilepsy
- Amnesty International
- Médecins Sans Frontières/Doctors Without Borders

Most of the INGOs are founded in western countries, therefore, some of their values are colonial or against the values of other continents and countries. For example, they may see as child labour what is not child labour, or they may promote 'rights' that are not rights at all in other communities.

International professional organisations

The main ones are:

- International Federation of Social Workers (IFSW)
- International Association of Schools of Social Work (IASSW)
- International Council on Social Welfare
- International Consortium for Social Development (ICSD)
- International Association for Community Development (IACD)
- International Association for Counselling (IAC)

Role players and roles at this level

- Secretary General of the UN – ensures unity and cooperation, leads the debating, creation and implementation of policies and represents the UN at continental and regional levels
- Heads of state or nations – represent their states or nations at the UN
- Government ministers – represent their states or nations at ministerial meetings of the UN
- AU – represents the continent at the UN
- International NGOs – represent their members at the UN

Specific roles of social workers and development workers

- AU workers – administer social services and development plans of the AU.
- Analysis or creation of development plans.
- Identifying and challenging colonial practices that could be impacting social functioning.
- Cultural development.
- Connecting this level with work that is happening at lower and higher levels.
- Research.
- Supporting, observing and monitoring elections.

Guidance: Using Ubuntu in the provision of social services at different levels

Like water is required for all parts of a tree, so is Ubuntu philosophy. Ubuntu is required at all levels of social service provision.

- Make Ubuntu the focus of social service planning.
- At the family level, Ubuntu help to understand relations and values.
- At the community level, Ubuntu shapes aspirations and interventions.
- At the societal level, Ubuntu shapes leadership.

- At the environmental level, Ubuntu defines the relationship between people and Country – it should be reciprocal and respectful for sustainability.
- At the spiritual level, Ubuntu shapes what people value.
- At the global level, Ubuntu solves global challenges by focusing on being human as opposed to focusing on the economy, influence and power – all these have resulted in colonisation, westernisation, poverty and unsustainability.

Summary

- There are seven levels at which social work and development services are provided.
- At each level participation of people or members should be prioritised, based on each's roles and responsibilities.
- Focusing on local, contextual and decolonising service provision is important.
- The first level is the family where services are provided per household.
- At the village level, services are provided per village.
- At the community level, services are provided per community.
- The other levels are 'country'/district/county, national, continental and global.

Further and advanced knowledge

- Regional Economic Communities (RECs)
- Sustainable Development Goals (SDGs)
- Spirituality services
- Environmental services
- Criticism and shortcomings of the UN
- Criticism and shortcomings of the AU

Questions for in-class assessments and examinations

Study the table below and answer the questions that follow.

Table 6: Levels and methods of social work (question)

Level of social work	Objective	Methods	Common Methods
Social work at the family level	Understanding, developing and protecting families and their members.	• Family social work • Social work with groups of people • Social work with individuals	Developmental social work Indigenous social work
Social work at the community level	Understanding, developing and protecting communities.	• Community social work • Community development	Environmental social work Spiritual social work
Social work at the country level	Understanding, developing and protecting the country (socially, economically and politically).	• Social development • Economic development • Political social work	Decolonised social work

1. Using the table as a framework for analysis, identify five key themes of social work at the different levels provided in this chapter.
2. What methods of social work can you add at each level of social work described in this chapter.

Potential questions for research

1. At each of the different levels, research is required. For each level, how would you go about the first stage of research? The stages of research are:
a. Problem identification stage.
b. Approvals, confirmations and ethics advice stage.
c. Data collection, analysis and conclusions stage.

d. Reporting and dissemination of findings stage.
e. Data use stage.
f. Review of findings and usage stage.
2. Throughout the process, the researcher is guided by the following principles. Which principle do you think is the most important and why?
a. Think and act ethically.
b. Think and act anti-colonially.
c. Think and act holistically.
d. Think and act respectfully.
e. Think and act justly.

Fieldwork ideas

1. The three forms of fieldwork placements suitable for Africa are Conventional placements: Community and developmental placements and Creative social work placements. For each level, develop one fieldwork activity using the template below.

Table 7: Fieldwork ideas (question)

Level	Fieldwork activity	Role players and institutions
Family level		
Village level		
Community level		
County or district level		
National level		
Continental level		
Global level		

2. Visit three potential fieldwork agencies and explore opportunities for fieldwork. Each agency should be at a different level. If you are not able to visit, you can send an email, social media inquiry or call and record the feedback.
3. Choose one component of fieldwork and discuss how they can work at the village level. Fieldwork has five basic components, SISSCR, that is:
    a. Student.

159

b. Institution of training.
c. Supervisors.
d. Service provider – agency providing social services
e. Community – the community where field education, innovation or activism takes place.
f. Regulator – this is the institution, body, and committee responsible for setting guidelines, regulations and standards.

Key terms and their meanings

African Union (AU) – the intergovernmental association of nations and states of Africa.

Community – a collection of villages or households in one geographical area.

Community-based organisation – an organisation created by members of the community for their welfare and development, is based in the community and operates at the community level.

Country – can refer to a geographical area under a Chief or King or a collection of such geographical areas that form a nation or state.

County – a large administrative area with multiple wards.

District – a large administrative area with multiple wards.

District/county-based organisation – an organisation created by members of the district/county for their welfare and development, is based in the district/county and operates at the district/county level.

Global macro or quinary – at the global level.

Household – the geographical place of a family.

International non-government organisation – an organisation for welfare and development which is not part of the government or intergovernmental system.

Macro or quaternary – at the continental level.

Macro or tertiary – at the national level.

Meso or secondary – at the community/ward and county/district levels

Micro or primary – at the family and village levels.

National non-government organisation – an organisation for welfare and development which is not part of the government system and operates at the national level, that is, it provides its services to all parts of the nation.

Non-government organisation – an organisation for welfare and development which is not part of the government system.

Province – the different divisions or regions of a country.

Regional organisation – an organisation for welfare and development which operates in one part of a country, continent or the world. Region means part of a geographical area, which can be a nation, continent or world.

State – the different divisions or regions of a country.

United Nations (UN) – the intergovernmental association of nations and states of the world.

Village – a collection of homesteads in one geographical area.

Ward – the smallest administrative area of a district/county with an elected official.

Ward-based organisation – an organisation created by members of the ward for their welfare and development, is based in the ward and operates at the ward level.

References and recommended readings

African Union (AU). (2023) About the African Union. https://au.int/en/overview. December 2023.

United Nations (UN) (2023). About us. https://www.un.org/en/about-us. December 2023.

Ayichi, D. (1995). In E. C. Eboh, C. U. Okoye, and D. Ayichi (Eds.), Models of rural development in Nigeria: With special focus on the ADPs. Rural development in Nigeria, concepts, processes and prospects (pp. 13–29). Enugu: Auto-Century Publishing Company.

Ollawa, P. E. (2011). On a dynamic model for rural development in Africa. *The Journal of Modern African Studies, 15(3), 457–480.*

CHAPTER 6

Botho as an organising precept for social services in Botswana: towards Africa's perspectives

Introduction

This chapter presents an in-depth description of *botho* as a philosophy of social development that can strengthen social work theory and practice. The chapter encourages discussions and debates on Ubuntu/*botho* as an African precept and its potential impact on the international social work profession. Following an introduction, the chapter presents highlights, objectives, and skills and competencies that learners will acquire. This is followed by a discussion of *botho* as an African philosophy on positive human relationships. This is done in the context of *Tswana* indigenous institutions, as well as social protection support systems. Further, the chapter discusses *botho* as a human ethic of care, social work, and spirituality to underscore the African connectedness to the spiritual world. Lastly, is a section on Afrocentric models of social work education and practice; the conclusion, and potential questions for research.

Objectives of this chapter

After studying this chapter, readers will be expected to have acquired knowledge on:

- *Botho* as an organizing precept for social work in Botswana.
- *Botho* as an African philosophy that guides interpersonal and /or social relationships.
- *Botho* within the social work profession in Botswana.
- Indigenous institutions that demonstrate the application of *botho* in social protection systems.

- The principle of *botho* as human ethic of care.
- The interconnectedness of *botho*, social work, and spirituality in promoting social functioning of people in society.
- Use and development of an Afrocentric model of social work in Botswana.
- Assessments that are suitable for the local context.
- Research questions and methods that are appropriate to the local context.
- Fieldwork, workplace-based and community-based learning that is contextual.

Skills and competencies addressed in this chapter

By the end of this chapter, readers will be expected to have acquired the following skills and competencies:

- To define the principle of *botho* as an organizing precept for social work practice.
- To demonstrate an understanding of *botho* as an African philosophy for guiding interpersonal and / or social relationships.
- To apply the concept of *botho* in the provision of social work services.
- To adapt the principle of *botho* in the provision of social protection services.
- To integrate *botho* in human ethic of care in interventions with diverse populations.
- To construct culturally relevant social work interventions underpinned by *botho* and spirituality to promote holistic care.
- To design Afrocentric models of social work within a socio-cultural context.
- Answer questions or assessments about the topic of this chapter.
- Create research questions and methods that are appropriate to the local context.
- Plan fieldwork, workplace-based and community-based learning that is contextual.

Botho

Botho in *Setswana* and Ubuntu in *isiZulu* denotes a deeper understanding of humanness in the African philosophy. The two languages are spoken in Botswana, Namibia, and South Africa; and are part of the family of languages known as Nguni in Africa. That dominant social work discourses originate from western culture is common knowledge in the social work literature. It is against that backdrop that social work scholars from non-western regions have long advocated for social work education and practice to be anchored on societal principles that are well understood and embedded in a culture within which social work is practised. The debate on the need to develop culturally relevant social work education and practice in Botswana started in the early 1990s. There is consensus among African scholars that *botho* represents the ideal that 'my identity as a person is only meaningful when I can co-exist respectfully and peacefully with others in my social environment'. A major challenge about *botho* as a discourse in Botswana literature is that it has not been well articulated. It remains an imagination in the minds of elders and others who embellish Tswana tradition and cultural wisdom. *Botho* underscores the importance of human interdependence and is consistent with social work's commitment to promoting positive human relationships in social interactions and transactions. This chapter seeks to examine *Setswana* principles that can help contribute to development of Afrocentric social work models in Africa.

Prior to colonisation, Africans had their unique value systems that guided human relationships and shaped collective efforts to address human needs in society. Botswana, like many African societies, was founded on an ethic of humanism that emphasised communitarianism as a guiding framework of social relationships. *Batswana* (the people), believe that an individual carries the identity of his/her family or clan and as such he/she should conduct themselves in a manner that reflects his/her community values. Thus, human identity becomes meaningful only when one can co-exist with others in his/her social environment. *Botho* underscores the importance of bonding, collectivism and a sense of belonging based primarily but not exclusively on kinship ties. There is a *Tswana* adage that says '*motho ke motho ka batho*' meaning "a person is only a person in community" (Hutton, 1996:7).

It is against this background that *Batswana* or *Tswana*, (as commonly used in history writings refers to the people of Botswana and those who speak the language), emphasise a "war of words" rather than physical violence to resolve interpersonal and community conflicts (*ntwa kgolo ke ya molomo*).

In typical *Tswana* norms, any two people that have a conflict should turn to their immediate environment (friends, family, and neighbours) for mediation. The intention is to preserve positive human relations and peace within the neighbourhood, community, and society. Even at governance level, Batswana believed that *"kgosi ke kgosi ka batho ba yone"* meaning 'a chief is a chief on the will of his/her subjects'. As such he/she was expected to rule fairly, equally, and justly for the common good of society. Thus, he/she was not expected to be authoritarian and unjust in his/her rule.

It is not the intention of this chapter to argue for a return to this pre-colonial past but to explore ways of blending local cultures and imported western and non-western cultures that characterised contemporary globalised nations. Further, it is also possible to imagine new African values based on our accumulated knowledge of global and local value systems as people of the world. The first recorded attempt to define *botho* in official discourse was in 1997 when the Government of Botswana adopted *botho* as a principle guiding the long-term vision of the country commonly referred to as Vision 2016. In that official document, *botho* was defined as:

> *The tenets of African culture - the concepts of a person who has a well - rounded character, who is well - mannered, courteous and disciplined, and realises his or her full potential both as an individual and as a part of community to which he or she belongs (Government of Botswana, 1997:5).*

Consequently, *botho* was adopted as a fifth national principle in addition to democracy, development,; self-reliance, and unity to guide the national development planning framework. Further, many formal organisations began to use the word *botho* in their strategic documents and service charters to reflect the paradigm-shift in service provision across all sectors. Unfortunately, not much has been done to document what this concept entails. However, it is commonly associated with an African philosophy of care that uses a combination of these words – benevolence, caring, collectivism, compassion, consensus, generosity, hospitality, interdependence, kindness, openness, respect, solidarity, sympathy, sharing, social harmony, and general sensitivity to collective over individual needs and aspirations (see Hutton and Mwansa, 1994; Mupedziswa, Rankopo and Mwansa, 2019; Osei-Hwedie, 1996; Van Breda, 2019).

The ethic of *botho* underscores the importance of human interdependence and is consistent with social work's commitment to promoting positive human relationships in social interactions and

166

transactions. This chapter seeks to examine *Setswana* principles that can help contribute to development of Afrocentric social work models in the country. We discuss the concept from its common usage in *Tswana* culture and attempt to demonstrate how it can be used as an organising precept for social work education and practice. We do not claim to know it all but hope to stimulate debate and expansion of this philosophy of African life in Botswana and beyond. It is our humble view that the concept of *botho* implies the need for internal transformation of one's character to embrace professional social work values in the context of culturally relevant social work practice.

Botho as an African philosophy on positive human relationships

Setswana language is part of the Nguni family of languages in Eastern and Southern Africa. The word *botho* or Ubuntu in isiZulu, denotes a deeper understanding of humanness common in the African philosophy (Mbiti, 2015; Nyaumwe and Mkabela, 2007; Rankopo, 2001; Twikirize and Spitzer, 2019) which describes the need for a community spirit of working collectively in mutually supportive and respectful ways (van Breda, 2019). It was popularised in South Africa during the Truth and Reconciliation Commission led by Archbishop Desmond Tutu to reconcile Whites, and Black people, and build a united nation with peaceful co-existing races in the post-apartheid republic (Ellastam, 2015; Maphosa and Keasley, 2015; Tutu, 1999).

The principles of Ubuntu resonate with universal values of human worth and dignity. Archbishop Emeritus Desmond Tutu (1999:34–35) explains that the meaning of Ubuntu is that 'a person is a person through other people. It is not "I think therefore I am". It says rather: "I am human because I belong". I participate, I share.' The concept highlights the interconnectedness of human society, with the implication that people should treat others as part of the extended human family. Noticeably, Allastam (2015) notes that, the interim constitution of the Republic of South Africa (1993) first spoke of the need for Ubuntu rather than retribution. The notion of *"Batho Pele"* (meaning 'people first') refers to a set of principles that promote service delivery in the public sector were founded on *Ubuntu*. This paradigm-shift in articulating Afrocentric models of social development began to spread to other parts of Africa, including Botswana.

In Botswana, the notion of *botho* emerged in social work education in the 1990s when the University of Botswana reviewed its curriculum to embrace indigenous ideas (see, for example, Hutton, 1996; Osei-Hwedie, 1993). There had been concerns among both local social work students and educators that the curriculum had not been sufficiently adapted to the Botswana context with one scholar publishing an article with the phrase "the agony of irrelevance" in reference to the dominant western discourses in the original curriculum (Ngwenya, 1993). It was during this time that Professor Kwaku Osei-Hwedie joined the University of Botswana and began to contribute significantly to efforts to indigenise African social work education and practice (see, Osei-Hwedie, 1990, 1993, 2001). Morena Rankopo, who is one of the authors of this book was part of this process having joined the Department of Social Work as a staff development fellow from the pioneer BSW class of 1986. Nevertheless, the indigenisation discourse has remained stronger at the level of idea generation and has resulted in a better understanding of African centred social work. However, there is still a scarcity of literature that articulates this notion of *botho* in the context of social work education and practice in Botswana. Even in neighbouring South Africa, where a significant population speak *Setswana* as their mother tongue, not much has been written on *botho* and social work (Sekudu, 2019). Thus, there is a need for both social work educators and practitioners to work together to produce literature that can be used in universities to shape social work discourses in the classroom.

Batswana believe that individuals are nurtured and shaped by the family, community, and cultural context in which they are raised. The very essence of humanness – social interaction, human skills of interpersonal communication, thinking, listening, making judgments about what is right or wrong, imagination, articulation and synthesising are all learned in the context of the family and community in which one resides (Hutton, 1996). Thus, Tswana culture socialises individuals to identify themselves with the larger extended family and community. Several authors who have written on the concept of *botho/Ubuntu* have consensus on the view that the concept has potential to become an African philosophical framework for social work to make it culturally relevant. This position is premised on the view that the dominant social work literature is founded on western culture and that in the same light other regions of the world should also articulate their culturally relevant frameworks to guide their local curricula (Mugumbate and Nyanguru, 2013; Mupedziswa et al., 2019; Osei-Hwedie, 2014).

Other scholars have gone further to suggest that *botho* is aligned to universal social work values and ideals that espouse positive human relationships, social connections, social capital, empathy, resilience, and

168

human dignity among others (Rankopo and Ose-Hwedie, 2001; Mugambate and Chereni, 2019; Twikirize and Spitzer, 2019). Thus, these African values may be universal human values that resonate well with the ecological model or person-in-environment perspective in the dominant social work literature. Based on the foregoing, African societies seek to promote less individualistic communities and societies where people become more interdependent on one another. Individuals are encouraged to look out for each other and support one another to achieve collective well-being. Our understanding of this notion is that there is still space for hardworking individuals to excel in their private space to amass more wealth than others who are less hardworking. The next section discusses *botho* as an integral part of community life among ordinary people.

Indigenous institutions, *botho* and social protection support systems

Villages in indigenous Tswana societies consisted of households including family members who shared a family name, a totem, and a clan. Individuals were raised in large extended families and all adults took responsibility for shaping the behaviour of children. All vulnerable population groups such as orphans, people with disabilities, the sick and the elderly were cared for within the context of the extended family. Extended families had clusters of households that constituted a ward and several wards made up a village. Poorer members of the family would be given a herd of small stock or cattle to care for and use the milk to support their members. Under the *mafisa* system, the livestock would be loaned to the poorer families to keep over an extended period. When they increase in number, the owner would set aside a few animals and give them permanently to the poor family. This is known as *go tshwaela*. Unfortunately, there was no formula of determining the number of livestock that could be inherited from this system. So, while it had potential to economically empower the poor, it could also be used as a tool for further oppression of the disadvantaged sectors of society.

At the community level, *botho* in Tswana culture was demonstrated through collective effort to grow crops on community land with the chief as the overseer. Selected age regiments would be assigned to plough the fields on behalf of the community. The harvest from these fields known as *masotla* is stored in granaries for the purpose of sharing these among vulnerable population groups who for some reason do not have relatives to support them (Ntseane, 2011). It is our considered opinion that social work practice has a lot to learn from such indigenous practices.

169

Communities had processes and mechanisms for ensuring that the needs of disadvantaged members of the community were met from the grassroots through informal social support. Thus, the community was in control of social interventions.

Social work educators and practitioners in Botswana must critically review these indigenous practices and processes to determine how they can be adapted to contemporary society. Botswana is a rapidly developing country and many of the conditions that prevailed during the pre-colonial era have changed drastically. Therefore, there is a need to dialogue with society on what *botho* means today. It is our genuine position that when a society cherishes certain values, it should find systematic ways to inculcate them in its people through formal and informal social institutions and systems. We need to see the *botho* principle being taught from preschool through primary, secondary, and higher education levels. Further, there should be community cultural centres that facilitate learning about *botho* to help visitors and expatriates working in the country to be assimilated.

Botho as a human ethic of care

Social work is a helping profession that requires acquisition of personal attributes and a commitment to serve and care for others. The concept of *botho* in many ways resonates with the values and ethic of care articulated in the social work profession. This chapter does not intend to discuss the issues around universality, internationalisation, localisation, and indigenisation of social work, for these have been ably discussed in the literature (Gray and Fook, 2004). We believe that while there are cultural differences across the globe where social work is practised, there are common grounds of agreement on what social work is and what it seeks to achieve in society. *Botho* seeks to develop personal attributes that place others before one's personal needs. The goal is to encourage family and community members to care for one another and thereby promote collective well-being.

In that regard, the notion is aligned to the human ethic of care found in all cultures across the world. Western societies evolved from communitarian societies that espoused similar values as the Africans. Further, the human ethic of care is often demonstrated by westerners in times of disasters that require emergency collective responses. This is a clear demonstration that human beings care about each other more than we care to imagine. However, it is the complexities of modern life that

170

perhaps make it difficult for this ethic of care to be realised to the same extent across cultures and between developed and developing countries (Gray and Fook, 2004).

Botho, social work, and spirituality

It is worthwhile to highlight that the issue of *botho*, social work and spirituality have received relatively little attention from social work educators in Botswana and at times appear to be actively avoided. Much of the scholarly literature on spirituality in social work tends to deal mainly with the relationship between religion and spirituality, focusing on definitional issues and on the importance of the spiritual and religious dimensions of people's lives (see, for example, Gray, 2005; Holloway, 2006). Given that social work is a secular profession, it has generated some controversy, particularly about inappropriate proselytization, the imposition of religious beliefs or activities on clients, and bias against various spiritual (Furman et al., 2004) or religious (Hodge, 2002) perspectives. As such, advocating for spiritually sensitive practice has not been translated in action across many countries including Botswana. Writers in this field lament the lack of training of social workers to deal with spiritual issues and debate whether spirituality should be taught in the social work curriculum (Gilligan and Furness, 2005). This chapter therefore argues for developing a broad theoretical and epistemological perspective on *botho* and spirituality in social work on the grounds that social workers' attitudes toward religion and spirituality do affect the way they practice. Moreover, clients are being positively affected by worker's attitudes, *botho* being one of those, and worker's ability to engage in religious and spiritual conversations in areas such as, but not limited to, depression and end of life issues.

Considering the foregoing, the critical questions that we must ask ourselves are: How can *botho* and spirituality be incorporated in the social work profession? What would happen where religion is no longer the structure within which people obtain guidance on morality? These are not easy questions to answer; however, to provide some answers, these questions require us to grapple with social theory, more especially the theory of modernity and its perspective on the indigenisation and secularization of society. Further, it requires social workers to investigate theories of reflexive modernity which attempt to deal with the fallout from modernity and its consequences for human beings (See, Gray, 2008). Inherent in much current social work and sociological thinking is the

171

notion that individuals can successfully mastermind their own lives and that morality is possible without religion.

Influenced by social theory, social workers accept that at least three aspects of modern society shape most people's lives in the western world: economic ideology dominated by industrial capitalism; political ideology characterized by the rise of the nation state, liberal democracy, civil liberties, human rights, and social justice; and cultural ideology in which rationality has replaced indigenous authority and given rise to a 'pluralistic society in which people are free to select from a number of life options' (Holden, 2002: 173). This chapter, therefore, contends that social workers in Botswana and elsewhere in Africa, should vigorously consider inclusion of *botho*/Ubuntu and spirituality in social work education and practice. In addition, social work practitioners must recognise that spiritual striving and religious experiences are additional aspects of the person's development.

Towards Afrocentric perspectives of social work education and practice

The Afrocentric paradigm is a culturally grounded social work practice-based model originating from North America. The model seeks to affirm, codify, and integrate common cultural experiences, values, and interpretations of social life that cut across people of African descent (Graham, 2002; Schiele, 1996, 1997, 2000). This perspective is like the views of African social workers who argue that African philosophies, history, and cultures must be used as a reference point for interpreting social and psychological phenomena to develop culturally relevant interventions of helping individuals, families, small groups, communities, and societies. Thus, the discussion of *botho* in this chapter seeks to contribute to this broader African centred paradigm that has become dominant in the past three decades.

Over the decades, scholars have debated the issue of whether social work should be universal or local, westernised, or indigenized and other such binary dichotomies (Gray and Fook, 2004; Rankopo and Osei-Hwedie, 2010). Some scholars have equally contested the universality of *botho* with some claiming it as an African principle (Tutu, 2004) while others rejected the proposition electing to view it as a global value embedded across many cultures and religions. Noticeably, Mugumbate and Nyanguru (2013) note that, Ubuntu as a philosophy is attributable to

172

blacks of Africa, especially sub-Saharan Africa. They further indicated that social work with individuals' endeavours to bring function on the life of dysfunctional individuals. Accordingly, it is worth noting that *Ubuntu* has several tenets that support the achievement of social work and in particular, case work. In gerontology, in African settings, it is the responsibility of children to look after elderly members of the family. Noticeably, social work education in Botswana as a discipline is over three decades old and in its infancy stage in terms of documenting culturally relevant models for social work education and practice. Based on folklore, it is stated that *botho* was a basic ethic of care in indigenous families which was translated into the care of needy or vulnerable family members including children, the elderly, people with disabilities and the poor. There is need therefore, to critically examine *botho* as an ethic of care as well as an organizing construct for social work practice and education.

On this note, the argument that runs down the gamut of this chapter is that there was an African social set up which was guided by *Ubuntu,* and this set up was destroyed by colonialism. Since then, western colonial social work was introduced and currently there is a clarion call by social workers towards Afrocentric social work and in this way, they are unfreezing the status quo (See, Kurevakwesu and Maushe, 2020; Rankopo and Diraditsile, 2020). This therefore means that *botho* must be used to make social work Afrocentric. Refreezing will need to be done once Ubuntu has been made part of the social work discourse and this can be through the promulgation of policies and making Afrocentric social work a permanent feature of social work curriculum. Thus, Afrocentric social work models are crucial in enabling blacks and Africans in other regions of the world to be treated with dignity and respect by non-African cultures. This would complete the principle of "non-judgmentalism" that upon which western social work has been founded. Our point is that "non-judgmentalism" within a culture is not the same where two or more cultures intersect. If that were the case, then Afrocentric social workers would not have been strongly advocated in North America and Europe.

Guidance: Using *botho* to guide social services

Botho is about community, reciprocity and relationships. As they say in Tswana culture, *motho ke motho ka batho.* Another proverb says, *dito makwati ditsewa mogobabangwe*, meaning we learn from others, reciprocally.

- Use *botho* to inform values and ethics.
- Use *botho* to craft social solutions.
- Apply *botho* to understand human aspirations.
- Use *botho* to understand how human beings relate and function.
- Use *botho* to design appropriate, culturally relevant and decolonial social interventions.

Botho recognises that social workers should value human dignity and worth of the person or clients they work with. *Botho* philosophy disapproves any form of anti-social behaviour, disgraceful and inhumane treatment of others. It encourages social workers to promote the idea of social justice for all. In individual casework, social workers find themselves working with people struggling with life stressors such as addiction, gender-based violence and other life-threatening problems. It is the ultimate duty of social workers utilising the *botho* precept to respect clients regardless of their presenting problem. The social worker must be able to separate the problem from the person, a process called depersonalisation. This helps to overcome labelling and stigmatisation associated with social problems.

It is believed that no person lives in a vacuum and no person is an island. Human beings have interpersonal relationships that are key to development and how they cope with life stressors. *Botho* philosophy guide social workers working in groupwork or systemic therapies to value and strengthen human relationships for the benefit of clients. It is understood that human problems emanate from the point where they interact with the environment, however, that same environment can be used as a safe haven for people facing different challenges. The obligation of the social worker is to positively influence human interaction and tap useful resources available in the community to help an individual.

Policy makers in Africa should strive to integrate *botho* in the policy making, implementation and evaluation process. This helps to give government direction to follow when crafting social policies that are culturally relevant and appropriate in addressing contextual social problems. Botswana has been hailed for integrating *botho* in national policy agendas. Social workers as experts in analysing social problems, they should craft and advocate for policy options that are undergirded by Ubuntu or *botho* principles. This helps in designing social protection programmes and projects that resonate with our cultural norms and values.

174

We reckon that an Afrocentric perspective of social work anchored on indigenous cultural values and principles this is an ambitious agenda which comes at a time when many developing nations are universalizing at rapid rates to generate qualifications and interventions that have a global appeal. This chapter has developed research questions below that seek to stimulate debate in this subject. We maintain that these questions are not easy to answer, however, they are worth debating to complete the diversity of cultures that social work seeks to serve. We propose that this debate be approached from the decolonisation perspective which seeks to deconstruct and reconstruct social work education and practice in non-western contexts. It is a project that requires academicians, practitioners, and social work learners to engage one another reflectively to ensure that the very essence of Africanism is accurately captured in the literature and conveyed in social work practice. We contend that *botho* may be more universal than is currently appreciated in the social work literature because it is widely portrayed in cultural and religious teachings of many societies.

Summary

- This chapter has defined the concept of *botho* and how it is used by African societies to shape and to guide interpersonal and social relations. *Botho* denotes the character of a person, the values, and the attributes expected of a citizen individually and collectively.
- *Botho* is more foundational in the preservation of mutual understanding, unity, love, social harmony, and care, not only for the person but for the property others. A person with *botho* is expected to be considerate, compassionate, benevolent, and respectful in their dealings with others.
- It promotes social justice, equity, and equality amongst members of a community or society. Thus, social workers using *botho* are expected to demonstrate humility, love, care, and commitment to serving their constituents.
- While this chapter has demonstrated the application of this philosophy in an African context, *botho* as a principle may be applicable to other cultural contexts. The term may be unique to Africans, but its essence might find universal application.

Questions for in-class assessments and examinations

- What are the basic tenets of an Afrocentric model of social work anchored on the concept of *botho?*
- How will such an indigenous concept fir into a rapidly developing socio-cultural environment?
- Can such an Afrocentric model appeal to the African continent with its vast ethic and racial backgrounds?
- Will such a model be easily accepted by the pacesetters of academic social work who trained in western contexts?
- Discuss the concept of *botho* as a precept for social work supervision.
- How can managers use *botho* to promote customer-centred services?
- Identify four social institutions that may be used to promote Afrocentric social protection programs.
- Illustrate how social work students may demonstrate *botho* in interactions with others in their social environment.
- Design an appropriate social work intervention drawing on the principle of *botho*.
- To what extent are Afrocentric social work models applicable to your fieldwork placement agency/programs/services?

Potential questions for research

- Explore the universality of *botho* (humaneness) as a cardinal principle of social work.
- How can *botho*/Ubuntu philosophy be integrated in social work education in your country?
- How can *botho*/Ubuntu be integrated in social work practice?
- Describe how *botho*/Ubuntu can be incorporated in social work models, perspectives, theories or conceptual frameworks?
- Examine how decolonization of social work can contribute to strengthening of Afrocentric social work models.
- Universalism vs localization: Interrogating 'humaneness' in a post-modern world.
- Reflections on Afrocentric social work education/practice: The case of Southern Africa.

176

- Decolonizing basic education: Towards development of botho as a civic value.
- Transformation of social protection policies through botho/Ubuntu.
- Building back better, botho and healthy families.
- Botho as a development paradigm to redress unemployment, poverty, and inequalities.
- Botho under siege? The trajectories of gender-based violence.

Key terms and their meanings

Afrocentric perspective – culturally grounded social work practice-based model that affirms, codifies, and integrates common cultural experiences, values, and interpretations that cut across people of African descent.

Botho – refers to "a process for earning respect by first giving it, and to gain empowerment by empowering others. It encourages people to applaud rather than resent those who succeed. It disapproves of anti-social, disgraceful, inhuman, and criminal behaviour, and encourages social justice for all" (Botswana Vision Council, 2016: 2).

Community development – a method of intervention that prevents and addresses long-term problems, challenges, threats, or issues and utilizes community assets, opportunities and participation.

Community – a collective of people who have a consciousness of a common identity, values, goals, and are willing to work for the collective good. They may reside within a defined geographic locality.

Decolonization – cultural, psychological, and economic freedom for indigenous people with the goal of achieving indigenous sovereignty. It entails the right and ability of indigenous people to practice self-determination over their land, cultures, and political and economic systems.

Spirituality – the human longing for a sense of meaning through morally responsible relationships between diverse individuals, families, communities, cultures and religions.

References

Botswana Vision Council (2016). A Long-Term Vision for Botswana: Towards Prosperity for All. Gaborone: Government Printers.

Ellastam, J. L. B. (2015). Exploring Ubuntu Discourse in South Africa: Loss, Liminality and Hope. *Verbum et Ecclesia, 36(2), 41-56.*

Furman, L. D., Benson, P. W., Grimwood, C. and Canda, E. (2004). *Religion and Spirituality in Social Work Education and Indirect Practice at the Millennium:* A Survey of UK (United Kingdom) Social Workers. *British Journal of Social Work, 34(6), 767-792.*

Graham, M. (2002). Creating Spaces: Exploring the Role of Cultural Knowledge as a Source of Empowerment in Models of Social Welfare in Black Communities. *British Journal of Social Work, 32, 35-49.*

Gray, M. (2005) 'Dilemmas of International Social Work: Paradoxical Processes in Indigenisation, Imperialism and Universalism', *International Journal of Social Welfare, 14(2), 230–237.*

Gray, M and Fook, J. (2004). The Quest for a Universal Social Work: Some Issues and Implications. *Social Work Education, 23(5), 625-644.*

Gray, M. (2008). Viewing Spirituality in Social Work through the Lens of Contemporary Social Theory. *British Journal of Social Work, 175-196.*

Hutton, M. and Mwansa, L. K. (1996). *Community, Social Development and Social Change. Social Work Practice in Africa.* Print Consult.

Nyaumwe, L. J. and Mkabela, Q. (2007). Revisiting the indigenous African cultural framework of Ubuntu: A theoretical perspective. Indilinga: African *Journal of Indigenous Knowledge Systems, 6:152-163.*

Ngwenya, B. (1993). The Evolution of Social Work in Botswana. In N. Hall (Ed). *The Social Implications of Structural Adjustment in Africa* (pp. 17-21). School of Social Work, Harare. Zimbabwe

Kurevakwesu, W. and Maushe, F. (2020). Towards Afrocentric Social Work: Plotting a New Path for Social Work Theory and Practice in Africa through Ubuntu. *African Journal of Social Work, 10(1), 30-35.*

178

Ntseane, P. G. (2011). Culturally Sensitive Transformational Learning: Incorporating the Afrocentric Paradigm and African Feminism. *Adult Education Quarterly, 61(4), 307-323.*

Maphosa, S. B. and Keasley, A. (2015). Disrupting the Interruptions: Reconsidering Ubuntu, Reconciliation and Rehumanization. *African Renaissance, 12:16-47.*

Mazama, A. (2001). The Afrocentric Paradigm: Contours and Definitions. *Journal of Black Studies, 31 (4), 387-405.*

Mbiti, J. S. (2015). *Introduction to African Religion.* Long Grove, IL: Waveland Press

Mugumbate, J. and Nyanguru, A. (2013). Exploring African Philosophy: The Value of Ubuntu in Social Work. *African Journal of Social Work, 3(1), 82-100.*

Mugumbate, J. and Chereni, A. (2019). Using African Ubuntu Theory in Social Work with Children in Zimbabwe. *African Journal of Social Work, 9(1), 27-34*

Mupedziswa, R., Rankopo, M. and Mwansa, L-K. (2019). Ubuntu as a pan-African philosophical framework for social work in Africa. In: Twikirize, J.M. and Spitzer, H. (eds). *Social work practice in Africa.* Kampala, Uganda: Fountain Publishers.

Osei-Hwedie, K. (1990). Social Work and the Question of Social Development in Africa. *Journal of Social Development in Africa, 5(2), 87-99.*

Osei-Hwedie, K. (1993). The Challenge of Social Work in Africa: Starting the Indigenisation Process. *Journal of Social Development in Africa, 8(1), 19-30.*

Osei-Hwedie, K. (1996). The Indigenisation of Social Work Practice and Education in Africa: The Dilemma of Theory and Method. *Social Work Stellenbosch, 32, 215-225.*

Osei-Hwedie, K. (2001). Culture and the Construction of Social Work Practice in Africa. *Journal of Culture Studies, 3(1), 231-240.*

Rankopo, M. and Osei-Hwedie, K. (2011). Globalization and Culturally Relevant social work: African perspectives on Indigenization, *International Social Work, 54, (1), 137-147.*

Rankopo, M. J. and Diraditsile, K. (2020). The Interface between Botho and Social Work Practice in Botswana: Towards Afrocentric Models. *African Journal of Social Work, 10(1), 1-5.*

Schiele, J. H. (1996). Afrocentricity: An Emerging Paradigm in Social Work Practice, *Social Work, 41 (3), 284-294.*

Schiele, J. H. (2020). The Contour and Meaning of Afrocentric Social Work. *Journal of Black Studies, 27(6), 800-1997.*

179

Schiele, J. H. (2020). *Human Services and the Afrocentric Paradigm*. Psychology Press.

Sekudu, J. (2019). Ubuntu. In: Van Breda, A. D. and Sekudu, J. (eds). *Theories for Decolonial Social Work Practice in South Africa*. Cape Town: Oxford University Press South Africa.

Twikirize, J. M. and Spitzer, H. (2019). *Social Work Practice in Africa*. Kampala, Uganda: Fountain Publishers.

Tutu, D. M. (1999). *No future Without Forgiveness: A Personal Overview of South Africa's Truth and Reconciliation Commission*. Rider, London.

Van Breda, A. D. (2019). Developing the Notion of Ubuntu as African Theory for Social Work Practice. *Social Work/Maatskaplike Werk, 55(4), 439-450.*

CHAPTER 7

Ubuntu and social development in Africa

Introduction

This chapter focuses on developmental social work, particularly the process of achieving it using the Ubuntu perspective. Authors have included Ubuntu principles that foster development, the role of social workers in the process and challenges faced in the process. Ubuntu oriented approaches allow social work students and practitioners to implement appropriate interventions in Africa. Such interventions are capable of tackling poverty currently affecting most families and communities of Africa. Key definitions will be provided first, followed by theories and then the process of developmental social work before the Ubuntu bowl is presented. At the end challenges will be discussed, and questions for assessments, research and fieldwork provided.

Objectives of this chapter

After studying this chapter, readers will be expected to have acquired knowledge on:

- The process of doing social work and social development.
- Ubuntu principles in social development.
- Key concepts of developmental social work.
- The utilisation of the Ubuntu bowl in the process of social work.
- Roles of social service workers, focusing on social workers.
- Assessments that are suitable for the local context.
- Research questions and methods that are appropriate to the local context.
- Fieldwork, workplace-based and community-based learning is contextual.

Skills and competencies addressed in this chapter

By the end of this chapter, readers will be expected to have acquired the following skills and competencies:

- Create social development activities using Ubuntu principles.
- Ability to differentiate welfare work, social development work, social work and development work.
- Ability to do community mapping of support systems available for clients from an Ubuntu perspective.
- Use developmental strategies to addressing social problems in Africa.
- Develop methods and use theories that are appropriate to and acceptable by an Ubuntu-dominated client system.
- Create questions and aims for teaching or learning, research and fieldwork within a developmental approach.
- Answer questions or assessments about the topic of this chapter.
- Create research questions and methods that are appropriate to the local context.
- Plan fieldwork, workplace-based and community-based learning that is contextual.

Theories used in this chapter

Social development theory

Social development is an integrated and holistic approach towards social work that recognises and responds to the interconnections between the person and the environment (Lombard and Wairire, 2010; Midgley, 2006). Unlike economic development theory which promotes modernisation, social development theory promotes wholistic development - social, economic, spiritual, environmental, or otherwise. While social welfare work and community work are about addressing the immediate needs of a family or community, social development focuses on both short and long term needs of society as a whole.

Kaseke (2017) notes that if social workers are to be key players in promoting social development, there should be a clear meaning of social development and how it can be operationalized. Social development has

182

much been presented on paper while practically many programs are still taking the remedial approach to service provision. These remedial services aim at addressing the *'here and now'* needs of people instead of their long term or permanent necessities. Social development is a pro-poor approach to welfare and service delivery meant to promote the participation of those who are socially excluded. The approach aims at achieving social and economic justice through strengthening communities' livelihood capacities.

Social development strives to promote social solidarity and active participation of citizens in matters that affect them. Mupedziswa et al (2017:19) argue that social development is an approach to address socio-economic challenges through participation, engagement, and involvement of different partners. The approach is developmental, progressive, and multi-dimensional as well as solution-focused in nature.

Midgley (2006) argues that social development must be progressive through projects, policies and plans that promote change. This forms part of a larger multifaceted process comprised of economic, social, political, cultural, environmental, gender and other dimensions that are integrated and harmonised. Social development is interventionist in that it requires human agency in the form of projects, programs, policies and plans that are implemented at household, family, community and national levels in order to achieve a number of developmental goals. The social development process is productive in that practice interventions function as investments that contribute positively to economic development. Social development is universalistic in scope and is concerned with the population rather than with impoverished, vulnerable, and needy groups of people. It also seeks to promote people's participation in development.

Ubuntu theory

Nzimakwe (2014) asserts that Ubuntu is a worldview of African societies and a critical factor which shapes the formation of perceptions around social conduct. This relates to value systems, beliefs and practices that capture the essence of what it means to be human. Ubuntu encompasses treating others with justice and respect in a reciprocal manner. Respect for Ubuntu would allow an individual to have the interconnectedness and enjoy the comfort of support from the surrounding environment. The approach becomes even clearer in the Zimbabwe context where collectivism and respect for cultural values can be used to get acceptance as well as support from the extended or nuclear families and community.

Social work process

Social work is a sequence of actions or tasks that are undertaken by practitioners so that they restore the social functioning (or prevent dysfunction) and enhance coping capacities of individuals, groups and communities. It involves engagement, assessment, intervention, and evaluation. Generally, this process is presented in a linear model, yet it is continuous, fluid, and cyclical and sometimes involves back and forth movements. Depending on the social work method used, this process can be of short, medium-term or of long-term duration. The number involved in the process varies based on the purpose, method used and levels of interactions that the practitioners intend to involve for effective interventions. Casework focuses on the person, family work focuses on family, group work focuses on three or more people while community work involves a community. Below is an illustration of the ideal social work process:

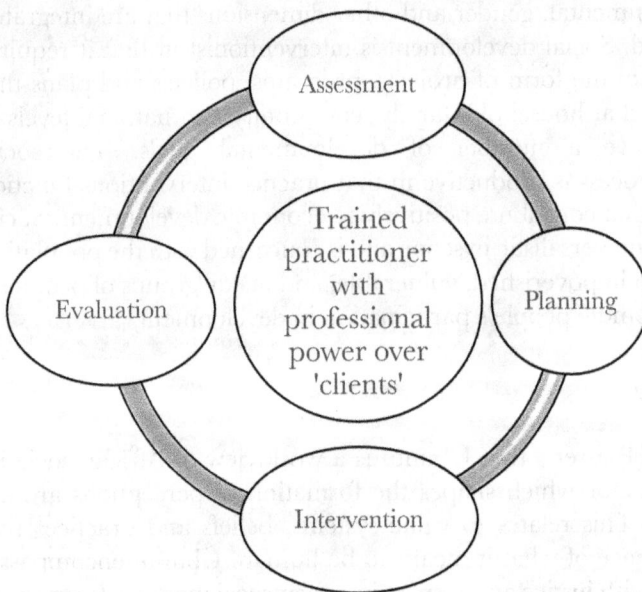

Figure 3: The social work process

The shortcoming of this process is that the practitioner has a lot of power at each stage. This leaves the individual, family, group or community weak in managing their current or future social problems. With this model, the individual, family, group, or community are referred to as 'clients. Another problem is that there is too much focus on managing the immediate welfare needs of the individual, family, group, and community as opposed to addressing social problems in a way that encourages participation and sees them as participants (not clients).

Differences between social work and social development

The difference between social work and social development should be well understood by social workers so that they effectively address challenges faced by their participants. Table 1 shows the differences between social work and developmental social work.

Table 8: The differences between colonial social work and development

Aspect	Colonial social work	Social development
Focus	Focuses on welfare.	Focuses on development.
Scope	Therapeutic and relational.	Policy and structural.
Level	Micro level of society (individual, family and group).	Meso (community) and macro (national and global) levels of society.
Philosophical background	Europe philosophies are prioritised.	Africa philosophy (Ubuntu) is prioritised.
Theoretical background	Implements methods and theories from the western countries.	Locally developed methods and theories.
Source of resources	Usually relies on external support systems at each level. Charitable.	Relies on available local resources at each level. Emphasizes self-sustenance and development.
Intervention mode	Stresses on social functioning and	Social, economic and policy intervention.

	socio-economic policy.	
Individuals, families, groups, and communities viewed as…	Clients	Participants
Practitioners	Social workers, family workers, group workers and welfare workers.	Social workers, community workers and development workers.

Decolonising interventions

The practice of social work in Africa was for a very long time guided by western theories that were far from much removed from the local reality. Twikirize and Spitzer (2019) note that Ubuntu is an African philosophical framework in social work that is rooted in collectivism. The problems that Africa faces do not emanate from individualized circumstances as some come from families and other societies or within communities. This denotes use of theories and interventions that speak to the needs of the local people. According to Mungai (2015), the Afrocentric approach in social work is based on Africa philosophies, history, culture, values and ethics. Use of these determinants informs the formulation and implementation of Ubuntu paradigm shift towards social work through which African cultures and values are taken into consideration. In African social work, there is need to value justice from Africa's viewpoint, collectivity, reciprocity, spirituality and interconnectedness of individuals and families within their local structures something that was affected by modernity as well as market forces (Mungai, 2015). According to Mtapuri and Mazengwa (2013), there is clear evidence from Zimbabwe that poverty alleviation strategies that are divorced from people's environmental and spiritual worldviews are doomed to fail. The wholesale importation of western theories, models and intervention strategies has led social work to become a borrowed profession that is fast losing relevance in the eyes of the generality of Africa's populace (Dziro, 2013). Use of these imported materials made life tough for social workers as their work is not normally considered under critical sectors for economic development. As such, very limited resources are committed for the same cause making interventions so difficult to implement that their failure is always at sight.

186

To make matters worse, the interventions attempted are far-fetched and divorced from reality. In short, this makes it a hurdle to address modern challenges faced by the local people that emanate from their indigenous systems. It is against this background that Africanisation of social work should address such an anomaly for attainment of social development amongst the social work clientele. According to Mungai (2015), the concept of *sankofa* (a symbolic a bird in Akan culture of Ghana that is looking back but going forward) is a way to go in the Africanization of social work. This entails that it is crucial for African social workers to take into considerations history, cultures, values, and available systems to come up with sustainable and prosperous interventions. There is a call for Africanization of social work through design, planning, implementation and evaluation of locally developed models for sustainable social development is the way to go if the profession is to regain its place amongst other 'professional giants'.

Ubuntu bowl concept in social work

The introduction of the Ubuntu bowl concept in social work strengthens the importance of the localization of the profession in Africa. A bowl is a round dish, basin or vessel that is open at the top and used to hold food or liquid. In the African context, the bowls were made of clay or wood based on locally available resources. Social workers in Africa should embrace the Ubuntu bowl that holds all principles and values useful in solving local problems. As such, the concept can be used in the assessment of a program, intervention or strategy and variance from the expected African standards. According to Zvomuya (2020), the the Ubuntu bowl consists of cultural diversity, social and environmental justice, value for family or the extended family systems and respect for the needs of future generations. African values include collectivism, reciprocity, spirituality and interconnectedness of all beings, beliefs, and humanity.

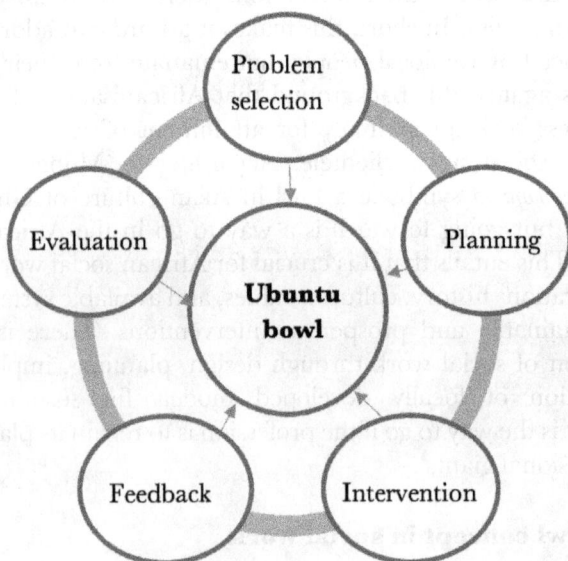

Figure 4: The Ubuntu bowl process

As presented in figure adopted from Zvomuya (2019), the Ubuntu bowl process is a whereby problems are identified and addressed in a comprehensive and Afrocentric manner. This is an intertwined approach towards tackling poverty in Africa in a sustainable way. At each stage of social work, it is important to refer to the Ubuntu bowl that forms the core of the African philosophy. Below is a tabular presentation of the Ubuntu cycle and the roles of developmental social workers.

	Stage	Useful Ubuntu values	Roles of developmental workers
1	Problem selection and clarification *(selecting a social need to focus on.)*	• Involvement of the community and leaders. • Humaneness	• Consulting community leaders and families on the problem. • Home visits for case assessment.

2	Planning *(developing case plans to address the identified and prioritized problem.)*	• Respect for spirituality and cultural diversity. • Value for family or extended family and other key stakeholders. • Respect for human rights.	• Engaging family members including extended ones. • Mapping clients' genogram and supporting system. • Community mapping on available stakeholders. • Advising on legal implications of proposed plans.
3	Intervention *(implementing developed case plans to meet the developmental need identified.)*	• Collectivism and interconnectedness of individuals at micro, meso and macro levels. • Respect of the environment.	• Including family and community members in counselling • Assigning tasks to family members in problem solving process. • Involving informal caring networks. • Linking clients to other relevant stakeholders and economic initiatives.
4	Feedback *(presenting outcomes of the implemented action plans.)*	• Respect of spirituality. • Interconnectedness • Cohesion	• Allow self-determination on alternative solutions to problems. • Getting feedback from family members on changes around the client. • Community dialogues on

189

			presented problems.
5	Evaluation *(determining the effectiveness of plans implemented in addressing the problem identified and meeting the developmental need.)*	• Needs of future generation. • Norm of reciprocity. • Social justice. • Inclusion of other culturally oriented solutions.	• Reflecting on the advantages and disadvantages of outcomes together with clients. • Allow for other cultural and religious practices. • Engaging community leaders on the problem and way forward.

Figure 5: Stages of intervention, Ubuntu values and roles of developmental workers

Impediments to using the social development approach

- Inadequate training.
- Limited resources.
- Migration and brain drain.
- Governments still focused on social welfare.
- Communities still expecting social welfare.

Case study: Departments of Social Development in Zimbabwe and South Africa

In 2021, the Government of Zimbabwe changed the name of the Department of Social Services and Department of Social Welfare to Department of Social Development whose aim is to (Government of Zimbabwe, 2021):

> *Reduce poverty and enhance self-reliance through the provision of social protection services to vulnerable and disadvantaged groups in Zimbabwe.*

190

The aim of doing this was to maximize developmental interventions. As the names themselves suggest, the department was not clear on its contribution about social development notwithstanding the fact that it employed most of the social workers in the country. Much focus in the Department of Social Welfare was to provide child protection and social welfare services to orphans, children living in poverty, children without protection, older people, people with disabilities and refugees. They provided education, health, food, counselling and cash so that selected beneficiaries are able to meet at least the minimum basic needs through programs such as Public Assistance, Harmonized Social Cash Transfer (HSCT), Food Deficit Mitigation Programme (FDMP) and Social Assistance. Being entrusted with the mandate to register private voluntary organisations (PVOs), non-governmental organisations (NGOs) and Community-Based Organisations (CBOs), the Department of Social Welfare would see most of the development partners coming to provide direct social welfare services. Provision of such services has not transformed vulnerable communities, as the process is just curative in nature. The renaming suggests that the department has now realised a niche of social workers not actively being involved in the social development processes of the country. A transition from 'social welfare' to 'social development' is a 'food-for-thought' for both social workers and their clients. It has been a trend that clients perceive social workers as mere providers of social welfare services (Zvomuya, 2017) and not active participants in transforming communities for social development. This is still the thinking amongst communities as they see anyone who provides charity as a social worker and expects to get such material benefits such as food handouts, cash, uniforms, and transport money and school fees from the department. Hence, the renaming of the department to present a social development element of its mandate and operations. This becomes the starting point in realignment of departmental core functions towards the provision of developmental social welfare services. With this renaming done, social workers ought to start implementing developmental social welfare programs. These programs are aimed at empowering social welfare beneficiaries towards poverty alleviation and shun dependency syndrome amongst themselves. According to Mundau and Zvomuya (2021), the call for developmental social welfare is one of the dominant agenda issues in social work. In developmental social welfare, the implementation of pro-poor projects and programs should be temporary and implemented only to save vulnerable populations from extreme poverty. To attain social development, training institutions need to provide developmental skills among social work students so that they impart the same to their clients. Such skills as creativity, risk and disaster management, project planning and management, climate change adaptation, entrepreneurship, and economic strengthening. This makes it easy for the Department of Social Development to get practitioners who have a wealth of knowledge in tackling the challenges faced by their clients. Imperatively, practicing social workers require some re-training so that their work immensely contributes towards meeting the aim of the department and promotion of social development in the country.

In South Africa, the Department of Social Development's mandate is to (South Africa Government, 2023):

> *Provide social protection services and leads government's efforts to forge partnerships through which vulnerable individuals, groups and communities become capable and active participants in the development of themselves and society. The social development function facilitates access to social grants and welfare services to reduce poverty and inequality, protect children, and empower women, youth and people with disabilities… The DSD continues to profile vulnerable households and communities to determine their socio-economic needs and create structures and enhance capacity in communities to reduce social ills. The department supports civil-society organisations that focus on initiatives that aim to improve livelihoods.*

Some policies used by the Department are:

1. Nonprofit Organisations (NPOs) Act – for regulation of NPOs.
2. White Paper for Social Welfare which sets principles, guidelines, policies and programs for developmental social welfare.
3. White Paper on Population Policy for South Africa which promotes sustainable development.
4. Social Assistance Act for the provision of social assistance.
5. Children's Act for the care and protection of children.
6. Older Persons Act for maintaining and promoting the rights, status, well-being, safety and security of older people.
7. Prevention of and Treatment for Substance Abuse Act for the establishment, registration and monitoring of in-patient treatment centres and halfway houses.

The South African Social Security Agency (SASSA), established through the SASSA Act is an entity of the department. The SASSA ensures effective and efficient administration, management and payment of social assistance. The agency administers and pays social assistance transfers to qualifying beneficiaries. Another agency is the National Development Agency (NDA) whose primary mandate is to contribute towards the eradication of poverty and its causes by granting funds to civil society organisations to implement development projects in poor communities.

Guidance: Using Ubuntu in social development

Social development is Africa's answer to its problems and the starting point is Ubuntu. Ubuntu shapes aspirations, and development will not happen if aspirations are misunderstood. Termites multiply quickly where there is wood and moisture but will struggle where there is not moisture and wood. Plastic and oil are very good products, but they choke sea life. To urbanise and modernise is not to develop.

- Use Ubuntu to transform social services, from modernisation and urbanisation to development.
- Use Ubuntu to support rural livelihoods and aspirations.
- Use Ubuntu aspirations to design human resource recruitment and retention policies.
- Development should focus on all levels of Ubuntu – family, community, societal, environmental and spiritual.

Summary

- The core tenets of social development are focus on human, family, community and societal development rather than welfare and aid.
- Social development supports Afrocentric models and strategies of poverty alleviation.
- Ubuntu ensures a stronger focus on the family and community.
- Ubuntu social work allows use of locally contextual, relevant, and sustainable interventions.
- Zimbabwe and South Africa are some examples that have embraced social development.

Further and advanced knowledge

In this chapter, two important concepts were the focus – social development and Ubuntu. It is important for readers to read more on these topics. While reading on Ubuntu, ensure that you identify Africa literature. This is because Ubuntu has been misrepresented by writers from outside Africa. A comprehensive coverage of Ubuntu is found at www.africasocialwork.net/Ubuntu.

Questions for in-class assessments and examinations

1. Participants or clients? Debate the most appropriate noun for people, households, and communities in social development. This can be done as an individual assignment, in pairs or small groups, in writing or orally.
2. Evaluate the current social development practices of South Africa in alleviating poverty among the poor.
3. Design a five-year strategy for the Department of Social Development of a selected country of your choice.
4. Create a job description of community development worker working in a rural village.
5. Create five tasks for a rural fieldwork placement for a final year student. For each task, provide a list of activities and success criteria for each task.
6. Design a poster with pictures that shows the Ubuntu principles that contribute to social development.
7. Write a speech for the Department of Social Development to be delivered to Chiefs of the local areas about what social welfare, social work and social development means.
8. Create a job description of a social development worker and a social welfare worker.

Potential questions for research

1. What strategies can be adopted to adopt Ubuntu and social development in childcare institutions?
2. Do a systematic literature review or an indaba on the role of Abrahamic religion (Christianity and Islam) in devaluing Africa worldviews as Ubuntu.
3. An evaluation and analysis of roles of Departments of Social Development.
4. How to make the work of non-governmental organisations and international organisations value Africa's worldviews.

194

5. How social workers can use Ubuntu as a tool to fight corruption and bad governance in developing countries?
6. Do an indaba with social development workers and beneficiaries on their experiences with a social development program.
7. Observe five community development projects and evaluate how social development was used, strengths and identify gaps.
8. Do a policy analysis of five social policies used by a government of your choice.

Potential fieldwork settings and ideas

1. The best placement for social development is one that allows you to be in the community especially in Rural District Councils (RDC) and Community Based Organisations among other grassroots settings.
2. Developmental social work is best practised in statutory welfare organisations such as the Department of Social Development.
3. Issues to take note of when going for attachment include needs assessment, creating solutions, community engagement skills, talent management and promoting participation.
4. Placements that are done in villages, involving village and community leaders would be most useful given that 75% of participants in social development come from rural communities.
5. Social development fieldwork requires innovation or creativity.

Key terms and their meanings

Development – (1) a process of achieving a family, community or society's desired goals in ways that meet their cultural, spiritual, social, economic and environmental expectations (2) the outcome of the process stated in (1).

Developmental social welfare – when social welfare services are provided to stimulate development.

Developmental social work – participation in economic production to increase social functioning of households, communities, and society. It focuses on development not welfare. Developmental social work includes human development (as opposed to human welfare), family development (as opposed to family work or welfare), community development (as opposed to community work and community welfare), social development (as opposed to social welfare), international development (as opposed to aid or international welfare). However, development often includes work, welfare, and development.

Social development – refers to interventions that prevents social problems and addresses all the social needs of an individual, group, family, community and society, in both the short and long-term. According to Kaseke (2001), social development emerged to address dissatisfaction with economic growth models that neglect of social factors. Hence, it refers to a development process, which includes the importance of social factors when addressing people's problems.

Social work process – refers to activities of working with individuals, groups and communities to deal with life challenges that can be social, economic, spiritual, environmental or otherwise.

Ubuntu bowl – refers to a combination of principles that represent an African way of doing things and oneness. According to Zvomuya (2020), the Ubuntu bowl consists of cultural diversity, social and environmental justice, value for family or the extended family systems and respect for the needs of future generations. Africa values include collectivism, reciprocity, spirituality and interconnectedness or wholism.

Ubuntu inspired process – refers to actions or interventions in line with Ubuntu principles.

Ubuntu – refers to a collection of values and practices that black people of Africa or of African origin view as making people authentic human beings. While the nuances of these values and practices vary across different ethnic groups, they all point to one thing – an authentic individual human being is part of a larger and more significant relational, communal, societal, environmental, and spiritual world (Mugumbate and Chereni, 2020).

196

Ubuntu social work – refers to social work that is theoretically, pedagogically, and practically grounded in Africa worldviews.

References and recommended readings

Chidzonga, M. A. (2017). A *Hunhu*-Ubuntu Informed Critique of Patriotic History Discourse and Chimurenga Nationalism. Dissertation submitted in Fulfilment of Master of Art, Dalhousie University, Halifax, Nova Scotia.

Council of Soci.al Workers (CSW) (2012). Social workers code of ethics. Statutory Instrument 146.

Dziro, C. (2013) Trends in social work education and training: The case of Zimbabwe. *International Journal of Development and Sustainability, 2 (2), 1423-1435*

Government of Zimbabwe (2021). Department of Social Development. Harare, Public Service, Labour and Social Welfare.

Hall, S. (1987). *Interviewing, Power or Knowledge and Social Inequality. A Handbook of Interviewing Research.* Thousand Oaks. Sage Publications.

Ife, J. (2010). *Human rights from below: Achieving rights through community development.* Cambridge: Cambridge University Press.

International Labour Organisation (1999). *Extending Social Security to all: A guide through challenges and options.* Geneva: International Labour Organisation.

Kaseke, E. (1994). *A Situation Analysis of the Social Development Fund.* Harare, Ministry of Public Service, Labour and Social Welfare and UNICEF.

Kaseke, E. (2001). Social Development as a Model of Social work Practice: The Experience of Zimbabwe. Harare: School of Social work. (published paper)

Kaseke, E. (2003). Informal Social Security in Eastern and Southern Africa, *Regional Development Studies,* 9, 1-10.

Kitetu, C. (2010). Organisational Networks of Kenyan Female Migrants in England: The Humble Chama Now operating at Higher International Levels accessed from http://codesria.org/IMG/pdf/CATHEREINE_KITETU.pdf

Lombard, A. and Wairire, G. (2010). Developmental Social work in South Africa and Kenya: Some Lessons for Africa. *The Social work Practitioner-Researcher, Special Issue, April 2010,* 98-111.

197

Lombard, A. (2010). The Implementation of the White Paper for Social Welfare: A Ten-year Review. *The Social work Practitioner-Researcher, 20 (2): 137–153.*

Mbuki, M. (2012). *Factors influencing participation of men in anti-poverty self-help groups: A case of Dagoretti District.* Nairobi: University of Nairobi Department of Education Management.

Midgley, J. (2006*). Development, Social Development and Human Rights: A Social work Perspective.* New York: Columbia University Press, 97–121.

Mtapuri, O. and Mazengwa, P. J. (2013). Of Spirituality and Poverty: A Zimbabwean Cultural Perspective: IndoPacific *Journal of Phenomenology, X (X), 10pp.*

Mugumbate, J. and Nyanguru, A. (2013). Exploring African Philosophy: The Value of Ubuntu in social work. *African Journal OF Social work, 3, (1), 2013, 82-100.*

Mundau, M. and Zvomuya, W. (2021). *Indigenising social work for social development: impediments and mitigations: Professional Social work in Zimbabwe. Past, Present and the Future.* Zimbabwe, Harare: National Association of Social workers

Mungai, N. W. (2014a). The challenges of maintaining social work ethics in Kenya. *Ethics and Social Welfare, 8(2), 170–186.*

Mungai, N. W. (2015). *Afrocentric Social work: Implications for Practice Issues.* New Delhi: Charles Sturt University.

Mupedziswa, R. Jacques, G and Mwansa, L. K. (2017). *Social work and Social Development in Botswana. Issues, Challenges and Prospects.* Botswana Millennium Development Goals Status. Gaborone

Muzondo, E and Rusero, M (2021). *Social Security in Zimbabwe: Professional Social work in Zimbabwe. Past, Present and the Future.* Zimbabwe, Harare: National Association of Social workers

Muzondo, E. and Rusero, M. (2021). Social Development Approach among childcare residential facilities: A case of Alpha Cottages, Masvingo, Zimbabwe. *Journal of Development Administration (JDA), 6(1), 111-119.*

Nahar, S. (2014). *The analysis of social development as a concept: A thesis submitted to the Department of Social work*: University of Texas at Arlington

Nzimakwe, T. I. (2014) Practising *Ubuntu* and leadership for good governance: The South African and Continental Dialogue, *African Journal of Public Affairs,* .30-41

198

Patel, L. (2012). Developmental Social Policy, Social Welfare Services and the Non-profit Sector in South Africaspol. *Social Policy and Administration. 46, (6), December 2012, 603–618*

Patel, L. (2015). Developmental Social Policy, Social Welfare Services and the Non-profit Sector in South Africaspol. *Social Policy and Administration. 46, (6), December 2012, 603–618*

Pawar, M. (2014). Social and Community Development Practice. http://dx.doi.org/10.4135/9789351507987-accessed 08 February 2021

South Africa Government (2023). Social development. Accessed on 10 November 2023 from https://www.gov.za/about-sa/social-development

Twikirize, J. M. and Spitzer, H. (2019) *Social work Practice in Africa: Indigenous and Innovative Approaches.* Kampala: Fountain Publishers.

Zvomuya, W. (2020). Utilization of Ubuntu bowl in social work Processes: The way to go towards attainment of social development in Africa. *African Journal of Social work, 10(1), 63 – 68.*

Zvomuya, W. (2017). Environmental Crisis and Sustainable Development in Zimbabwe: A Social work Perspective. *African Journal of Social work, Volume 7(2), 36-44.*

Zvomuya, W. (2017). Environmental Crisis and Sustainable Development in Zimbabwe: A Social work Perspective. *African Journal of Social work, 7(2), 36-44.*

CHAPTER 8

Community work and community development in Africa

Introduction

This chapter introduces community work and community development from an African Ubuntu perspective. The chapter then defines community work and community development and lists their objectives, guiding principles and ethics. Theories of working with communities are provided. These are *ujamaa*, Ubuntu and the developmental approach that promotes social and economic development. Strategies and examples of community work and community development are provided (mostly from Zimbabwe), followed by the process and pillars of community work and community development. Readers will also find useful templates and detailed case studies. At the end of the chapter, it is expected that readers will have both theoretical knowledge and practical skills to conceptualize, plan, initiate, implement, review and close a community project in African contexts.

Objectives of this chapter

After studying this chapter, readers will be expected to have acquired knowledge on:

- Definitions of community work and community development from an indigenous perspective.
- Theoretical foundations of community work in Africa.
- Objectives, guiding principles and ethics or values in community work and community development.
- Process of community work or community development.
- Models and pillars of community work.

200

- Strategies community work and community development.
- Assessments that are suitable for the local context.
- Applying Ubuntu in community work and community development.
- Research questions and methods that are appropriate to the local context.
- Fieldwork, workplace-based and community-based learning is contextual.

Skills and competencies addressed in this chapter

By the end of this chapter, readers will be expected to have acquired the following skills and competencies:

- Do a community work and community development audit of a selected community.
- Identify community needs or problems that require community intervention.
- Identify the pillars of community work and community development of a specific community.
- Identify economic and social drivers to community well-being and promote them.
- Identify appropriate and indigenous intervention methods for a selected community.
- Develop an intervention or implementation plan for a selected community to generate community well-being.
- Ability to intervene and implement community programs that achieve self-help.
- Offer capacity building to communities through the transfer of knowledge and skills for their empowerment, liberation and well-being.
- Support and encourage the establishment of growth-oriented community social enterprises that are both sustainable and market driven.
- Ability to nurture community enterprises and local projects that meet community needs and are based on social and economic responsibility.
- Review or evaluate a community development program.

- Ability to develop a project sustainability plan that determines project continuity.
- Answer questions or assessments about the topic of this chapter.
- Create research questions and methods that are appropriate to the local context.
- Plan fieldwork, workplace-based and community-based learning that is contextual.

Definitions of community work, community development and development

Community is a collective of people who have a consciousness of a common identity, values, goals, and are willing to work for the collective good. They may reside within a defined geographic locality and share a common identity. It comprises households who usually form a village or neighbourhood.

Community work and community development are some of the methods used in social work studies, community studies or development studies. These social work methods focus on identifying social problems, and addressing challenges, threats or issues experienced by a community as compared to casework which focuses on an individual. The community or development worker is usually a catalyst; he/she does not impose decisions on the community. Rather, the worker mobilises the community members to participate in all projects and empowers them to achieve a mind-set for self-help. There is a slight difference between community work and community development as shown in the two definitions below from Khomba and Kangaude-Ulaya (2013):

> Community work is a method of intervention that addresses immediate, short and medium-term problems, challenges, threats or issues and utilises community assets, opportunities and participation. The assets can be human, family, environmental, spiritual, or otherwise and can also come from outside. Community work focuses on short-term welfare and addresses immediate needs, it is often reactive. Community work can be done on behalf of the community. For example, during a cyclone, community welfare needs will include safety, shelter, food and health. These can be provided by community workers. Community development is a method of intervention that

202

prevents and addresses long-term problems, challenges, threats, or issues and utilises community assets, opportunities and participation. Community development focuses on long-term well-being and addresses long-term needs, it is often preventive, and it empowers and builds capacity. Community development cannot be done on behalf of the community. For example, after a cyclone, community well-being needs will include prevention of property damage and loss of life during cyclones in future. This can be done by the community on its own or working with community development workers and other stakeholders.

Development is a process of ensuring that a community has all the tangible and non-tangible goods, infrastructure and services required to satisfy their short- to long-term needs. A developed community has all the tangible and non-tangible goods, infrastructure, human expertise and community services required to satisfy their short- to long-term needs.

Community work and community development share a lot in common. Both are concerned with community welfare and well-being. The two methods depend on the community as a key to the success of an intervention. The African theory on the same explains this better in that *'simba rehove riri mumvura'* (the power of fish is in the water that unsound it. Literally, this means that great individuals, great communities and great entrepreneurs all succeed through the push, pull and support from their communities.

Goals of community work and community development

The goals of community work and community development include:

- Identifying community problems and community viable projects, community challenges, threat or issues.
- Building awareness around communities of potential problems and viable projects that exist, the challenges and threat or relevant issues and ways to prevent, solve or take the opportunities available to them in their community.
- Identifying community resources and mobilizing participants and stakeholders to generate well-being utilizing local resources.
- Solving or preventing problems, challenges, threat, or issues.
- Empowering or building capacity of the community to solve problems, challenges, threat or issues.

203

Guiding principles, ethics and values in community work and community development

- *Ubuntu - ndiri nekuti tiri* (I am because we are).
- *Simba rehove riri mumvura* (the power of the fish is water around it).
- Understanding and respecting community aspirations.
- Focusing on community needs, problems, challenges, threats and issues.
- Multi-stakeholder approach.
- Developmental socio-economic approach.
- Empowerment or capacity building.
- *Machobane* principle – this means sustainability e.g. when farming, you can rotate, intercrop, or use organic manure.
- Self-drive for self-reliance.
- *Ujamaa*, meaning community pulling together as one family, collective participation of all.
- *Umuganda* meaning coming together for a common purpose.
- Importance of leaders, including indigenous leadership and aged people.

African theoretical foundations of community work and community development

- *Ujamaa* is about creating a community identity, working collectively, decolonization from western methods (independence), self-reliance, building community cohesion, local production and well-being. *Ujamaa* also means and supports a *multisectoral approach*. Although this theory existed since times immemorial, it was popularized by the former President of Tanzania, Mwalimu Julius Nyerere who asserted that a community or nation will achieve more if they pull together.
- *Ubuntu* theory also informs community work and community development. Ubuntu community work and community development refers to social work that is theoretically, pedagogically and practically grounded in Ubuntu. *Ubuntu* promotes communityhood and an admiration for the dignity of others. Community work and community development resonate with the African saying *ndiri nekuti tiri* (I am because we are).

204

Ubuntu embraces the solidarity, justice and cohesion of the community and builds sustainable communities through teamwork and service to others, above all and valuing interdependency.

- The African developmental approach, credited to Professor Edwell Kaseke who wrote much about it during his time at the School of Social Work, when it was still under the University of Zimbabwe, is an important model in community work and community development. Kaseke (2001a) said social development seeks to ensure that individuals have access to resources necessary for meeting basic needs and in conditions that do not undermine their self-esteem. In Kaseke's developmental work model, the roles of workers include creating opportunities for economic productivity (e.g. farming, irrigation, mining, fishing, off-farm income generating projects, self-employment and enterprises); lobbying and advocacy for social justice; mobilising local savings; improving people's economic productivity skills; mobilising the rural communities to improve infrastructure such as roads, bridges, clinics and schools; assisting communities to develop development projects (proposals, plans, funding and feasibility) and ensuring that communities contribution is valued, pursued and recognised. This means that development is driven from the micro and macro levels, and from the economic and social perspectives.
- Other theories include *ukama* (African family theory), *umuganda* model, *mtundu* (community) model, indigenization theory, decolonization theory, African assets theory and bottom-up theory.

Process of community work or community development

1. Problem/Project identification/Auditing: This is a baseline survey in the community to identify all their development pillars and needs. Identification is achieved by doing a community audit or survey. The audits and surveys are achieved through community needs assessment, community observation by the worker, using existing research data, focused group discussions, consultation or a combination of all these.
2. Planning: the plan explains the activities in detail, offering practical steps. It is consultative and the input of a variety of stakeholders is important. It must be aimed at addressing on

community needs. The plan must be sustainable, measurable, achievable, results based and time-bound (SMART).

3. Implementing: Using the frame developed at planning, the implementation process follows these steps (i) initiate the project (ii) implement the project activities, (iii) monitor closely and evaluate stage by stage every step and outcomes of the projects (iv) identify areas to improve (v) initiate and renew project for improvement or prepare the community for closure and self-reliance/close the project and hand over implementation to the community.

4. Reviewing: do a final evaluation or review of the project or program and share lessons. Plan the next phase or the program using results of the review.

5. Sustaining: develop a plan about how the program will continue or end in a *machobane* (sustainable) way that leaves the community responsible for continued implementation.

Africa social, economic, cultural and political background

Africa is a continent endowed with land for agriculture, mining, and water for fishing. Most of Africa's population live in rural communities and most of the people living in urban areas have a permanent rural home or connection. This makes it important for community workers and community development workers to plan from a non-elitist urban approach. The elitist approach has its roots in colonisation, where white people developed services for urban communities using western modernisation approaches founded on their culture and values. The elitist approach resulted in segregation, apartheid and creation of reserves where black people were forced into small pieces of unproductive land. Colonization took many forms – spiritual, religious, political, environmental, cultural, psychological, and educational.

Seventy five percent or more of African people are believed to be living in rural communities with little to no income, with most living in abject poverty. For income and livelihoods, many Africans work on the land – farming, mining, fishing and doing other economic activities.

African culture is centred around the family, village and surrounding community. Families are much larger in size, they include the extended family, that is members of the clan or tribe. Africa has a rich cultural

206

heritage of family life, dance, music, food, marriage, childcare, Ubuntu, *ujamaa* and others. Africa's spiritual heritage is also rich.

Politically and administratively, Africa has dual systems because of colonisation. The first is the indigenous system of governance. In Zimbabwe, they include *Samusha* (Village Head), *Sadunhu* (Sub-Chief), *Ishe or Mambo* (Chief) and at the top will be King, for example the Rozvi King and the Ndebele King, both whose kingships were destroyed during colonisation but are reviving. In countries such as The Kingdom of Eswatini, Ingwenyama (King), currently holds executive powers like that of a sitting president. Different systems and different names are used in other countries. The second is the western form of politics and governance, and in some countries, the Arabic form. The indigenous system works together with western systems of ward, sub-county, county or district, province and state. Western democracy, as a system of politics and governance, has produced mixed results. It has promoted stability and cohesion in some communities, but it has also resulted in disharmony, violence, death and loss of sovereignty.

It is also important to state the role of the African Union (AU), and regional bodies for South, East, Central and West Africa. The AU and these other bodies set policy directions that influence individual national policies. Examples include the African Charter on Human and Peoples' Rights, African Charter on the Rights and Welfare of the Child and African Union Convention on Preventing and Combating Corruption. Regional organisations include the Arab Maghreb Union (AMU), Common Market for Eastern and Southern Africa (COMESA), Community of Sahel-Saharan States (CEN-SAD), East African Community (EAC), Economic Community of Central African States (ECCAS), Economic Community of West African States (ECOWAS), Intergovernmental Authority for Development (IGAD) and Southern African Development Community (SADC).

Due to colonisation, community development was developed based on western values but it failed to address the challenges of poverty facing most Africans (Kaseke, 2001). This resulted in a call to decolonise the theory and practice of community work and community development. The strategies, theories, examples, explanations, case studies and definitions in this chapter are therefore rightly presented from a decolonial perspective.

Strategies and examples of community work and community development

Economic strategies

Nhimbe/Jakwara (Zimbabwe), Harambee (Kenya) or Ubudehe (Rwanda)

Nhimbe is also known as *ikibiri* in Burundi and *msaragambo* in Tanzania, *bulungi bwansi* and *gwanga mujje*. These are rotational work parties or community mutual assistance arranged at village or multi-village level. The community join hands to support each other for no economic reward. Rich farmers *(hurudza)* and poor community members have an opportunity to join hands and share. This is associated with wild joy and a lot of melodious singing, merry-making and rejoicing as people work, share good food, mostly locally brewed beer, small grain *sadza* or *matoke* and meat. Usually, this process invites surrounding village heads and their members to participate. Village heads are respectable people during this community activity and food sharing is based on village participation. *Nhimbe* has several benefits including pulling labour together, helping would be needy villagers, transferring skills from *hurudza* to others especially the young, motivating others to work and promoting community cohesion through sharing and working together. In Rwanda, it is called *ubudehe*, meaning mutual assistance. It is done differently, depending on community culture, so it varies from country to country but also community to community. These strategies, if used effectively, increase production.

Japato (food for work)

Japato is a model of local participation in the building of local infrastructure such as repair of community roads, bridges and water points as a form of building local infrastructure and community development. The sponsors (government or non-governmental organisations (NGOs)) give the community work to do in their community in return for food, money or development resources. It is also considered as a model for social assistance to able bodied but desperate households who require assistance with food. Food for work programs is usually organised by government utilising government community development officers together with the support of social welfare officers whose role is to make the necessary assessments to determine which community benefits. also use this method.

208

The local village heads take responsibility to list benefiting community members or households and take on supervision of the work progress including monitoring and evaluation to determine sustainability. If used effectively, food for work programs is economically viable for the sponsors and community.

Mukando/Stokvel/Chama (rotational savings)

This is a practice developed well across Africa and each country has its different forms of community savings and lending. It is a very functional and successful social support system that has seen many families educating their children. The *stokvel* is a terminology used to describe rotational savings and practised largely in South Africa and *chama* is used in East Africa especially Kenya. *Mukando* is a term applied in Zimbabwe where both men and women practice it. This involves a group of people contributing a fixed amount of money from their salary or income during agreed times or on agreed date and then take turns to receive all the contributed money one at a time. This can involve a group of trusted friends of up to 10 people. In the villages, women do *mukando* to raise money for school fees, kitchen utensils or groceries. *Mukando* can be tied to an enterprise such as beer brewing or market trade, where after a day, week or month's income, members give an agreed amount to one member at a time. Another format is where one member would brew beer for sale, all the members are obliged to attend, pay their contribution of *mukando*. This kind of practice is called *mutudu*. Several fundraising activities would be arranged on the day including dancing competitions and selling delicious food. The expenses one member accumulates are usually recorded and in their turn of *mukando*, the benefiting member would match the expenses to strengthen the saying that *kandiro kanopfumba kunobva kamwe* or *kandiro enda kandiro dzoka*, that is, one good turn deserves another.

Family crafts and artisanship

This is a type of community development that is wholly in-built within the community. Craft skills for artisanship are passed from grandmother to grand-daughter, grandfather to grandson, from father to son and from mother to daughter. The resources are natural, and the skills are locally acquired through community internship and indigenous apprenticeship arrangements. The skills transfer process can be done in many other forms, for example, from father to daughter depending on the nature of skill. Crafts and craftsmanship skills have the potential to change the shape of

209

the entire community through successful crafts sales and setting up community enterprises based on crafts. The Chimanimani Gudyanga community is endowed with large forests of baobab trees from which they harvest the bark *(gavi)* which is used to make a variety of crafts that are sold along the Mutare - Masvingo highway. There are several other examples of family crafts and artisanship passed from generation to generation.

Employment creation or employment services

To improve the wellbeing of individuals, families and the community, generating sustainable employment opportunities at community level is a good option. This can be self or formal employment. This can be done by government or community-based organisations. Opportunities include putting people directly into employment or starting with internships. Another option is to promote and improve family crafts. There are several other options including career guidance services.

Income generating projects (mabhindauko)

This involves a group of people in a community coming together to implement an enterprise that can give them income. There are several types of income projects. Small income generating projects created at community level can grow into successful community enterprises that become sustainable and are driven by market demands hence grow through addressing community demands. They must be tapping the economic potential of the community, i.e. benefiting from locally available resources to sustain themselves. Community enterprises should have access to training programs and mentorship that will provide upgrades from technical skills *(craft making)* to business skills *(entrepreneurship and financial literacy)*. These projects usually have 2-10 members.

Mushandirapamwe (cooperatives)

These are large income generation projects although *mushandirapamwe* can be done for social reasons. It involves more than 10 people putting their resources together to run a project. There are several projects to choose from including retail cooperative shops, housing cooperative, cooperative garden, cooperative college or school, cooperative mining or fishing or tourism or cooperative transport business. Shops. A savings or banking account can be opened. The popular bus company, *Mushandirapamwe* was a result of such a cooperation.

Development and improvements of markets

Finding markets and market improvement are a key strategy in growing community social enterprises as they struggle to become sustainable. Income generating projects when they reach the sustainability level, they need to be supported to venture into viable markets, value addition ventures.

Road construction or rehabilitation

Roads are part of a vehicle for community development and marketing of locally produced goods. The improvement of roads in a community enables the easy movement of goods and services. Hence, road construction is part of community development with the potential of raising the standards of infrastructure in the community and for community well-being.

Village industries, value addition and processing

This strategy is about developing the community's capacity to process and add value to products from their communities. An example is Zvinoda Madzimai, a group of women that grows peanuts, then process it into peanut butter for sale. Others process honey into fine honey, maize into mealie meal and *maputi*, vegetables, timber, bark into dyes, harvesting and packaging local teas, minerals, fish, cotton into yarn, making juices, making beer, making wines, sunflower into oil, and fruits.

Investments and savings support

One economic strategy desirable for communities is investing and saving. Investment means using available resources with an aim to produce and generate more resources. Savings means putting resources aside to support more production or as insurance. Communities have several ways to invest and save, some of these ways need to be strengthened. Investments are always associated with risks. Some people in the community invest in livestock, but diseases and drought are often challenging, so there is need for strategies to protect livestock as an investment. Others use banks, but

211

there is inflation, and banks can close. Others invest in assets or in water to improve agriculture. Others invest in formal and informal education and training of their children or themselves. Therefore, the role of development workers is to ensure that investments and savings are effective, and that they are protected.

Social welfare grants and cash transfers

This strategy of giving deserving people a monthly grant for a short or lengthy period has been used in many African countries. The grants come from the government or non-government sector. However, a key weakness of these grants has been their size, most too little to make any significant impact on the life of the people, their families and communities. Grants that are too small promote dependency, but those that are linked to economic growth and development provide a sustainable solution to poverty among community members.

Educational strategies

Family and community education

In Africa, education takes place in the family and community although formal education takes place in schools. It is important to improve family and community education and not just formal education. Formal education in-classrooms came later by white people, before them people learned and were taught in families and communities. The education that is available in the family and community includes family and community learning to speak, learning to walk, physical education, history, civic education, political education, sexuality, marriage, work ethics, income skills, food preparation, crafts, music, storytelling, farming, mining, fishing, environmental care, childcare and many others. Knowledge of stars and the sky (astronomy), knowledge of the mind (psychology), knowledge of society (sociology), knowledge of the animals (veterinary), knowledge of treatment and health (medicine and public health) and many others were taught in families and communities. As community development workers, it is important to strengthen these and find strategies to revise them if they were lost.

212

School construction or improvement

Education is a key social service and the improvement in the sector is a critical form of community development and a major component of community work. In some instances, whole new school structures are needed i.e. in new and overpopulated settlements. Education forms a key component of the social services in the community, hence school development committees (SDCs) play a significant role in the improvements of the education system. Community social workers take the responsibility to establish these social enterprises, social groups whose role is to drive social development in the community. The community is motivated to play a significant role in the construction of school structures, i.e. through individual household contribution to school construction. In other areas food-for-work parties have been seen to provide for labour in the school construction and contribute to one of the key social works core mandates of social development. But the other important aspect of educational improvement is its focus on the provision of the intellectual capacity that allows people to contribute to their life sustaining acts to achieve well-being. Another educational program is early childhood education. This is an important community development strategy that prepares children for education. It can be implemented through construction of early education centres, classrooms or providing resources needed and teachers, community, and learners.

Child work in Africa

Child work a form of learning and training which has socio-economic benefits. Child work is not a new thing, it happens even in developed countries. The important thing is to be able to regulate it and in Africa there are several ways to regulate child work. One strategy is to ensure that the work is fit for the age. The second is to ensure that children work with adults. The third is to ensure that length and amount of work is fit for age. The fourth point is to ensure that work is done for learning, and parents are always ready to advise, mentor and even re-do the work not done properly by children. The fifth strategy is to ensure that other forms of learning, such as classroom education do not get in the way of learning at home, but also that home learning does not get in the way of classroom learning. Schools often want to override home learning, and if not checked schools become spaces of unlearning. As children grow, their workload increases, and they are given a responsibility to mentor and train others. Children who fail these roles of working and mentoring others are considered lazy, and they become a burden to the family, and their own families in future. No one child requires this kind of stigma. It is important also to distinguish child work from child labour. The is a clear distinction between child labour and child work. Child labour is when you deprive a child of their childhood, is dangerous to their physique, or interferes with learning and schooling. Child work is about children performing age-appropriate duties within their homes under the care of their parents. There is no exploitation. The intention is mentorship, traineeship and apprenticeship which exposes children to social and economic roles at their age, in the next age and in adulthood. Perhaps, we should recast this opening sentence. I believe that Africans should be able to see child labour where it is e.g. in commercial farms.

National Youth Service

This strategy has been used successfully in Nigeria, Kenya, Seychelles and other countries. Zimbabwe's attempt to use this strategy failed because it became a political program. Ideally, this service teaches young people African work ethics and promotes pride in one's heritage and culture. Different strategies are used, ranging from learning history, training in paramilitary and security work and learning vocational skills through apprenticeships and national service. It is available after secondary school, after high school, after college or after university for periods ranging from 3 months, 6 months to one year.

Vocational skills training

Training young people in skills they can use to get income is important. This can be done as part of independent training but also in collaboration with colleges. Seeking internships or apprenticeships from companies or skilled individuals is another strategy. Useful skills include building and construction, farming, mining, fishing, horticulture, driving, carpentry, processing, retailing and many others.

Decolonisation and Africanism education

African countries suffer from the effects of colonisation. These effects include dependence, poor self-esteem, lack of innovation and lack of belief in one's culture and ways of life. There are several ways to decolonise, and

214

it is everyone's responsibility to do so. One strategy for any community or institution is to come up with a decolonisation plan and follow it. The plan can cover areas like education and art but also removing colonial symbols and names. Teaching children to take pride in their families, communities and countries is an important way to achieve this.

Social strategies

Voluntary work parties

This is a model of community development where community leaders identify a community challenge and encourages community members to fix it on a voluntary basis. These may include a broken bridge, building a clinic, repair to a dip-tank, and usually those kinds of tasks undertaken by our urban municipal authorities. It carries the authority of the village head or the local chief, hence non-compliance would be seen as improper. Tasks are usually performed on a rotational basis and as per village by village. These voluntary parties under the jurisdiction of the village head act as the indigenous local

Zvipo (donations)

Zvipo are donations made to the community-by-community members or by people from outside. They can be given voluntarily or after a fundraising effort. They are usually in the form of money, crops or livestock but can also be bricks, cement or other foods. The donations are used for welfare or development. The role of workers is to mobilise zvipo.

Community committees (boreholes or water)

These are committees formed to protect and maintain water sources. They ensure water is clean and equipment is not vandalised. In urban concentrated areas which water is often a challenge, there are boreholes or water source committees to maintain order and to share water.

Girinka

The girinka concept is that one cow is given to a poor family by a neighbour. Usually, it is given to a first-born calf. The intention being to ensure that everyone has cattle. This process cements and strengthens community connections and bonds (Kalinganire, Gilkey, and Haas, 2017). Similar projects have been done in Zimbabwe, for example the Heifer-Zimbabwe Project or the Presidential Heifer Project. In Zimbabwe, a donation or *chipo* of a heifer is given to one deserving family with the hope, understanding and agreement that the first calf dropped is to be given to their deserving neighbour. The project is intended to bring about social change and create cohesion between the participating communities. The heifer project in Zimbabwe has proved to be a success and just needs to be replicated at a large scale.

Umuganda (community day), *ubunyarwanda* and *itorero ry'igihugu*

Umuganda is a form of collective community development in East Africa, mainly Rwanda (Kalinganire, Gilkey, and Haas, 2017). In Kinyarwanda language, it means coming together for a common purpose. Once every month, all of Rwanda engage in community work and development. It is a mandatory nationwide community day held every Saturday of the month. This is a national project where businesses, workers, villagers, politicians, and children take part in making the country a better place. The activities vary from repairing, planting, cleaning, building and many others. Other concepts from Rwanda include *ubunyarwanda* which means national pride in national citizenship, cooperation, and cohesion and *itorero ry'igihugu* which means aiming to be good, live in peace and harmony, strong sense of cultural values.

Zunde raMambo

This is a granary managed by the Chief or Headman of an area. Before Zimbabwe's last Rozvi King was killed around 1868 it was the responsibility of the monarchy to ensure that there was a granary to store food to be given to the extremely poor or to be used during time of crisis. The monarchy's Chiefs (*ishe* or *mambo*) and Sub-Chiefs (*ishe* or *sadunhu*) assisted in this regard. They were in turn supported by *samusha*, village heads. The *zunde* works like this: members of a community contribute labour (farming, mining, agriculture, fishing or other) and the proceeds are handed over to the Chief for custody in a granary (*zunde*). The matriarchy was usually responsible for storage but also contributed to distribution. For farming, each village head who constituted the Chief's Court or *Dare* is mandated to allocate a piece of land equivalent to a hectare or less, where

216

every villager participates in growing food. At harvest time the entire harvest would be stored into the *zunde* for future allocation to destitute households and children who needed support.

Support groups

These are made of about 10 members or more who are affected by a similar or related issue. As members, they design a strategy to address the issue they are facing. Such groups include disability groups, victims of violence groups, minority groups, parents' groups, aged people groups, HIV/AIDS patients, and many others. The role of workers is to ensure such groups are formed and that they receive appropriate support to meet their needs.

Sharing child responsibility in the extended family

When children lose their parents permanently through death or through imprisonment, migration or incapacitation, the preferred strategy is 'fostering' within the family. Another strategy is to support the children while in their homes. Adoption of children by families who are not related to the child by blood, including families from other races, is not supported in Africa. Those from outside Africa who have been able to do it have used financial influence, deception and were supported by colonial laws. Institutionalization of children has been popular, driven by several factors but it is unAfrican and results from several disadvantages for children, families and the community. The preferred strategy is to care within biological families and extended families.

Sharing child responsibility in the community

In African communities, child upbringing is a shared responsibility. The maxim that an *African child is everyone's child*, or *it takes a village to raise a child*, hence every child belonged to the village. This was figuratively translated in such a way that every respectable man or woman of the village had the authority to control and discipline an errand child in the village and still report to the biological parents without any questions raised. There are several ways of achieving this including rotational childcare and identifying bad behaviour from any child in the community and deal with it or report it to parents. For community workers, the role is to ensure that every member of the community can not only raise their own but other's children.

Family and community guidance and mentoring

In African communities, families and communities provide guidance and mentoring especially to young people, but also adults who are having social issues, such as domestic violence. There are people in families who have these roles, for example, *tete* (father's sister) and *sekuru* (mother's brother). In the absence of *tete* and *sekuru*, roles are played by sisters and brothers as well as grandmothers and grandfathers. The role of workers is to ensure that families use these resources and to ensure that the whole community builds the capacity of its *tete* and *sekuru*. Their other important role is to provide culturally appropriate counselling, sex education and marriage support. Before marriage *tete* and *sekuru* do a pre-marital interview to ascertain suitability of the marriage, existence of true love and to rule out existing family affinities (*ukama*). Their roles do not end here, they do check-ups regularly.

Child protection committees

Protecting children requires everyone to be involved. Children are vulnerable to rape (by family members and non-family members), malnutrition, hazards and lack of education. It is the role of families and communities, including their courts, to identify vulnerable children and address their vulnerability. But in other communities, especially farming, mining and urban communities, family and community are very weak, resulting in family and community roles of child protection not being played. In that case, child protection committees become important. These committees do not work in all communities, is used carelessly they cause more conflict than contribute to development.

Ceremonies and celebrations

Ceremonies play an important role in any family and community. They bring people together. They give people a sense of hope and purpose in life. There are several forms of ceremonies that workers can promote and support, these include birth ceremonies, child naming ceremonies, marriage gifts sharing ceremony (*roora*), marriage celebration

218

(*mapururudzo/mapemberero/ mhemberero*), ceremonies to heal or support the sick, harvest ceremonies, rain ceremonies (*mukwerera*), death ceremonies, transition to adulthood ceremonies and many others. These ceremonies build results in stronger families, people's resilience, and oneness. Workers should encourage, promote and support them instead of suppressing, replacing and ignoring them.

Jenaguru, pfonda and related ceremonies

These ceremonies are usually done at night, so it is important to ensure the security of children and young people. This means there is need for adult supervision to ensure that there is no violence, rape and use of drugs and alcohol. *Jenaguru* is a night play under the full moon, it involves one or several villages. It involves plays, games, singing, dancing and many forms of educational entertainment. *Pfonda* is done at night too and involves same activities as *jenaguru*.

Community social responsibility

This is a situation where companies and institutions support community work and development. It is a voluntary service but a good corporate culture. For example, mining companies reinvest socially in the communities they do mining work or any other extraction work by supporting schools, roads, and recreation. This improves the community form where they get land to mine and workers, but also improves the families of their workers and the workers themselves. They can donate funds or resources for the community to use, they can sponsor community events or provide the necessary services, for example, road construction. Roads are part of markets and marketing strategy.

Online groups and communities

Technology makes it possible now for people to communicate in groups or online communities. There are several technological applications that could be used, they keep changing and new ones keep coming in. These groups can be used to connect families and communities. The downside is that they come at a cost, and users need a level of literacy to be able to use some of them. Some of the applications have inappropriate content. Until Africans contribute to production of these technologies, and creation of online content, most of them will remain not suited to African communities.

Dare and indaba

Dare is a decision-making committee or court made up of three or more people. A dare is used to plan events, prevent or solve problems. It can be at family, community or societal level (discussed later). *Indaba* is a decision-making committee or court made up of ten or more people. It is used to plan events, prevent or solve problems. It can be at family, community or societal level.

Family council or dare

A family council is decision making body of a family. It exists at the immediate, extended and tribal family levels. The chair is usually the oldest member of the family, but chairing can be delegated to a neutral member of the family, for example a nephew, a family friend or a cultural leader. Family councils plan for the family's development, handle ceremonies, prevent and solve challenges.

Agricultural and environmental strategies

Chisi and Chief's fines for environmental degradation

Chiefs and headman have an obligation to guide against environmental degradation. Besides environmental awareness, they also punish wrongdoers. This ensures environmental sustainability. Lack of it has come back to haunt rural and urban communities. Every community had its sanctions and the village head and the chief both had the mandate to punish through fines or sanctions for those involved in environmental degradation and random cutting down of trees without their authority. In observing tradition and keeping up with local rituals and values every community, village heads observe a day of rest called *chisi* – a day to rest from any environmental and agricultural work in Zimbabwe and the chief and village head sanction anyone who does not observe the sanctity of the day.

Water harvesting

Water is a crucial commodity in a community. Water is life as many people say. Water drives community development and is a crucial strategy without which we have many poorer communities. Majority of rural communities rely on rainfed agriculture, hence for whole six-month rural communities are unproductive because of dry seasons. Community workers and community development workers can promote water harvesting for example constructing dams, sinking boreholes, shallow wells, deep wells, sand wells, springs, roof tanks, rock wells, reservoirs, or tunnels.

Livestock rearing

This strategy involves livestock like cattle, goats, sheep and poultry. Pigs are also reared, but in some communities, they are forbidden. Cattle is an animal of great importance as it provides a source of draught power, food, money, investment, and social value. Cattle provide nutrition through milk and meat for communities but also manure for gardens and fields. Most importantly cattle are used in rituals. They provide meat during funerals; it is a tradition that at every funeral of an elder person, a beast has to be slaughtered. It is used in many other rituals, such as *magadziro*, known as memorial service one year after the death of an adult person. At weddings cattle are slaughtered. Cattle is a symbol of wealth in the community and the well-to-do have many cattle and they can use them as source of income. However, rearing cattle involves a lot of effort. They need pastures, water and to be protected against diseases and marauding animals like hyenas and lions. Other strategies to increase survival of cattle include building dip tanks, planting grass, trees and water harvesting. Other projects related to this include keeping bees for honey, fish and crocodiles for meat. Others also keep rabbits.

Cooperative farming

Zvinoda Madzimai in Zimbabwe is an example of a cooperative and agricultural committee established at the community to achieve desired common goals. Cooperatives and Agricultural Committees work at the village level and usually under guidance of agriculture extension worker and other development workers. Workers are often part of the team that scaffolds development-oriented committees through the provision and the drive towards social change, towards social development and the

221

empowerment and liberation of the community to attain their well-being utilizing their own means. Other support services to cooperatives or any other growth-oriented community initiative has often been private companies providing community social responsibility programs. These may be mining companies operating in the local community and offer to support the community through some developmental donations. Other development organisations like ZOIC also procure funding from social investors to support cooperatives, agricultural committees, or even educational committees to improve their well-being. This can be through the support i.e. providing agricultural commodities to enable Zvinoda Madzimai in their ground nut farm production. Development practitioners take a leading role in identifying these potential projects. They have the skills to interact with the committees and cooperatives to single out their needs and motivate them to come up with growth-oriented community improvement projects that can be supported. Support to committees and cooperatives can come in different ways and the community may come up with an integrated combination of community requirements related to agriculture, education hence community projects like adult or early child learning, career guidance can be part of the community requirements.

Field days, prize giving days, shows or master farmer awards.

Field days are a very important way of promoting agricultural productivity in communities. This is a day where farmers gather to see a selected field and learn how the owner has managed it. It could also involve agricultural shows of crop produce from several farmers. Shows are organised at village or district level but also regional and national level. The Harare Agricultural Show is an example of a successful farmers' show. Field days also include prizes and awards. The master farmer award is usually given to a person who has progressed a lot in their farming.

Farming and agriculture demonstrator, brigades or guides

Demonstrators are often government workers who are trained to train both small and large farmers. They can be supported with training, transport, and incentives. Brigades and guides are usually initiated by NGOs to support farmers. Brigades or guides are trained in farming. They use their skills in the same manner demonstrators do. Campaign for female

222

Education (CAMFED) has trained and used young female guides to help improve agriculture.

Recycling

There is a lot of waste that is generated, especially in urban communities. Strategies to promote recycling are many, and some of them generate income. Community workers and development workers need to be aware of more strategies, and they should link these to environmental management.

Machobane Farming System (MFS)

This is a system of farming developed by Dr James Jacob Machobane in Lesotho in the 1950s. It increases productivity by using organic manure, intercropping, and rotating crops. Machobane promoted farming throughout the year to spread risk and increase production. The MFS addresses issues of declining soil fertility, small land size and climate variability. It is also known as *Mantsa Tlala*, or expeller of hunger. This was based on scientific research on Basotho farming practices done by Dr Machobane which showed that MFS was cheaper, sustainable and yields were 3 times more than conventional farming promoted by white people.

Madzoro (rotational livestock herding)

A whole community can organise cattle herding (and goats and sheep) in ways that allow community members free time to focus on their economic, household and other livelihood activities. A community of at least 10 households who are mutual friends organise *madzoro* between themselves. This is a way of allowing themselves an opportunity to organise their household work while the nine other households take turns herding cattle. This allows each household a total of 9 weeks before their turn comes. This a show of community cohesion and mutual support which is good for community work. It is also known as *jana* or *jangano*.

Protecting animals from unnecessary killing, beating, and hunting

In Africa, animals can be slaughtered for food or ritual purposes, and this is acceptable. White people like to do hunting games in Africa, but this results in unnecessary killing of animals for trophies. This should be avoided no matter how much money they pay and how much tourism they bring. In western culture, they take animals and make them pets that they live with in their homes. The animals are introduced to fertility control, breeding and their diet is altered. According to African tradition, these are barbaric practices. In Africa, animals can be used as pets but not to that level of staying in homes, they are given the freedom to remain animals. Animals used for farming and hunting should be protected from unnecessary pain and overworking.

Tourism and recreational facilities

There are other communities that are endowed with natural resources or man-made structures that are wonderful to watch. Tourists from other parts of the country, regions or continents can visit to see these features. Examples include *Masvingo eZimbabwe* (also known as Great Zimbabwe) and *Mosi oa Tunya* (colonial name Victoria Falls). Community workers and community development workers can promote tourism, by both local visitors but also regional and international to get more foreign currency. Where tourism features are not there, they can be developed and promoted.

Psychological and spiritual strategies

Another role of community workers and community development workers is to support communities spiritually and psychologically. These include strategies to deal with fear, anxiety, mental health, loneliness, loss, hopelessness, exclusion and stigma. These can be caused by disasters, conflict, death, illness, and unemployment. There are several ways of achieving this including promoting cultural events.

Death ceremonies

Death ceremonies provide comfort during time of grief. The death of a community member is not an individual family's concern but one that the community show solidarity. Every household is represented, and families bring food to assist the bereaved family. Members of the community take over the responsibility for the burial process and there is a lot of psycho-social support that happens during a funeral, including dancing, singing, speeches and drumming. In Chewa and Nyanja culture of Malawi, Nyau masked dancers entertain people and perform spiritually supportive rituals. In some communities, after a month the bereaved household prepare food to thank the community for their support and a death ceremony called *manyaradzo*, literally where it is intended to assist the family to get over the bereavement. After a year, another ceremony called *magadziro* is done to ensure that everything is fine with the family and to provide final bereavement support. *Magadziro* provides closure to the family and community because all the remaining assets of the deceased are shared, and the deceased is accepted as having joined fellow deceased beings in the spiritual world. These rituals vary from place to place but they are all meant to provide spiritual, social and psychological support. Other strategies that provide spiritual and psychological support include performances, rite of passage ceremonies for teenagers.

Chema

Chema are contributions made by relatives, friends, and community to support a deceased person's family. These could be in the form of money, food, transport, and other resources to support during and after the funeral.

Sports, recreation and entertainment strategies

Sports come in various forms, some are done for social benefits, some for physical benefits and some for economic benefits as a career. Strategies for community work and community development include providing sporting facilities, coaching services, and sporting kits. It is important to select the kinds of sport people identify with and accept culturally. Sports where people expose naked bodies are usually not preferable. The same applies to entertainment. In urban communities, recreational parks and spaces are a useful strategy. In Dakar, Senegal they have mass exercise parks or spaces for the public where exercise equipment is installed for free use.

Pre-migration, in-migration and post-migration training, education, and awareness

With many people in Africa migrating to other countries, including overseas, to look for employment, it is important to teach people about the physical and psychological hazards involved. There are many, whether people have migrated formally as students or workers, as refugees or as so-called illegal migrants. The first challenge is that of being duped. People

225

have lost money after being promised jobs in South Africa, overseas in America, Europe, China or Middle East. The second challenge is of being smuggled and sold to cartels of fake employment agencies. The third one is unemployment and underemployment. Others fail to find jobs, but others find jobs they are overqualified for. Others get underpaid or end up in risk jobs such as prostitution and thieving. The fourth challenge is that of being acculturated and assimilated into non-African cultures. This affects adults as well as children. As people step out of Africa, the pressure to change their values becomes more. This includes the pressure to marry into other races, which has numerous psychological challenges for the couple and families, but more so for their future generations who will grow up divided between two races and cultures. Others say multiculturalism is good for the world, but there are more ideas against it. It perpetuates assimilation of smaller races into white culture, and causes more conflict in African families. The fifth challenge with migration is the potential for permanent migration which weakens African communities. African minds, the able-bodied and future generations get lost in Europe or America as diasporans, and by the same process their contribution to their *musha*, community, country and continent gets lost if they do not send remittances back home. It would be important for pre-migration training, education, or awareness to address all these issues to help African communities before they migrate but also for those who have already migrated. The post-migration period is when people return to their country and homes, it helps them to settle and continue with their lives in their communities.

Legal, administrative, political and security strategies

Dare and indaba

Dare refers to a court. In Rwanda they are known as *gakaka* and *indaba* in South Africa. In African communities, *dare* are organised from lower levels upwards. Dare is useful in communities because they resolve conflict, reinforce good behaviour, punish bad behaviour and make communities safe by dealing with violence and unfair behaviour. *Dare* is there to protect vulnerable members of society and reduce misuse of power. The first *dare* is called *dare repamba*, which means a family court. In this court, parents and all children and close relatives solve any misunderstanding that happens at the family level. It is often chaired by *baba*, *mai* or *tete*. This is followed by *dare remhuri* (also called *dare remusha*. This court is made up of

226

members of the extended family or tribe. The third level is the village dare (*dare remusha*). Others call this *dare ra sabhuku* but the noun *sabhuku* is derogatory, it was used by colonialist to mean village secretary but the roles of *samusha* are more than secretarial. The fourth court is *dare raIshe* or *sadunhu*. This is the local, sub-chief or headman's court. The fifth court is *dare raMambo* (Chief's court). The final court is *dare raMambo wenyika* (the King's court). The King's court in Zimbabwe was affected by colonization but there are communities working for its revival. These courts work with courts that came after colonisation: magistrate's courts, labour courts, family courts and others. The indigenous courts should not be ignored, often community workers rush to work with the police and magistrate's court.

Promoting political participation

Community work is political and politics is development with power. It involves influencing people to make informed choices. Community work and community development try to increase the political participation of communities. Political engagement empowers the worker and that of the communities they serve. It is also about convincing people to address issues relating to self-help, building community infrastructure, hence maintain their own dignity, freedom and sustainability. Both urban and rural community work experts organise and influence national commemorations and political events, i.e., Zimbabwe celebrates Independence Day every year in April and all communities recognise that as a political event and day to remember and do something in remembrance. Therefore, across different countries, *uhuru* parties are celebrated jointly and in harmony. It is a time to recognise the work of government in service to their communities. There are also times when communities are demonstrating against certain actions of government, hence social action is a community political strategy to communicate their feelings to government. Community action involves mobilization of the community intended to send out a message to government. Usually this happens with repressive governments where there are no open channels for communication. Community workers and development workers engage in planned community organization and community action, to fulfil one of the core mandates of the profession. It involves appealing to the community to participate on a variety of issues such as voter education, leadership campaigns, fundraising, workshops on campaign strategies, communication and out-reach, and many other areas of political mobilization.

Formation and empowering associations

In Zimbabwe, residents' associations, community associations, farmers associations, miners' associations, fishers' associations, workers associations, political parties, commuters' associations, and consumers associations are all examples of forms of political and community action. There is strength in numbers.

Neighborhood watch committee and community policing

These are local committees in villages, mining areas, farms, or towns responsible for security surveillance and community policing. They usually work with national security but also private security companies. The people who are selected to provide the service are usually volunteers from the community, but they can also be paid. National police usually provide basic training, equipment, and support. When the neighbourhood teams work with police, this is called community policing. Other strategies of community policing involve forming youth clubs, children clubs, suggestion boxes and victim friendly units.

Vigilante groups

In some communities, crime reach unacceptable levels that people organise themselves to deal with thieves (*tsotsi*), burglars, cheaters and conman who use several strategies to steal, including force, firearms, rape, spraying with chemicals, beating or hitting, false messages and many other tricks. When this happens, and there is inadequate security from the police, people organise themselves to fight crime as vigilante groups.

Development committees

In Zimbabwe, these are called Village Development Committee (VIDCOs) and Ward Development Committees (WADCOs) and are linked to local government. The award is composed of several villages. Their role is to identify needs, plan development, implement plans and link with local government which in turn links them with national government. In Ethiopia, they have farmers committees and residents' committees.

228

Health, food and nutrition strategies

There are several strategies community workers and community development workers can use to promote health and nutrition. These include building health infrastructure, such as building clinics, health education, prevention, village health workers, village birth attendants, indigenous healers, herbs, nutrition gardens, nutrition clubs and many others.

Community and village health workers and birth attendants

Community and village health workers (*mbuya utano* for women or *sekuru utano* for men) are part of the primary health care system. They play an important role of ensuring universal health access through health education, reporting, referrals and dispensing approved medicines. Community-based birthing is very common in rural and remote communities, where community trained village birth attendants, usually old grandmothers *(mbuya nyamukuta)* have managed that aspect of community health. They have been trained and are now a recognised service in the formal government-led community health system. Majority of colonial rural clinics did not have sufficient accommodation for expectant mothers to stay at the clinic before birthing. This has resulted in the increase of deaths of both mothers and baby at childbirth. These primary health workers need support with protective, communication, emergency equipment but also training in first aid. The facilities also need improvement, and this includes their treatment rooms and accommodation. Incentives for them another option since they spend significant amounts of time volunteering for the health system instead of working in their fields, gardens, markets, or homes.

Nutrition and herbal gardens and clubs

These groups grow crops that enhance nutrition. They do this through home gardens in urban and rural areas, urban farms and cooperative gardens. They also grow plants like *moringa* that have herbal properties.

Indigenous and religious healers and herbalists

They have knowledge of plants that are used to make medicines or can be used as medicines without processing. They also have knowledge of procedures like wound care, repairing broken bones, fertility, common colds and many others. In Zimbabwe they are regulated under the Indigenous Healers Act; they have an office at the Ministry of Health and they have a council – Indigenous Medical Practitioners Council. Local healers are easily accessible to the community, and they are often consulted first before people go to clinics. They need to be supported, as they can influence health education and practices.

Chirambamuriwo (beef committees)

It involves members of the community putting their resources together to buy cattle, slaughter them and share the meat. This contributes to family food but also nutrition. It is also a way of marketing cattle where there are no buyers or where individuals are not able to buy a beast on their own.

Food relief (kutambirisa)

This is a common strategy used by government, non-government organisations and corporates. It involves sourcing food and delivering to communities in need. The food can include cereals, oil, grain, water and beans. There is a strong debate about what should be prioritized giving food, supporting agriculture or building water sources. What do you think?

First aid and occupational hazards training

Life is full of hazards at home, in the community, on farms, on roads, at school and in workplaces. Besides these hazards, there are also health conditions like asthma, heart attack, epilepsy and sugar diabetes that require people to have skills to manage them. It is therefore important for communities to have skills for first aid, lifesaving, and risk management. When hazards occur, such as road accidents, mining accidents (e.g. makorokoza), workplace injuries, house fires, domestic violence, cyclones, suicide attempts and many others, those around should be able to reduce injury, harm, loss of life and loss of property.

Mental health awareness

There are lots of mental health (urwere hwepfungwa) issues in the community. If they are not resolved, they result in depression or death. Some of these

230

mental health issues *kushishikana, kufunganya* or *kudzamirwa* (stress), anxiety, *kurwara nekufungisisa zvakadzama* (depression), *kusarudzwa kwakanyanya* (stigma), *kuona kana kunzwa zvinhu zvisipo/mamhepo* (hallucinations or seeing things or hearing voices), kutya kwakanyanya (fear), *kupenga* (psychosis), *kufunga manyepo* (delusions), kurashika pfungwa (delirium or schizophrenia), *hasha dzakanyanya* (too much aggression), *pfungwa dzekuda kufa* or *kuzviuraya* (death or suicide ideation), *kupera pfungwa* (dementia), *kutamba nepwere* (dementia), *kudzungaira* (too confused), *makaro makuru* (compulsive behaviour), *kushaya unhu* or *zungairwa* (personality disorder), *kusagadzikana* (hyperactivity), *dununu* (hypoactivity), *makunakuna* (incest), *kuita bonde nemhuka* (sex with animals, bestiality), unusual abnormal sexual behaviours or *kudhakiswa* (drug or alcohol abuse). The role of workers is mainly community public education to help people to prevent and manage these disorders. Knowledge on the biological nature of these conditions helps communities to understand them. In turn this helps to reduce accusations of witchcraft.

Reproductive mentoring, education and awareness

Reproduction is an important component of African culture. It is highly valued. There are systems in place already for reproductive mentoring, education, and awareness but some need to be supplemented because of several reasons, including the disintegration of families and communities. Issues to deal with include fertility, which when not available or dealt with properly, results in violence or divorce. Another issue is sex before marriage, which causes a lot of disharmonies in families and communities. Another issue is abortion, which usually is associated with sex before marriage. Yet another issue is HIV and AIDS which interferes with reproduction and can be passed to the foetus or the newborn. How can workers deal with these issues? They need to ensure that available systems are functional, if not, they do community awareness or promote school-based programs to target young people.

Sanitation improvement

There are several methods that have been used to improve sanitation in both urban and rural communities. Sanitation awareness is one of them. Another is to promote, support and construct public and home toilets.

Clean water provision

Water is an important resource. Clean water is even more important. Community workers and community development workers need to work with local communities to identify, enhance and protect clean water sources.

Less useful and inappropriate strategies

It is also important to share with readers strategies that are less useful, harmful, and inappropriate in the African context. Most of these strategies are built on western culture, cause more conflict, mistrust and violence in families and communities instead of solving it. These include, but not limited to, the following:

1. Scouts, girl guides and brigades and church related camps and activities that dwell much on non-African values and culture.
2. Places where alcohol, sex and western-themed movies or films are accessible.
3. Donation of books from western countries. Most of the books are irrelevant and still carry colonial themes.
4. Donation of used or low quality (dubbed *zhing zhong*) or inappropriate clothes, toys (e.g. white dolls), food, art and technology. Other communities only eat *remba*, kosher, halaal or vegetarian foods, especially meat. These are cultural values that should be respected.
5. Use of community workers from outside the country, especially white. Avoid using community workers who do not understand the community's language, culture and values.
6. Activities that expose people's naked bodies involve touching or altering people's bodies and decorating bodies. These include tattooing, skin lightening and some hair styles like long or plaited or dreaded hair for men. Generally, hair is to be kept short and clean.
7. Activities related to or promoting gays, lesbians, homosexual, same sex marriage and bisexuals. The practice is culturally unacceptable in Africa, and illegal in countries like Zimbabwe.
8. Adoption of children by families who are not related to the child by blood, including families from other races, is not supported in

232

Africa. Those from outside Africa who have been able to do it have used financial influence, deception and were supported by colonial laws. The preferred strategy is 'fostering' within the family. Another strategy is to support the children while in their homes.

9. Programs that do not adequately consider the needs of less powerful groups in communities such as women and children are likely not to increase disadvantage of these groups.

10. Institutionalisation of children has been popular, driven by several factors but it is unAfrican and results in several disadvantages for children, families and the community. The preferred strategy is to care within biological families and extended families.

11. Western concepts and practices of human rights, majority age, child labour, spirituality, land, health, dating, sexuality, democracy, gender, home and family. African families are large compared to western families, and polygamy is acceptable in many communities. The African permanent home is *musha*, the one in the rural village, the one in towns is temporary and can be disposed anytime When people visit *musha* often, it's not being careless with money, it is part of why they work.

12. Strategies that encourage more political or tribal polarisation. However, workers need to be mindful of community differences and their impact on their work and development.

13. Dangerous or hazardous games like boxing or Karate.

14. Child adoption is inappropriate in African cultures. The *musha* approach supports children to grow up in their homes or in homes of their blood relations.

15. Ignoring the presence or roles of leaders, aged and gatekeepers should not be ignored, these include *samusha, sadunhu, Ishe,* war veterans, politicians and spiritual leaders.

16. Activities that are seen to promote laziness and dependence.

17. Do not use Black American culture and urban African new cultures as representative of African culture. There are differences. What people usually see in the media is not African culture but media representation of it.

18. Social welfare or social assistance grants that do not have an economic or developmental incentive have several disadvantages.

19. Prisoning young children in conflict with the law which has several disadvantages. There are several methods to divert them from the prison system.

20. Performances or works of art, music, dance, language and writing that demonise Africans or promote non-African values, thinking and practices.

Models of community work or community development

Sanga Development Foundation (SDF) multi-stakeholder community development model

The SDF model helps to understand the pillars of community work and community development. The model has 7 pillars that contribute to development of the Sanga community as shown in Figure 1.

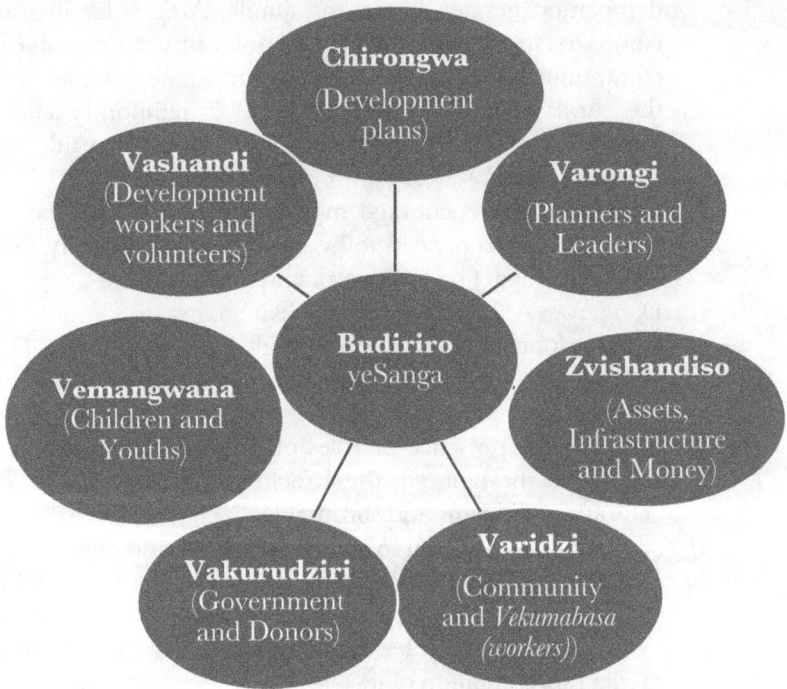

Figure 6: Stakeholders in development

This SDF model puts the community (Sanga) at the centre of development. The community is the stokeholder, the main pillar of development.

234

Zvinoda Madzimai community social enterprise model

This model puts the concept of culture and community participation at the centreof community development and is summarized in thematic terms (ZOIC 2009). The themes are:

Theme 1: Culture is central to successful entrepreneurship designs.
Theme 2: Social networks are the glue that holds society and entrepreneurs together.
Theme 3: Social capital is the human factor and anchor of rural business success.
Theme 4: Creative thinking as the ART for building successful enterprises.
Theme 5: Building on innovation and creativity to sustain rural entrepreneurship.
Theme 6: Information communication technology (ICT) as an entrepreneurial mover
Theme 7: Meeting and mating of ideas and cultures causes entrepreneurial progress.

From the two models, the pillars of community work and community development are:

1. Community.
2. Culture.
3. Innovative work or development plans.
4. Planners.
5. Community leaders.
6. Assets, infrastructure and money.
7. Members working or living outside the community, in towns or diaspora.
8. Government.
9. Non-government agencies.
10. Children, youths and other interest groups.
11. Development workers and volunteers.
12. Social capital and social networks.

Pillars of community work or community development

The community

The community is a collection of households in a specific geographical area. They are the people experiencing problems, challenges, threats or issues and they have development needs or aspirations. There are several types of communities, including but not limited to these 10 factors:

1. Village
2. Suburb
3. Town
4. Group of villages
5. Farm community
6. Mine community
7. Fishery community
8. Refugee camp
9. Shanty town
10. Social media groups

A community has opportunities and strengths, such as willingness to change situations *(self-drive)*, land, water, minerals and vegetation, community knowledge and labour and community cohesion. But a community also has problems, challenges, threats, or issues, including:

1. Lack of adequate social services like water, health, security, food, roads, communication, transport, education, agriculture, markets, and many others.
2. Lack of social and economic development.
3. Poverty.
4. Human abuse rights issues.
5. Lack of participation in national development processes (marginalization).
6. Lack of work and self-development plan.
7. Unemployment and lack of income.
8. Lack of cohesion (conflict with family or community).
9. Degradation of natural resources (climate change).
10. Lack of support from local and national government (marginalisation).

These problems, challenges, threats, or issues can be classified as economic, social, psychological, political, environmental and spiritual. The community can form a Community Association (CA). A CA has a written constitution (can also be unwritten), leaders and a plan. A residents' association or villagers' association is an example. In other communities, a community centre is provided by the local authority or by the government. The centre should have at least an office and a meeting room. Others use the residence of their leader as a community centre. In other communities, you find members who are working outside the community. These include those working in schools, police stations and other workstations outside their community. These are usually members of the civil service. Then there are others working in growth points, towns, farms and mines. Others work in nearby countries and in Africa as a while others work outside the continent, usually termed overseas or diaspora. While these people do not regularly stay in the community, they have land and homes, and they aspire for the development of their community. Most are willing to contribute their knowledge, experience and remit back home.

Community leaders

Leaders are part of the community. The leaders include village heads, area chairpersons, elected officials or Chiefs. The leaders are expected to drive the process of work or development in their area. However, at times this does not happen because they lack knowledge, skills, resources to do so. To address this challenge, the leaders can be trained, and this role falls on community workers and other development welfare workforce. Another solution is to train volunteers who will work with them. In most cases, the government or non-government agencies provide the necessary workforce.

Local and national government

Local and national governments play an important role in community work and community development. The local government includes the elected leader of the ward or county and the district, municipality, or country authority. The national government includes the elected Member of Parliament, government officials from health, social services, agriculture, women, youths, education and others. The roles of National and local Government are that national government takes responsibility for national budgets for which local government receives its own share of budget. The Constitution of Zimbabwe Amendment (No.20) Act of 2013

237

provides for devolution, a situation where local authorities have some level of autonomy regards financial planning and budgeting.

Community planners

Without planners, community work and community development will not easily take off. The duty of the planners is to collect ideas from community and stakeholders and put those ideas into a plan. This is a written document agreed by the community. Planners can be leaders, workers, community members, volunteers, or organisations. Communities have their own indigenous planning structures, that organise the social, economic, and political plans. In Zimbabwe, these are called Village Development Committee (VIDCOs) and Ward Development Committees (WADCOs) and are linked to the formal and political structures of the district.

Community workers, community development workers and volunteers

Workers are employees of government or non-government agencies who are trained, qualified and experienced. They may hold a certificate, diploma, or degree in community work, social work or development studies. Workers in community work or community development work as one or more of the following professionals: Community Worker, Community Development Worker, Community Social Worker, Community Organiser, Community Developer, Community Youth Worker, Community Researcher, Project Officer/Coordinator, Community Mobiliser, Gender Officer, Disability Worker, Aged Support Worker or Community Childcare/Development Worker. Volunteers may be from the community or outside, and they provide their time and energy and at times resources to drive work and development. Some responsibilities or duties of workers and volunteers include:

1. Identification of community needs and those in need.
2. Linking community needs with government programs.
3. Community advocacy and planning to improve community well-being.
4. Resource mobilization and refer clients to community resources.

5. Building community capacity and strengthen community organisations.
6. Creating community groups of purpose and social enterprises.
7. Stakeholder identification and participation.
8. Ensuring community ethics, values, culture and beliefs are respected.
9. Decolonising community work and development.
10. Advocate for local government, national government and non-government support.

Workers and volunteers require several skills, knowledge and competency, including, but not limited to:

1. Knowledge of local protocol, culture, values, beliefs and practices.
2. Communication skills including speaking in local language.
3. Community awareness skills.
4. Leadership skills.
5. Networking skills.
6. Fundraising and resource mobilisation skills.
7. Needs analysis skills.
8. Skills to refer to services and services providers.
9. Planning skills.
10. Cultural skills.
11. Employment or income creation skills.

Children, youths, women and other interest groups

Children and young people represent the future of the community. They should be included in the process of community work and community development. When planning and organizing, it is important to know that children and young people enjoy play, art, short meetings and short documents. They want to be appreciated and to be entertained. They can be easily bored so when planning, community workers must plan with their needs in mind. Other interest groups include women, people with disability, aged, cultural and minority groups and community organization must be able to mobilize each of these groups and develop programs that are unique to each of them. Zvinoda Madzimai (meaning what women wants) group in Gutu is an example of the women's group that has been successful in meeting the needs of. Comprehensive community development must embrace the needs of different groups.

NGOs are part of the community interest groups. They include private voluntary organisations, foundations, and trusts. They can be local, national, regional and international. Some are self-funded, others are funded by donors, businesses or governments. Others are social and development investors, relief organisations, churches and other agencies that aid in cash or kind. NGOs are an important stakeholder who bring in resources, experience, and knowledge to the community. However, they usually have their own covert interests socially, politically, and otherwise. Some want to convert people to enlarge their organisations or churches, and to ensure the dominance of their beliefs. Others want to change local culture in the name of 'modernisation'. Others use strategies that result in more harm, conflict, and disharmony in communities. Others are fly by nights; they just come to do short term projects and disappear.

The plan

An important pillar in all community work or community development activities is the plan. This is made by all the community, stakeholders, leaders, volunteers and workers. It is the guide upon which the programs are implemented. Further, it provides the broad roadmap for interested social and economic investors. The process of developing a plan should be developed with the support of the community leaders, while it is driven and led by the community-based organization or the community workers. The work plan or development plan contains the following:

1. Introduction and institutional background
   - A description of the institutional/organisational, background and context.
2. Description of the community
   - this must include the land, the people, the natural and human resources to steer the program.
   - The village, district, province, up to the national level, vital statistics, includes the number of households, total population, number of villages and natural resources, the political situation and leadership structures.
3. Environmental analysis/issues/challenges

240

- an analysis of identified list of problems, potential programs, the community economic and social drivers, challenges.
- analysis of Strengths, Weaknesses, Opportunities and Threats (SWOT analysis).

4. Strategy to deal with challenges
   - strategic pillars of the organization – the strong legs/pillars of the organization.
   - priority list of programs or projects identified or to be created to solve the problems, challenges, threat or issues.
   - list of potential solutions, projects or programs.
   - analysis of solutions that have been used before to support the strategy.
   - stakeholder mapping and their roles, identification of potential support resources required.
   - identification of existing resources.
   - identification of more social investors and stakeholders.

5. Logical frame (log frame) and implementation plan and structure
   - a schedule or time plan that details out the project time frame.
   - list of objectives, activities to achieve them and expected results.
   - a description of how the community, leaders and stakeholders are involved in the listing the problems, challenges, threats or issues and mostly in the implementation structure.
   - profile and names of project leaders, volunteers and professional workers and their roles in supporting the project.
   - listing and mapping of stakeholders' roles and contributions.

6. Budget and resources needed for the project.

Social capital and social networks

Social capital and social networks play an important role in community work and community development. Social capital refers to the social resources that a community has, for example, cohesion. Social networks are a form of social capital on their own, and these include the friendships a community has with nearby communities and other stakeholders. The connections a family or community have increased their sources of funding, support, markets and influence. Examples of social capital include *Ubuntu* that increases justice and familyhood, *ujamaa* that increases labour, *umuganda* that increases communityhood and *machobane* which increases sustainability.

Templates to use in community work or community development

Template 1: Mini community audit questionnaire.

Item	Response
Name of community.	
Description of community.	
Community needs that were identified (current situation or problems). It is important to use numbers here, but you can also describe.	
Describe the current plan.	
How long will be the next plan and when does its start and end?	
What is the plan for fundraising and stakeholder mapping?	
What financial resources and assets are needed for each activity and are available?	
What human resources are available for community work or community development? What are the economic and social drivers in the community?	
What are the likely challenges and opportunities?	

Template 2: A tool to identify community problems and needs

The 6-stage process of identifying community needs or projects is as follows:

1. Problem or needs triggering – there is something that triggers a community, organisation, government, or worker to realise that there is a need, and a project is required. In community work, the triggers are usually sudden and not anticipated but in community development the triggers are usually anticipated. Triggers could be droughts, accidents, cyclones, deaths, hazards and others.
2. Community mobilization and sensitization – this involves concept and issue discussion and problematization of issues which could be in the form of theoretical paper presentations, community discussions, consultations or listening to stories.

242

3. Problem or needs clarification – this could be in the form of short community dialogue sessions, community group discussions, group and individual verifications of the problem issues.
4. Project selection – the community with stakeholders will create a list of potential projects then select a project that can effectively address the current need.
5. Project piloting and verification – this could be in the form of a short project to test feasibility, methods and participation. The tester or pilot project is implemented with close monitoring and documentation. At times there is no need to pilot.
6. Approval and replication of the piloted project to address the identified needs.

Community intervention or implementation plan

Template 3: Community intervention and implementation plan

Item	Response
Name of community.	
Leader's title and name.	
Description of community and its economic and social drivers?	
Community needs.	
Names of planners, workers and volunteers.	
To address the needs, what will be done (what is the strategy and the activities)?	
Who will do what? stakeholder plan and program/project management structure.	
When will each activity start and finish? (timeline or schedule or log frame).	
Does the community have current or expired development plans?	
Assets, infrastructure and money/resources available.	
Members working or living outside the community, in towns or diaspora.	
What are possible intervention methods? Which ones were selected by the community?	
Government, non-government agencies in the area?	
Children, youths and other interest groups – an analysis.	

What needs have been identified for this community? How was each need identified? Participation must be very strong with community aspirations and community buy-in.	
What needs are short-term (urgent or immediate), medium-term or long-term?	
What are the likely challenges and opportunities? (SWOT analysis for strength-weaknesses-opportunities and threats).	
Sustainability Plan - what happens when the end of the project is reached? Do you exit, renew or what? Is this sustainable? Outline a Sustainability Plan.	
How will be activities be monitored, evaluated and how will the project be reviewed?	

Template 4: Evaluation or review questionnaire

Item	Response
Name of community project, activity, or program.	
Name of person or agency or committee doing the review or evaluation.	
Description of how information for the review or evaluation was collected.	
Situation before the project or activity was implemented (the baseline).	
What has changed or not changed?	
What to positive changes?	
What limited or affected success?	
Assess the planning and plan.	
Assess the implementation.	
Assess the monitoring and continuous evaluation.	
Was sustainability ensured?	
Assess participation.	
What could be done next time (recommendations)?	
What could we do differently/in another way.	
What are the likely challenges and opportunities?	

Stages to follow when meeting indigenous leaders

Template 5: Protocol or stages to follow when meeting indigenous leaders.

1. Identification – identify the leader or leaders of the community you want to work with.

2. Intermediary – find an Elder to act as an intermediary if you are not known to the area. Ask them to explain local customs and protocols including payment of a court gift.

3. Introductions – it is recommended to be introduced through an intermediary.

4. Court gift – the gifts vary from place to place and could be cash or livestock.

5. Meeting the leader – in other cases, you will be asked to present your issue through one or more representatives of the leader even if he or she is there?

Local customs and protocols may include greetings, gifts, clapping hands, removing hats, removing shoes, kneeling, no revealing clothes for both men and women, accepting food or drink, head cover for women, no cameras or other technologies, sitting on the floor, not writing or note taking, not arguing, addressing the leader by their title or clan name and many others.

Case study

Initiating a community development project in Ethiopia

Case study 1: Initiating a community development project in a kebele (ward) in a rural woreda (district) in Ethiopia.

My name is Kassa. I am a social worker in Tigray region of Ethiopia. I have worked as a caseworker and groupworker for 6 years in an urban community. As a caseworker, my work involved assessing the needs of individual clients who visited the office of the non-government agency Kassa worked for. At times, there were about 8-12 clients from one community, and Kassa usually formed a group to work with them as a team. Both casework and groupwork were not well received by the clients, they were not sure of the benefits, what they wanted was help as quickly as possible. The agency had clear outlines and strict rules of the casework and groupwork strategies I could use. The methods were out of touch with the clients, for example, I could not easily include their families in the client's plan. After 6 years I decided to leave this agency as it had become more controlled by its managers who were trained in Britain and had little respect for methods relevant and acceptable in the Tigray communities. It did not take long to find a job but there was a problem because I got a community work job. Since I graduated, I have never practised community work. The government agency I worked for was starting a community program to get communities more involved and socio-economic development. There was not much time to prepare as my first assignment was in two weeks' time, in a rural community. The community was made up of about 6 farmers associations. After thinking about this, I spoke with my boss at the government department, and he told me the first thing was to know what had already been done in the community which I did only to find out there was not much community work and development. When I told my boss, he said then it is important to approach the leaders. We did that in my second week at work, but I was not even the leader of the team that visited the community because of protocol and government and in the community. My boss said protocol was very important otherwise the community would not accept the worker and the community development project. We were received warmly but they were interested in what the government would bring. We could not make any commitments even though some of my colleagues wanted to. When we left, it was clear that they were not sure why we wanted to do but they had agreed to a meeting of all leaders in the next two years.

Sanga community in Zimbabwe

Case study 2: Research on Sanga community of Nyashanu country in Buhera district in Zimbabwe

Research was done by Mugumbate and Daka in 2020 to document projects that were carried out between 1980 and 2020. Why is it necessary to research these projects? First, these projects have not been documented, meaning that current and future generations have limited access to how these projects were run. By documenting these projects, the community

246

will be provided with a source of information to use to understand food production, welfare, income, and development. The research came up with two methods of classifying the projects. The research identified 20 projects that were categorized into IFVCN, that is **I**ndividual development projects; **F**amily development projects; **V**illage development projects; **C**ommunity development projects and **N**ational projects as shown in figure 5 (Mugumbate and Daka, 2020).

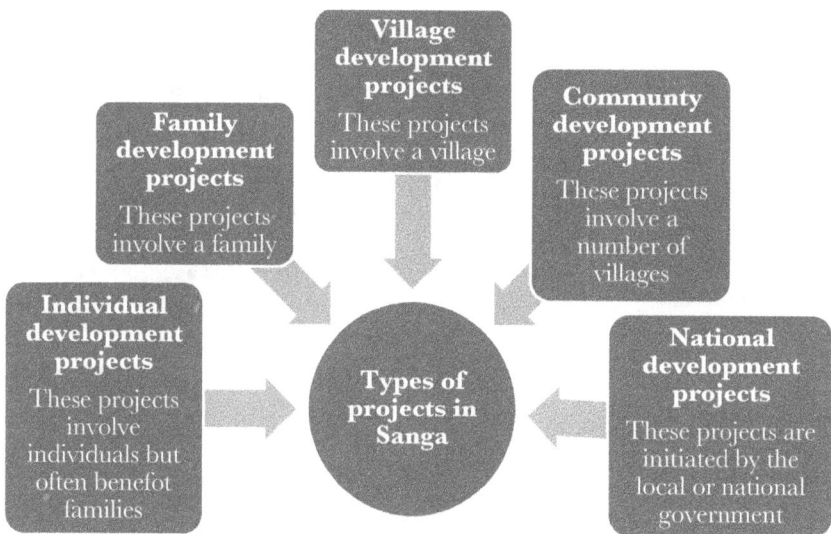

Figure 7: Classifying projects by level using the IFVSCON approach

The projects were also divided into **IMPRESS** as follows:

- **I**ncome and cash crops projects – watermelons, tomatoes, vegetables, and cotton.
- **M**anufacturing projects – weaving, pottery, molding, welding, and carpentry.

247

- **P**rocessing projects – brewing/beer making, peanut butter-making, oil extraction, bakery and grinding.
- **R**earing of livestock projects – poultry, goats, cattle, and rabbits.
- **E**nvironmental, conservation and water projects – dams, wells, gully covering and planation.
- **S**ales and retail projects – tuckshop and cosmetology.
- **S**ervices projects – school construction, market and road making (Mugumbate and Daka, 2020).

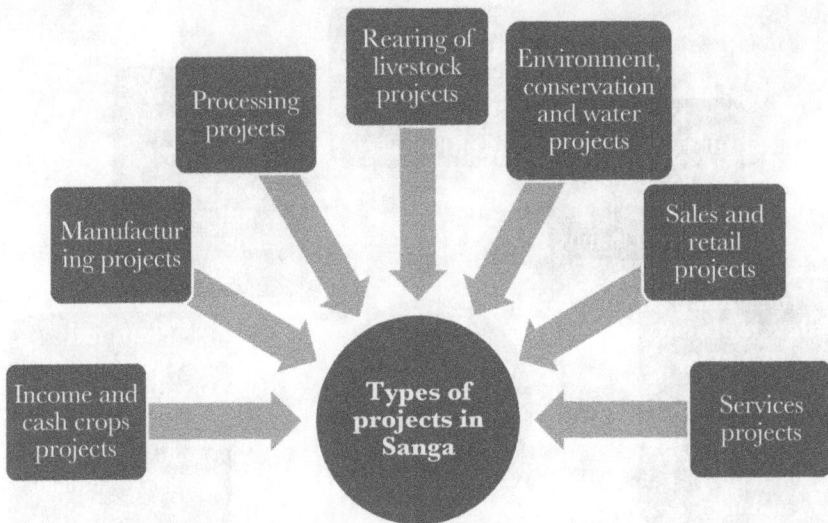

Figure 8: Classifying projects by type of activities.

Zvinoda Madzimai Peanut Butter Making-Project

Case study 3: Zvinoda Madzimai (What Women Desire) Peanut Butter-making Project.

The project seeks to advance community entrepreneurship through processing and value addition. It is an example of a community growth-oriented project or cooperative. The project is run by the Zimbabwe Opportunities Industrialization Centers) as one of community projects in

Bikita and *Gutu* involving village women cooperatives. *Zvinoda Madzimai* was started by a group of 25 village women from *Chirimubgwe* village (*musha*) and Manyanye village under Headman (*sadunhu*) Nerupiri and Chief (*Ishe*) Gutu. They both benefitted from a donation of $85 from their local Member of Parliament way back in 1988. The group of 25 women traded or loaned the money amongst themselves in the form of a community micro-lending scheme that targeted the community mainly government employees, and largely teachers through a money lending scheme. Members would borrow and pay back with a 10% interest rate per month. The cash transactions became complicated as the group traded more money and this resulted in a split. Groups are always prone to internal dysfunction, hence the need for intervention. Some *Zvinoda Madzimai* group members viewed the practice of loaning cash as complicated and demanded that their shares be reimbursed. The group cohesion, syntality and common vision was lacking hence the imminent split as group. The members came together to disburse the proceeds and the original group collapsed. A minority group of 10 re-converged and continued as *Zvinoda Madzimai*. They ventured into buying grocery items and retail of items largely those commonly utilized by women in their households, such as cooking oil, bath and washing soap and other items most preferred by the household. Hence the name *Zvinoda Madzimai*.

When a social worker met the *Zvinoda Madzimai* group, a new process of problem and project identification was initiated by the social worker. Having listened to their story and understanding where and how the group started, more sessions for group cohesion and group leadership skills were taken in order to strengthen the vision and mission re-building. Ideas to venture into other community projects were incorporated and the group grew to venture as an agricultural cooperative and chose groundnut farming involving 150 village women and men farmers. The community had an estimated population of 350 households. The community has 10 schools, seven primary schools and 3 high schools up to advanced high school level. Two gravel roads link the community with Masvingo town only 40 km away.

Working through a ZOIC social worker the group received funding for their groundnut farming project and value addition from WK Kellogg Foundation of the USA. The same project was replicated in Bikita with a group known as *Tagona* Peanut Butter Processing all focused on identifying community based, but growth-oriented initiatives with potential for growth.

Zvinoda Madzimai is an example of a successful community-based development program, with potential to grow and whose focus is long term

249

sustainability of individual farmers, households, and the community at large. The benefits have accrued to everyone in the system of the community structure. Young post ordinary level (secondary school) graduates have found jobs at the new milling factories established at the village level. The ten (10) group members have become the owners of a very successful village industry which became registered as a Private Limited Company.

Value addition and peanut butter processing was their brand as a growth-oriented community initiative. Social workers play a significant role in the transformation of growth oriented and potential village industrialization through encouraging formation of social enterprises such as *Zvinoda Madzimai* that are both sustainable and market driven to ensure they meet community needs and are based on fiscal responsibility. The *Zvinoda Madzimai* and other W. K. Kellogg Foundation funded projects were community-based experiments designed to test viability and replicability of community growth-oriented initiatives, hence focus on rural industrialization through technological advancement and value addition.

Questions for case study 1, 2 and 3

1. What protocols are observed in your own country or community?
2. What do you think happened in the second meeting in case study 1?
3. What are the shortcomings of casework and how does it differ from community work?
4. What have we learned from Kassa's account?
5. How do you think Kassa did to understand community needs? What do you think the needs were?
6. Create a chart that shows a stakeholder map of a community of your choice (name of community and the stakeholders likely to be included in a development program).
7. Write a history and profile of your own community?
8. What do you think are the local protocols in Sanga community?
9. Identify the leaders and planners in Sanga community?
10. Looking at Sanga, what are its strengths and opportunities?
11. What could be sources of knowledge on this community? Discuss these. Think of research, leaders, agencies, community members,

your own knowledge as a professional, historical documents and many others).
12. Create a chart that shows a stakeholder map of this community.
13. Appraise the two classifications of projects in Sanga.

Guidance: Using Ubuntu in community work and community development

Communityness is the main value of Ubuntu. Therefore, Ubuntu can be applied in any technique or method of doing community or development work. A mountain gets mist from other mountains, and it reciprocates by giving others mist.

- Ubuntu protocols should be used to maintain or create relationships with the community.
- Use Ubuntu to assess community needs and aspirations.
- Use Ubuntu frameworks to plan interventions.
- Use Ubuntu to evaluate programs.
- Use Ubuntu for training.

Summary

- In this chapter we valued indigenous African knowledges, theories, practices, examples and ideas that have been sidelined in favour of western or urban ideas.
- Communities have potential to solve their problems, challenges, threats, or issues. However, this usually does not happen because they have immediate challenges to deal with, others lack resources, mobilisation skills, knowledge, resilience, and experience required to plan, initiate, and implement programs and to sustain them.
- Both community work and community development are interventions that seek to address problems, challenges, threats, or issues at community level.
- The theoretical foundations of African community work and community development are *ujamaa, Ubuntu* and developmental approach.
- Culture and innovation are central to successful community entrepreneurship and successful community ventures.

- Improved relationships, group cohesion, group syntality, social capital and improved social networks are the glue and anchor that holds society together.
- Objectives, guiding principles and ethics are vital components in community work and community development.
- There are different strategies of community work and community development in Africa addressing economic, social, psychological, political, environmental, and spiritual objectives of communities. In this book we provided over 60 examples but also over 20 strategies that are harmful or less useful.
- The community is at the centre and is an integral part of community work and community development.
- The pillars of community work and community development include work plans, development plans; planners; community leaders; assets, infrastructure and money, members working or living outside the community, in towns or diaspora; government, non-government agencies; children, youths and other interest groups; and development workers and volunteers.
- Process of community work or community development is identification of pillars; planning; implementing; reviewing and sustaining.
- Use of local resources, coupled with participation, use of technology and innovation result in successful community working and development.

Further and advanced knowledge

This chapter introduced community work and community development. To improve theoretical knowledge and practical skills, more training and practice is required. Such training includes fieldwork in a community work agency; process of community work and community development; needs assessment/project identification; researching with communities; decolonising communities, project planning and management; developmental work and socio-economic development.

More reading on the integrated *musha/nyumba* theory is recommended. This was covered in the theories chapter but covered in depth in Taranhike, D. S. (2021). Integral Kumusha: A Case of Buhera – Towards

Questions for in-class assessments and examinations

- What are the three African theories or theoretical foundations underpinning community work and community development? Discuss any two.
- How is community work different from casework or individual work and groupwork?
- How does community development contribute to developmental social work and social development?
- Use the needs analysis template to understand the needs of a selected community.
- Do a community work and community development audit of a selected community. Identify community needs that require community intervention. Use the relevant template.
- Identify the pillars of community work and community development of a specific community of your choice.
- Identify appropriate intervention methods for a selected community of your choice.
- Develop an intervention or implementation plan for a selected community of your choice.
- Discuss, step by step, how you could plan, implement, review and end a program in a rural community?
- Review or evaluate a community development program that has been implemented in your community.
- Use 10 slides to create a lecture about sustainability of community work and community development projects to be delivered to volunteers.
- Use 10 slides to demonstrate the full cycle and stages of community problem/project identification.
- Create an audio speech to be delivered to local community leaders about different methods of community work and community development. Remember the importance of local protocol and language.
- Use 10 slides to demonstrate to the project leaders, local community leaders and project volunteers on leadership skills and group cohesion.

253

- Discuss any 2 indigenous laws or rules from indigenous leaders, 2 national laws or policies from a government, 2 regional policies from a regional body and 2 continental policies from the African Union that contribute to community development.
- See case studies for more questions.

Potential questions for research

- What is the most effective model of assessing community needs?
- What are the strategies to enhance and sustain community development projects?
- What are the indigenous methods appropriate for the community?
- A bottom-up approach to developing African community work and development theory.
- Analysing the African cultural leadership and management approaches.
- How to enhance ujamaa and Ubuntu approaches to community development?
- Development of community work and development models?
- Comparative analysis of the western and African cultural leadership skills
- Improving or increasing participation of marginalised groups
- Evaluate the process of community work or community development
- Impediments and opportunities to sustaining development
- Research could also focus on livelihood strategies, income, markets, peace, governance, and natural resources (land, water, air, fisheries, oceans, minerals, vegetation, and others)
- Management and nurturing growth-oriented community social enterprises

Key terms and their meanings

Community development – a method of intervention that prevents and addresses long-term problems, challenges, threats or issues and utilises community assets, opportunities and participation. Community development focuses on long-term well-being and addresses long-term needs, it is often preventive, empowers and builds capacity. Community development cannot be done on behalf of the community.

Community work – a method of intervention that addresses immediate, short and medium-term problems, challenges, threats or issues and utilises community assets, opportunities and participation. The assets can be human, family, environmental, spiritual or otherwise and can also come from outside. Community work focuses on short-term welfare and addresses immediate needs, it is often reactive. Community work can be done on behalf of the community.

Community – a collection of households in a specific geographical area.

Developed community – a community that has all the tangible and non-tangible goods, infrastructure and services required to satisfy their short- and long-term needs.

Development – a process of ensuring that a community has all the tangible and non-tangible goods, infrastructure and services required to satisfy their short- to long-term needs. A developed community has all the tangible and non-tangible goods, infrastructure, human expertise and community services required to satisfy their short- to long-term needs.

Developmental approach – a process of development that prevents and looks at needs in the long term as opposed to welfare.

Developmental social work – a process of development that balances social and economic development.

Entrepreneur – an adventurous person with innovative skills and willing to take risks by investing in a risky project and shows great risk mitigation skills to succeed in their venture.

Family: a collection of social units made up of a father, one or more mothers and children who are from a common ancestry and share one *musha* (permanent home).

Growth-oriented project – a project identified at the community and shows all potential for growth and sustainability based on utilization of local available resources and active local participation.

Homehold – a home and people living on it. A home can have one or more households. A home can have one or more families.

Household – a house and its occupants (applies to urban houses that are often single).

Integrated *musha/nyumba* theory – a theory for of centring socio-economic development on permanent homes found in rural villages. See theories chapter.

Participation – a process whereby beneficiaries of community projects make decisions about their needs, priorities and interventions in line with their aspirations.

Social capital – these are the social resources that a family or community has, for example, Ubuntu that increases justice and familyhood, ujamaa that increases labour, *umuganda* that increases communityhood and *machobane* which increases sustainability.

Social enterprise – a community-based intervention originally started as social activity and grant funded initiative with capacity to raise income. Social enterprises are income generating projects that have escalated to another level of enterprise.

Social work – an academic discipline and profession that embraces and enhances long-held methods of addressing life challenges in order to achieve social functioning, development, cohesion and liberation using diverse African indigenous knowledges and values enshrined in the family, community, society, environment and spirituality (African Journal of Social Work, 2020).

Ubudehe – a collective cultural value of working cooperatively. Similar concepts in some communities include *nhimbe* (Zimbabwe), *ikibiri* (Burundi), *msaragambo* (Tanzania), *bulungi bwansi* and *gwanga mujje* (Uganda) and *harambee* (Kenya).

Ubuntu – a collection of values and practices that black people of Africa or of African origin view as making people authentic human beings. While the nuances of these values and practices vary across different ethnic groups, they all point to one thing – an authentic individual human being is part of a larger and more significant relational, communal, societal, environmental, and spiritual world. the term Ubuntu is expressed differently is several African communities and languages but all referring to the same thing. In Angola, it is known as *gimuntu*, Botswana (muth*u*), Burkina Faso *(maaya)*, Burundi (Ubuntu), Cameroon *(bato)*, Congo *(bantu)*, Congo Democratic Republic *(bomoto/bantu)*, Cote d'Ivoire (maay*a*), Equatorial Guinea *(maaya)*, Guinea *(maaya)*, Gambia *(maaya)*, Ghana *(biako ye)*, Kenya *(utu/munto/mondo)*, Liberia *(maaya)*, Malawi *(umunthu)*, Mali *(maaya)*, Mozambique *(vumuntu)*, Namibia *(omundu)*, Nigeria *(mutunchi/iwa/agwa)*, Rwanda *(bantu)*, Sierra Leonne *(maaya)*, South Africa (Ubuntu/*botho*), Tanzania *(utu/obuntu/bumuntu)*, Uganda *(obuntu)*, Zambia *(umunthu/*Ubuntu) and Zimbabwe *(hunhu/unhu/botho/*Ubuntu). It is also found in other Bantu countries not mentioned here (Mugumbate and Chereni, 2020). Ubuntu community work and community development refers to interventions theoretically, pedagogically and practically grounded in Ubuntu.

Ujamaa – cooperating and pulling together as a community to achieve self-help.

References and recommended readings

African Journal of Social Work (AJSW) (2020). Statement of Policy. Harare, National Association of Social Workers (NASWZ).

Bohwasi, P. (2000). Advancing entrepreneurship in Gutu: Zvinoda Madzimai Women's Group

Bohwasi, P. (2014). A study of community entrepreneurship in Zimbabwe with special reference to rural areas, Masvingo Province. Unpublished PhD thesis submitted to Woburn Business School, Aldersgate University College.

Dhlembeu, N. (2014). Post qualifying training manual for Probation Officers, an assignment for the Department of Child Welfare and Probation Services and the Council of Social Workers. Harare: Council of Social Workers.

Kalinganire, C., Gilkey, S., and Haas, J. L. (2017). Social work practice in Rwanda: The challenge of adapting western models to fit local contexts. In Mel Gray (Editor) *The Handbook of Social Work and Social Development in Africa*. London: Routledge.

Kaseke, E. (2001). Social development as a model of social work practice: the experience of Zimbabwe. *School of Social Work Staff Papers*. Harare, School of Social Work.

Khomba, J. K., and Kangaude-Ulaya, E. C. (2013). Indigenisation of corporate strategies in Africa: lessons from the African Ubuntu philosophy. China-USA Business Review, 12(7), 672-689.

Mugumbate, J. R. (2019). *Kunzwisisa budiriro (Understanding Development). Chinyorwa chevadzidzisi nevadzidzi*. Training Manual. Buhera: Sanga Development Foundation (SDF)

Mugumbate, J. R. and Chereni, A. (2020). Now, the theory of Ubuntu has its space in social work. *African Journal of Social Work Special issue on Ubuntu Social Work, 10 (1), v-xvii*

Mugumbate, J. R. and Daka, A. (2020). Projects and initiatives for food production, income, welfare, livelihoods, and development in Sanga community, Buhera, Zimbabwe: a study of projects from 1980-2020. *SDF Research Report 2, 1-20*. Sanga: Sanga Development Foundation.

Rutikanga, C. (2019). A Social Work Analysis of Home-grown Solutions and Poverty Reduction in Rwanda: The Indigenous Approach of Ubudehe. *Social Work Practice in Africa Indigenous and Innovative Approaches*. Edited by Janestic Mwende Twikirize Helmut SpitzerKampala, Fountain Publishers

Zimbabwe Opportunities Industrialisation Centers (ZOIC) (2008). Filling a need - The story of Tamuka Garments Chimanimani, a Development Venture Capital approach. Report. Harare: ZOIC

Zimbabwe Opportunities Industrialisation Centers (ZOIC) (2009). Creating sustainable livelihoods opportunities, Strategic Plan 2010-2015, ZOIC strategic plan workshop, Opportunity House, Harare, Zimbabwe

CHAPTER 9

Using Ubuntu outside Africa: insights, knowledge, values and strategies for the African diaspora

Introduction

This chapter presents Ubuntu values and social work practice, migration and settlement with the African diaspora. The aim is to equip social workers and development workers with knowledge and skills to effectively support African families, communities and individuals living in the diaspora. The Ubuntu values are essential and are observed by many African community groups and families as a way of maintaining their African heritage and practice. Ubuntu social work is distinguished as a social work practice that is theoretically, pedagogically, and practically grounded in African community knowledge and practice. Ubuntu practice has been preserved as oral literature which has passed from generation to generation through storytelling, poetry, song, art, dance, and many other forms. Maintaining indigenous positive values, including spiritual values, can assist young people and their families in addressing their social problems.

Objectives of this chapter

After studying this chapter, readers will be expected to have acquired knowledge and skills in the following areas:

- Ubuntu values when working with Africans who have migrated outside the continent.
- Migration and settlement issues for families who want to migrate outside Africa.

- Migration challenges such as raising children or family in western cultures.
- Working with the African community groups in the diaspora.
- Assessments that are suitable for the diaspora context.
- Practical application of Ubuntu outside Africa with African diaspora and non-African populations.
- Research questions and methods that are appropriate to the diaspora context.
- Fieldwork, workplace-based and community-based learning is contextual.

Skills and competencies addressed in this chapter

By the end of this chapter, readers will be expected to have acquired the following skills and competencies:

- Knowledge, values and strategies that are useful for African people and particularly students studying social work to become social workers.
- Confidently answer questions or complete academic and practical assessments related to the use of Ubuntu with the African diaspora.
- Able to develop meaningful research questions and methods that are appropriate to the local context.
- Effective planning of fieldwork, workplace-based and community-based learning that is contextual.

Goals of social work with diaspora families and communities

The following are some of the important goals for social workers working with African people in Diaspora.

- To assist individuals, families, and community groups to settle better by providing support services and empowerment.
- To remind people from African background about Ubuntu values and other indigenous practices that are useful to families and community.

260

- To help social work students to learn better ways of supporting and engaging with individuals, families and community groups using Ubuntu values and practices.
- To advocate on behalf of vulnerable individuals and families to access support services.
- To support young people, families and individuals in their transitioning and settlement journeys.

Skills and competencies addressed in this chapter

By the end of this chapter, readers will be expected to have acquired the following skills and competencies:

- Problem identification and application of social work skills and practices.
- Identification of mental health related issues.
- Ability to apply intervention skills.
- Knowledge and capacity to support individual clients and families
- Identification of migration and settlement related issues for migrants.
- Ability to apply case work and case management skills.
- Ability to identify African theories related social work practice.

Migration

Human migration is the movement of people from one place or country to another with the intention of settling permanently or temporarily. Migration can be involuntary or forced and be for different reasons, such as insecurity, slave trade, deportation, human trafficking, war/displacement, and ethnic cleansing. Although the changes brought by migration and settlement difficulties can be challenging, the community spirit of Ubuntu plays a significant role in supporting African migrants and keeping families together. Ubuntu values such as love, truth, compassion and understanding of humanity – are expected to be displayed by every elder in society. These elders want their young people to learn the values and spirit of Ubuntu. African social workers who work with young people from African community groups also promote Ubuntu values. Social workers should have a clear understanding of Ubuntu values and their importance and apply them through their social work practice. Social

261

workers aim to serve communities, individuals and families in addressing social problems and meeting their own needs. They promote the protection of human rights, dignity, and integrity. Drawing on the complex migration and settlement challenges experienced by many African families who have migrated to the western world and lost the beautiful values of Ubuntu at the family and community levels, social workers and development workers should consider Ubuntu values when supporting such families for their intervention to be meaningful and effective. Parents are experiencing a high level of difficulty in rearing their children because young people are adopting individualistic life faster than their parents, most of whom have grown up in communal societies with the values of Ubuntu (Abur, 2019).

Young people

Young people and families from African backgrounds who have migrated to western countries are caught between two cultures. In countries such as Australia and United States of America, a good number of young people from the African community are in contact with the criminal justice system, having become involved in criminal activities, engaged in drug/alcohol consumption, and disengaged from their families and community (Abur, 2019). Many are confused, finding themselves torn between western culture and their own; they find it increasingly difficult to stick to their own African values. People are easily influenced to abandon their own values and take on the values of the host society to allow them to fit in the system. This has been one of the complex issues facing parents and young people in African communities in Australia. Raising children in Africa is something done by the community: parents are assisted by their extended family members and community members in moulding teenagers. This means that Ubuntu values are important in African society. The values of Ubuntu are rooted in humanity and caring and supporting one another as human beings, both collectively, as a society, and within our families.

Guiding principles, ethics and values in doing social work with the African diaspora

The following are some Ubuntu principles, ethics or values applicable to social work students while supporting or working with the African diaspora.

- To apply all relevant ethical practices of love, caring, peace, truth-telling, empathy, respect, dignity, happiness, internal optimism, kindness and inner goodness and compassion while working with clients by avoiding any issues/discussions that may trigger some difficult past experiences.
- To facilitate and provide an understanding of family values and cultural values.
- Respecting cultural heritage of family, individuals and community groups while working with them.
- To foster social justice practices by supporting and empowering individuals, families and community groups to have a voice in decision making process concerning issues to their lives.
- Support community leadership and create leaders within the community by empowering and encouraging young people to consider positive leadership in the community and families.

African theoretical foundations of social work

There are good African theories that are applicable to social work. They are safe and useful in African society. African theories are mostly developed in Africa and by African writers based on African cultures and practices. These theories consist of the following:

- Afrocentrism theory
- Collectivism theory
- African family theory
- Individual-in-family theory
- Ubuntu theory
- Indigenisation theory
- African migration theory
- African mentoring model

The African theories outlined above are essential reading for social workers and development workers seeking a deeper understanding of the Ubuntu approach. Social work students and social practitioners and development workers must thoroughly study the presented African theories and explore others to deepen their understanding. They should also aim to develop new theories that expand the African body of knowledge.

Social issues, challenges and problems among diaspora families

Many social issues are encountered in the diaspora when families are settling in western countries or their new countries. These social issues include cultural shock and change, parenting problems/raising the children in new culture, housing issues, unemployment, racism and discrimination, mental health due to settlement difficulties, language problem for those who do not speak English, social change, and social isolation. Some of these challenges are commonly found with families and individuals because of migration and settlement difficulties. The disconnection with environment and spiritual practice or indigenous practices including food and other cultural activities are also missed.

Raising children in the diaspora

Raising young children without Ubuntu values or family values is problematic in many ways and may result in conflict within the family. One of the great proverbs from the Eastern African states this beautifully: when two elephants fight, it is the grass that suffers (Jabs, 2007; Walker-Dalhouse and Dalhouse, 2009). When two elephants, who are the parents, in this case, keep fighting, regardless of who wins the conflict, the people who suffer the most are the young people of that family. For instance, some parents are denied access to their children by their estranged spouse, maybe because they want to punish their opponent psychologically by denying him or her access to their children. Are children part of the conflict? Well, children are victims regardless of whether they are part of the conflict or not. Children will always be the victims. However, Ubuntu values and family principles are very useful in keeping families together and helping parents to raise children with positive attitudes and morality.

In western culture, the women are commonly responsible for the children. She decides if she wants her children to have access to their father or not. The law encourages and supports shared responsibilities when it comes to accessing children. Both parents are entitled or have the right to see their children. A parent can only be prevented access to their child/ren when they are perceived as a threat to the wellbeing of the young person. A parent can be denied access with the aim of protecting the child/ren or young person from harm. Do African-Australian parents understand and respect what the law says? The answer is maybe not. Many parents do not understand why the law supports the idea of both parents having access to children in the event of separation or divorce. However, one of a child's most fundamental rights is to know both of their parents. It is selfish to deny a child access to their parents where there are no threats or risks identified.

In some cases, some men in the African community in western countries perceive themselves as powerless in the case of divorce or separation. Women have more power when it comes to decision-making in Australia because the responsibility mainly lies with women and is based on how the government supports families (Abur, 2019). Men have little say when it comes to financial decisions in the family, except when the man is working and independent and free to make financial decisions. These social challenges relating to families and youth in the African community are also confirmed in previous research (Abur, 2018, Abur, 2012). There is frequently an incongruity between different generations' awareness of their new environment and differences in their expectations of how young people should negotiate the settlement landscape.

The social changes brought about by migration and settlement difficulties have a huge impact on families and individuals within the African-Australian community. Gender division in families, intergenerational conflict between parents and teenagers, separations and divorces are some of the social issues confronting parents and their young people. Some men have lost their family responsibilities in Australia and this has caused problems in relationships, leading to high rates of separation and divorce in the community. Women have taken responsibility for caring for children on their own, and this leads to another layer of problems, as many youths become rebellious against their families and ultimately become involved in criminal activities (Abur, 2019). This is widely reported in the media, such as in the activities of the so-called 'Apex Gang' in Melbourne (Crane, 2016).

The number of families separated or divorced has increased in the African-Australian community because males, who are indigenously considered the head of the family, are unemployed and cannot provide for their families (Abur and Spaaij, 2016). Many young people who are incarcerated in Melbourne, Victoria, have somehow dropped out of school and have less connection with their family members, instead relying on peer groups for support (Abur, 2019; Abur and Mphande, 2019). Social and intractable conflicts often arise because of social situations and disagreements on social issues, such as parenting, financial management and disputes over party celebrations or hearsay/gossip (Jabs, 2007). The best thing communities can do to assist vulnerable families and young people is to create support services where casework and in-home support services are provided to vulnerable families. By providing family support, services will be able to increase parenting confidence and capacity, strengthen family relationships and promote better opportunities and outcomes for children (Abur, 2019). Parents do have an influence on the lives of their children. If the parents support the young person to engage in school and associate with the right people, the young person is likely to be influenced in a positive manner (Walker-Dalhouse and Dalhouse, 2009).

Mental health issues in countries of origin

Mental health is an area which is frequently neglected in many African countries. Indigenous beliefs and attitudes still play a significant role in influencing the treatment of mental health illnesses in society (Gureje and Alem, 2000). There are no good mental health policies and institutions built to address mental-health-related issues in society. Many people are affected by war, poverty and a lack of necessary medical services, often leading to serious mental health problems. In addition to poverty and lack of good services, there are physical deprivations and hardships that lead to high levels of trauma. Traumatic events, such as witnessing execution and the death of loved ones, and different forms of abuse, such as torture, rape and oppression, as well as looting and widespread destruction, can have a profound emotional and psychological impact on families and individuals, and it has been widely recognised that many refugees suffer from varying degrees of Post-Traumatic Stress Disorder (PTSD) (Abur and Mphande, 2019). There are no proper mental health assessments and services put in place by governments to address this; however, there is a great need within the community. Systems also need to be put in place to address other serious mental health problems, such as schizophrenia, psychosis, bipolar

266

disorder, mood disorders and dementia (in older people). Mental health is one of the subjects that need to be taught properly to social work students to prepare them to manage mental health patients or clients when they are working in the field.

Ubuntu values versus western values

In theory, Ubuntu is a collection of values and practices that many African nations observed as a guiding value for their families and community groups (Mugumbate and Chereni, 2020). People of Africa and/or of African origin view Ubuntu as making people authentic human beings. While the nuances of these values and practices vary across different ethnic groups, they all point to one thing, an authentic individual human being is part of a larger and more significant relational, communal, societal, environmental, and spiritual world (Muchanyerei, 2020; Mugumbate and Chereni, 2020). Ubuntu is a widespread African worldview which upholds the values of intense humanness, caring, sharing, respect, compassion and associated values, ensuring a happy and qualitative community life in the spirit of family (Mabvurira, 2020). Many African social workers incorporate Ubuntu principles into their practice in the field of social work. The values of Ubuntu assist social workers in decision-making in complex situations that require ethical consideration (Mabvurira, 2020). It is the responsibility of any generation to tell their stories based on their experiences and their local knowledge within society. "A person is a person through other persons. None of us comes into the world fully formed. We would not know how to think, or walk, or speak, or behave as human beings unless we learned it from other human beings. We need other human beings to be with us and to be human" (Muchanyerei, 2020, p. 60). Ubuntu represents authentic values in African communities (Nabudere, 2005). Ubuntu is usually expressed in maxims such as 'You are what you are because of other people', 'I am because we are' or 'I am what I am because of you' (Samkange and Samkange, 1980). Every individual is viewed through their family and the family is viewed through the community. Individualism is not valued. There are powers held by different age groups within families, the community, and the society (Lutz, 2009). These powers are used to shape others to become authentic human beings. In simple terms, we need other human beings to live with us and to be human (Tutu, 2004).

Ubuntu theory values the connection and relationship between individuals within the family unit and the community relationship of people within communities (Mugumbate and Chereni, 2020). The African community is a communal society where people share responsibilities when it comes to community issues or family issues. For instance, there is a famous saying in African: "a child is raised by the whole village". The idea is that every person or adult has a role to play in taking care of children by nurturing, mentoring and teaching them to be responsible people that can or will play significant roles in their communities. Ubuntu is commonly practised and expressed in different African languages across the continent (Mugumbate and Chereni, 2020).

The concept of Ubuntu is also about sharing and caring for other people or vulnerable people in our society, which is also a core value of social work. One of the problems with Ubuntu as an African Indigenous knowledge is that it is not documented but has instead been transmitted from generation to generation through storytelling (Louw, 2006). Elders in the community tell complex and positive stories to young people as a way of passing on their indigenous knowledge. Elders share stories of leadership and explain how issues are solved within the family and community and between different community groups (Mabovula, 2011; Sanusi and Spahn, 2019). In many African community groups, everyone is expected to play a significant role in society and in the family. The expectation of supporting one another is attached to moral values, such as compassion, as well as cultural values. This also links in with issues of social justice and inequality in society, as well as respecting human dignity (Abur, 2019). Some people in society feel discomfort when seeing poor people struggling to access services, while other people enjoy the privilege of accessing these services. It is the same case in countries where other people have more power over others, as is often the case with native-born Australians and migrants. In many countries around the globe, migrants or refugees face xenophobia and different levels of discrimination. However, Ubuntu values and practices challenge the notion of segregation and tell us to consider one important thing: humanity. We are born in society, we live in society, and we must contribute positively to society by supporting one another regardless of our social, political and cultural backgrounds. Some African individuals and families in western countries are trying to do what is expected of them by society; however, some have adopted an individualistic lifestyle and have no connection with their families back home in Africa or even in the western countries to which their families have migrated. Maintaining indigenous African culture and connection with family members back in Africa is a dream of many grown-up Africans who are living in the western world. However, parents are challenged by

268

younger generations that have little or no understanding of African family values. The challenges of migration and settlement have caused dysfunction in many families. African family values are not regarded as important anymore; many parents now find they are restless at night, thinking about the future of their children in the western world.

What are the consequences of losing indigenous values? In recent years, using Australia as an example, many young people from African backgrounds have been incarcerated or put in the care of child protection services. Part of the problems is the loss of the African values of Ubuntu and family values due to migration and settlement. Social changes have brought different levels of complexities to some families. The complex situation of migration and settlement has severely affected families and young people in the African-Australian community (Abur, 2019). Divorce and separation rates have risen among parents from African-Australian community groups who are living in western countries. For instance, some families in African community groups in Australia are headed by a single mother. In addition, some of these parents are struggling with their own personal mental health problems, such as trauma from previous life experiences in war-affected areas, difficult life experiences in refugee camps and chaotic lifestyles due to transitioning from place to place (Abur, 2019). These issues make parenting more challenging and complex for single parents (Abur, 2018).

Divorce and separations are not a new phenomenon in the western world, but some African-Australian families have struggled with this social change. It is a complex situation among African-Australian families because there is a high level of conflict and ongoing tension involved between the two sides of the family. Sometimes, relatives and friends from both sides of the conflicts are also caught up in the conflict. However, the real victims are the young people, who are left under the care of a single parent. Ubuntu values have a strong link with social work values and practice. Both Ubuntu values and social work values are about the promotion of caring and supporting vulnerable individuals and community groups; promoting human dignity and social justice; respecting individual experiences and stories; supporting vulnerable children and women in society; and promoting peace and non-violent communication between individuals, family members and community groups (Mugumbate and Nyanguru, 2013). Ubuntu values and social work practices encompass family values, community values, spirituality and environmental values. These are observed and maintained in many African communities. Ubuntu practice exists in the form of oral literature, passed from generation to generation through storytelling, poetry, song, art, dance and many other forms (Mugumbate and Chereni, 2020). Ubuntu philosophy promotes teamwork, team spirit and collaboration between individuals, community groups, family members. It promotes and deepens understanding and cohesiveness in society. Some differences between Ubuntu worldviews and western worldviews:

- Sense of community: The Ubuntu worldview holds strong values about community belonging and social cohesion as a collective responsibility of all members of the community. Communality is very important as compared to the western values of a liberal society.
- Lifestyle: The Ubuntu worldview holds that individual lifestyle is dependent on other people, such as family members and other community members. However, the western worldview holds that individuals can determine their own lifestyles depending on their desires and dreams, not according to community and family expectations or demands.
- Parenting: Ubuntu practice holds that parenting is the responsibility of the family, relatives and community members. Children are brought up or cared for by community members. In the western worldview, however, parenting is the responsibility of parents and close relatives, such as grandparents; the community is not involved in parenting decisions or directions.
- Values: The Ubuntu worldview holds that families and communities must hold on to their values and practice. This means that community and family values are very significant in any decision-making about your life and career direction. However, the western worldview does not impose community values and family values on individuals. The practice is very liberal; people have the choice to make decisions without community and family influences.
- Languages: African communities emphasise their indigenous languages, which give them ways to communicate with their family members in Africa. However, in a multicultural society like Australia, indigenous languages are not prioritised. Instead, the English language is prioritised. This takes children further away from their clan because their family members do not always speak English.

- Social change: The Ubuntu worldview is connected to indigenous African values and practices. However, the western worldview has adopted or is undergoing many social changes in terms of gender, marriage, sexuality and family.
- Connection with family: According to the Ubuntu worldview, family connection is a basic relationship that every individual should have, and they should hold it strongly. However, the western worldview considers family connection to be a choice for individuals.
- Gender: The Ubuntu worldview sees gender issues very differently. Indigenous values and practices still hold a strong position in the community. However, the western worldview has embraced different concepts of gender.
- Spirituality: African communities are highly spiritual, and their spirituality is exercised in several ways, including belief in God, connection with deceased people (whether these are family ancestors or unrelated people), belief in the Bible or Quran and worshipping, fasting or praying
- Majority age: In African society, a child remains a child until they start their own family. In Australia, children seem to be free as soon as they start earning their income, which might be as low as 15 years. They can easily move out of their family home. The expectation in African families is for the child to move out when they marry.

The differences presented above result in several forms of conflict within African families in Australia. Social workers, who are often of white race, use western ideas to solve conflict arising from these differences. This does not solve these challenges in most cases, hence the need for adopting indigenous practices in addressing such forms of conflict. Communities know best about their problems and the solutions to those problems. The African indigenous concept of Ubuntu is important in connecting people with their societal norms and values. Many African people have a wealth of knowledge and skills regarding Ubuntu values and practices within their own community groups and in their own community languages. Having local knowledge and skills in your local community is fundamental. Local knowledge involves skills that people have developed or accumulated over a period and continue to develop, passing knowledge and skills on to younger generations (Mugumbate and Chereni, 2020). Social work services in many contemporary African communities are provided by family members, community members and religious groups, but they are now gradually becoming organised by governments and other non-governmental organisations.

Positionality and social work practice

It is pivotal, from an academic perspective, to understand the relationship between different social issues and power in society. Positionality is a concept that is related to intersectionality: factors such as power, culture, gender, ethnicity and class, which influence us as human beings. People act and respond differently to different situations based on their positionality and experiences (Franks, 2002). Social workers in practice and teaching field in Australia and the United Kingdom have, at some point, witnessed some passive or active discrimination or "the white privilege" enjoyed by social workers of the white race. Courtesy of the anti-oppressive and anti-discriminatory policies introduced by the western countries to recognise the global majority or people from minority groups, these social workers have now been empowered to voice out against racism and other forms of discrimination against African diaspora. Some of the social workers have worked with families and young people from African backgrounds, allowing them to understand the complex issues facing families and young people in African diaspora communities using their homegrown Ubuntu values and principles for effective interventions and support.

Implications for social work

Social work is one of the professions that works closely with young people and their families. In the academic field, social work is a discipline and profession that supports vulnerable people in society. The role of social work is to address life challenges and bring social change, function, development, cohesion and liberation from oppressive issues in society. Understanding Ubuntu philosophy for African people can have a great influence in assisting young people and families from an African background. In social work, the best thing that can be done is to provide appropriate assistance and information that can make a person or vulnerable family change their lives by taking a positive direction in their decision-making on things that matter to them. Social workers working with migrant families and young people should promote the positive values

272

of Ubuntu to young people and their families while working with them. This will help young people to value their parents' and their community's cultures by connecting them with positive values and indigenous beliefs. Therefore, the recommendation for social workers or other professional workers working with young people and families from migrant backgrounds is to be open in engaging people in their positive values. Social workers should consider cultural issues and values such as family connection/structure, religious/spiritual connections, and the expectations/responsibilities of the family. Young people who are at risk of engaging in criminal activities or experiencing drug- and alcohol-related issues can be assisted by social workers to connect with their faith community group/faith leaders to assist them in understanding the consequences of negative behaviours.

Strategies for social workers working with diaspora families

The following are some useful strategies for African migrants and their children to consider when they are settling in a new community or country. Some of these strategies includes mentoring young people to learn about their own culture and social activities of their parents alongside western culture. Some parents may consider bringing their own relative to assist with management of young people or parenting. Social work should consider the following strategies:

- Supporting families with an African heritage to keep their cultural values and practices.
- Reading more about Ubuntu values as they are very useful for African families in living in western world.
- Psychosocial education meant to help families to:
  o Promote responsible behaviour.
  o To be conscious about the future and potential distractions around.
  o Valuing your family and culture of your people regardless of your education background.
  o Seeking assistance from right people before the problem becomes out of control.
  o Teaching children about their African values.

Case study

A social worker is working with a single mother of five children, three girls and two boys. They migrated from South Sudan to Australia and settled in Melbourne city with a hope of changing their life situations after many years of suffering from war and displacement related difficulties because of war and displacement. However, a mother found herself being faced by settlement challenges including, cultural change, parenting children in the western culture. She expressed her frustration to the social worker that "I am losing control of my children because of the child protection system in this country. My children are not listening to me anymore. I want to go back to Africa. I wanted to take my children back to Africa. I do not want them to die in jail here. Children are brought up differently in Africa. I live in fear of the child protection system here. I was brought up differently in the village. We listen to our parents and elders in the village. This is not the case in this western world. Here, many young African people lost their direction and cultural values. They do not care about family values anymore. This is an individualised society; teenage children do their own things, and they do not care about their parents. Sometimes, family relationships are not working.

Questions for case study

Based on the case study above, discuss the following questions by answering each question according to social work practice.

1. Why does the mother want to go back to Africa with her children?
2. What are the cultural issues or cultural changes in this case study?
3. Why are teenagers not listening to their African parents?
4. What are the migration and settlement challenges in this case study?
5. From a social work perspective, what are the support services needed by the single mother and her children?
6. Are the ambitions for migrating families fulfilled in the diaspora?

Guidance: Using Ubuntu outside Africa

If you uproot a plant, and plant it with the soil around its roots, it will grow, will not wilt, and will be health. It you wash the soil from its roots, it will not thrive. This is the scenario of Ubuntu philosophy amongst the Africa Diaspora. Therefore, it is critical for social workers supporting African families to be culturally sensitive, have cultural competency and consider tailoring Ubuntu values in all their social work interventions. Below are the seven (7) stages that outlines a clear process to put into practice Ubuntu philosophy when supporting the African Diaspora:

Cultural competency training

Organisations employing or engaging social workers, students or development workers working with African diaspora should make it a mandatory for all employees or staff to train on African cultures, histories and experiences to enhance their cultural competence. A meaningful training needs to impart knowledge on the impact of the "the white privilege" on African colleagues and families who are of African heritage, increases the engagement of African diaspora with services and social workers and development workers being culturally sensitive to the needs of the African diaspora. Social workers and development workers need to get a clearer picture of "traditional relationships" in the African context, their interconnectedness, issues of spirituality when it comes to mental health and parenting a child.

Identify family tree

Understanding family tree of an African diaspora is key in mapping available resources and support system for the care of children or adults in needs of care. Each social worker or development worker should, during the introductory home visits, develop a family genogram of each individual family he/she is working with. Whether resident in the same country or not, a three-generational genogram is helpful for each African family involved with the child or adult services. This family tree is useful in tracking members of the family or extended family who can support the client financially by identifying an economic support network, emotionally or spiritually. When supporting African diaspora, it is important to remember that most of the support network is back home in Africa, but they remain important part of the plan who can be contacted and even take care of their relative child or adult.

Completing culture and identity work

The third important stage in supporting the African diaspora is completing culture and identity work. This entails capturing or taking note of the main language they use at home, how a child and adults in the family like to be identified as, what they value as important to them, what is their heritage, who is important to them in their family tree, what are the relations like within their household and members of the extended, what do they believe in and their religion. It is common that for some African diaspora who have established in the UK, Australia or Canada, whether with permanent residence or citizenship or without, to cut ties with their families within western countries or back home. Nonetheless, social workers or development workers ought to uncover what the elders of that family believe as their family culture, this becomes the basis for social workers or development workers to support parents/guardians in coming with a plan to instil these values in the young people or blend it with the existing interventions to promote their culture and identity.

Ascertain immigration status

The immigration status of African Diaspora has an impact on their access to public services and support. For example, in the UK, this determines whether the family has recourse to public funds or not. Financial issues have been a source of social issues among the African diaspora, especially those who have just migrated as with no recourse to public funds. This means they must fork out money from their pockets to fund childcare costs, health surcharges, no benefits to rely on for survival in times of crisis, all this may lead to neglect amongst children. Therefore, using Ubuntu philosophy, social workers should be compassionate for such families consider through exploring, explore available non-public support, for example, charity shops and food banks in the UK.

Involving family members in family conferences and meetings

Although families have a right to choose who they want to be part of their support network, African families rarely overlook the support from their

276

extended families. Therefore, social workers and development workers should explore further the family network, through the family tree or other social networks including the church, friends and work colleagues and they should make efforts to involve this network in their case management processes. Considering the African diaspora have support network back home in Africa, in this era of social networks and internet, it is critical to connect the support network remotely using telephone or online applications.

Using culturally responsive practice

The sixth stage in Ubuntu-driven social work or development practice entails using culturally responsive interventions with the African Diaspora. Social workers or development workers must consider cultural practices of each individual family to meet their cultural needs, however this needs to be done in line with national and regional laws. For example, use of music from respective African countries that the family or child likes in therapy or sessions, this convinces the African family that they are being recognised which strengthen the relationship between social workers and their clients. Therefore, all the cultural responses or practices should be clearly documented, all variances with the law be explained to the family and adjustments together with referrals to appropriate services being made accordingly, especially on areas around physical chastisement for disciplining children or forms of domestic abuse or abuse in general between couples which are borne of contention.

Support African heritage and culture

A strategy to achieve Ubuntu-driven interventions with the African diaspora is supporting their heritage and culture. This means respecting their traditional holidays, traditional activities, fund them where possible, provide opportunities for connection. For example, supporting a young person from Africa or with African heritage, including parents if appropriate, to attend a music gala of artists from their countries. Not attending to their homes or contacting them when they have important events in their lives is a sign of respect for the African diaspora. Giving them compassionate leave, not expecting them to attend meetings when grieving or upon death of a member of an extended family should not be underestimated as this means a lot to their lives. This practice promotes sustainability of the interventions made, revives the connection that the family has with its African origins and empowers them to be who they are.

Summary

This chapter presented the Ubuntu philosophy and discussed its connection with migration and settlement, family, raising children, mental health and social work. It described the differences between Ubuntu worldviews and western worldviews, practical application of Ubuntu when working with African diaspora the implications of positionality practice in social work. The chapter also suggests that Ubuntu values and practices are important for African communities living in the western world. Ubuntu is a tool to promote the wellbeing of children and vulnerable community members. The African ideas of allowing the whole village to raise a child mean that the welfare and protection of children is a duty of society – it is shared by all. This makes every adult person in the village more likely to take on the responsibility of protecting, caring, teaching and guiding children. There is a need to promote local knowledge, skills and strengths at both the practice and policy levels. Social workers need to keep championing the idea that community members have vast experiences, skills, and knowledge about local issues, and these are more significant than those belonging to outsiders. Ubuntu philosophy is well described by our great leader Nelson Mandela that "the spirit in humanity that profound African sense that we are human only through the humanity of other humanity beings". There is no better way to summarise the Ubuntu values to the world. It is about connection, showing love to other human beings, caring and delivering services to vulnerable human beings.

Further and advanced knowledge

Further reading and learning of African philosophy, African social work theories, decolonising social practice and migration and settlement challenges are recommended for students, social practitioners and social development workers to advance their knowledge.

Questions for in-class assessments and examinations

- What is your understanding of Ubuntu values?
- Find a detailed lived experience of Ubuntu that has been shared by someone and draw a mind-map or framework of what Ubuntu means to the person. You could also interview

278

someone with lived experience of Ubuntu or share your own lived experience.

- How can Ubuntu values or practices assist African parents in living in the diaspora with their young people?
- What are the migration and settlement challenges?
- What role do social workers play in supporting families and individuals?
- What are the youth issues based on the case of the family provided in section 14 of this chapter?
- Describe Ubuntu parenting practice and why it is important from an African perspective?
- What is your understanding of positionality?
- What are some of the useful and safe African theories discussed in this chapter?
- In the case provided in section 14, the mother mentioned that she fears the child protection system. Describe the western child protection system? What makes it scary?

Potential questions for research

- What are the collective indigenous values for African families in the diaspora and how do they differ from western society?
- What is social work skills that are suitable for African families living in the diaspora?
- Describe and analysis settlement issues that affected families and youth from African backgrounds living in diaspora.
- Are African indigenous values and taught helpful to young people living in western countries?
- Migration processes are full of many challenging issues to overcomes. What are the common challenges in migration and settlement?
- Would African families living in the western countries benefit from Ubuntu values? How and why?
- What are common mental health issues encountered by individuals and families during settlement and how individuals and families access support to overcome these mental health issues?
- What are the differences between raising children in Africa and raising them in the western countries?

- Ubuntu values seem to be more important in many African communities, what are the common principles of Ubuntu?

Key terms and their meanings

Case management – a collaborative process that involves assessing, planning, implementing, coordinating, monitoring, and evaluating the options and services required to meet a client's health and human service needs.

Case work – a direct service, provided by social workers or community service workers to their individual clients. Case work resolves issues of resources, social and emotional problems.

Child protection – about protecting children and young people from harm caused by abuse or neglect within the family. Therefore, the role of child protection workers is to promote children's wellbeing and protect them from harm or abuse.

Diaspora – refers to population of people who are dispersed from their original country or homeland to a foreign country.

Migration – the movement of people from one place to another place with an intention of settling, permanently or temporarily, at a new location (geographic region) because of different reasons such as conflict and economics.

Family – comprised of nuclear, immediate, extended and tribal family members rather than being limited to a nuclear family consisting of a mother, father, and children.

Western – with characteristics of or made up of ideas founded on philosophies, values, cultures and religions of people of European ancestry.

References and recommended readings

The following reading materials are recommended for further reading.

Dhlembeu, N. (2014). Post qualifying training manual for Probation Officers, an assignment for the Department of Child Welfare and Probation Services and the Council of Social Workers. Harare: Council of Social Workers.

Abur, W. (2019). *A new life with opportunities and challenges: The settlement experiences of South Sudanese Australians*. Africa World Books Pty Ltd.

Kalinganire, C., Gilkey, S., and Haas, J. L. (2017). Social work practice in Rwanda: The challenge of adapting western models to fit local contexts. In Mel Gray (Editor) *The Handbook of Social Work and Social Development in Africa*. London: Routledge.

Kaseke, E. (2001). Social development as a model of social work practice: the experience of Zimbabwe. *School of Social Work Staff Papers*. Harare, School of Social Work.

Mugumbate, J. R. and Chereni, A. (2020). Now, the theory of Ubuntu has its space in social work. *African Journal of Social Work Special issue on Ubuntu Social Work, 10 (1), v-xvii*

Abur, W., and Mphande, C. (2019). Mental health and wellbeing of South Sudanese Australians. Journal of Asian and African Studies, 55, (3), 412–428, doi/10.1177/0021909619880294.

Abur, W, and Spaaij, R. (2016). Settlement and employment experiences of South Sudanese people from refugee backgrounds in Melbourne, Australia, *The Australasian Review of African Studies*, 37(2), 107.

Abur, W. (2012). A study of the South Sudanese refugees' perspectives of settlement in the western suburbs of Melbourne. Unpublished master's thesis. Melbourne: Victoria University. http://vuir. vu. edu. au/22013.

Abur, W. (2018). Settlement strategies for the South Sudanese community in Melbourne: An analysis of employment and sport participation, Victoria University.

Abur, W. (2019). *A new life with opportunities and challenges: The settlement experiences of South Sudanese Australians*, Africa World Books Pty Ltd, Perth, Australia.

Gureje, O., and Alem, A. (2000). Mental health policy development in Africa, *Bulletin of the World Health Organization*, 78, 475–482.

Jabs, L. (2007). Where two elephants meet, the grass suffers: A case study of intractable conflict in Karamoja, Uganda. American Behavioral Scientist, 50(11), 1498–1519.

Khomba, J. K., and Kangaude-Ulaya, E. C. (2013). Indigenisation of corporate strategies in Africa: Lessons from the African Ubuntu philosophy. China-USA Business Review, 12, (7), 672-689

Louw, D. J. (2006). *The African concept of Ubuntu. Handbook of restorative justice: A global perspective*, 161–174.

Lutz, D. W. (2009). African Ubuntu philosophy and global management, *Journal of Business Ethics, 84(3), 300 - 313.*

Mabovula, N. N. (2011). The erosion of African communal values: A reappraisal of the African Ubuntu philosophy. *Inkanyiso: Journal of Humanities and Social Sciences, 3(1), 38–47.*

Mabvurira, V. (2020). Hunhu/Ubuntu philosophy as a guide for ethical decision making in social work. *African Journal of Social Work, 10(1), 73–77.*

Muchanyerei, B. (2020). An Ubuntu definition of the family in migration and childcare issues: The case of Zimbabwe. *African Journal of Social Work, 10(1), 58–62.*

Mugumbate, J. R., and Chereni, A. (2020). Now, the theory of Ubuntu has its space in social work. *African Journal of Social Work, 10(1).*

Mugumbate, J., and Nyanguru, A. (2013). Exploring African philosophy: The value of Ubuntu in social work. *African Journal of Social Work, 3(1), 82–100.*

Nabudere, D. W. (2005). Ubuntu philosophy: Memory and reconciliation. Texas Scholar Works, 1–20.

Samkange, S., and Samkange, T. M. (1980). *Hunhu* or Ubuntu: A Zimbabwean Indigenous political philosophy. Salisbury: Graham Publishing.

Sanusi, Y. A., and Spahn, A. (2019). Exploring marginalization and exclusion in renewable energy development in Africa: A perspective from western individualism and African Ubuntu philosophy. *Energy Justice Across Borders*, 273.

Tutu, D. (2000). No future without forgiveness: A personal overview of South Africa's Truth and Reconciliation Commission. London: Rider Random House.

Walker-Dalhouse, D., and Dalhouse, A. D. (2009). When two elephants fight the grass suffers: Parents and teachers working together to support the literacy development of Sudanese youth. *Teaching and Teacher Education, 25(2), 328–335.*

CHAPTER 10

Training and academic fieldwork for social services

Introduction

In this final chapter, we look at social work education and fieldwork. Education is a form of training which involves developing an educational philosophy, developing a training program, developing training methods, gathering training resources, selecting of trainees, delivering the training, assessing skills and knowledge gained and graduating. Within training, there is a skill building method where trainees go to the field to observe, learn and perfect skills. In social work, this is called fieldwork, placement, or attachment. Research refers toa process of setting a knowledge generation philosophy, identifying knowledge gaps, creating research methods, implementing the methods, collecting data, analysing, reporting, using the findings and reviewing it.

Objectives of this chapter

After studying this chapter, readers will be expected to have acquired knowledge on:

- Africa's theories of education and training.
- Domains and levels of social services training.
- How to publish educational and research resources.
- Assessments that are suitable for the local context.
- How fieldwork is conducted.
- Research questions and methods that are appropriate locally.
- Contextual fieldwork, workplace-based and community-based learning.
- Using Ubuntu in education and training.

Skills and competencies addressed in this chapter

By the end of this chapter, readers will be expected to have acquired the following skills and competencies:

- Components of academic programs.
- Outcomes of academic programs.
- Using African knowledge in teaching and learning.
- Using African knowledge in publishing.
- Using African knowledge in fieldwork.
- Answering questions or assessments about the topic of this chapter.
- Creating research questions and methods that are appropriate to the local context.
- Planning fieldwork, workplace-based and community-based learning that is contextual.
- Identifying common mistakes when designing academic programs.

Theories of education and training

The African theory of education (ATE) and African philosophy of education (APE) are the main theories of education and training. Other theories include pan-Africanism, Afrocentrism, developmentalism, Ubuntu, indigenisation, orature and decolonisation. ATE teaches us that education should not only be academic, but it must also serve a relevant purpose and must be relevant and useful to our communities. APE teaches us that our communities have a role to play in education, in fact, before modern day education, learning was happening in our communities, especially experiential learning. Both ATE and APE emphasize Ubuntu, that is, education is not only about the learner, but their interaction and interdependence with their family, community and society at large. Ubuntu education uses the family, community, and environment as sources of knowledge but also as teaching and learning media. The essence of education is family, community, societal and environmental well-being. Interaction, liberation, participation, recognition, respect, and inclusion are important aspects of Ubuntu education. Methods of teaching and learning include groups and community approaches. In short, Ubuntu shapes the objectives, content, methodology and outcomes of education.

284

African indigenous education model (Omona, 1998)

Table 9: Africa indigenous education model (Omona, 1998)

Principle	Meaning
Preparationism or preparedness (*obwetekatekyi* in Rukiga Language in Uganda).	Prepare children for future economic, social, political, and cultural roles in in the family, the tribe or the clan, community and society.
Functionalism (*omugasho*).	Education must serve a function to the learner, family, community and society in which it takes place.
Communalism (*kukorera hamwe*).	Sense of community, cooperative learning, and the view that it takes a whole community to teach.
Perennialism (*ekimazire obwire bureingwa*).	Valuing knowledge from the past or looking back to what African philosophers said.
Holisticism (*kutwara ekintu hamwe*).	Which means valuing knowledge of the past or looking back to what African philosophers said.

Nziramasanga educational model

In 1999, Dr Caiphas Tizanaye Nziramasanga led a commission in Zimbabwe that recommended what an African education should look like. Excerpts from the Commission's report are provided below, verbatim (Nziramasanga 1999, p. 24). The commission concluded that education should be based on the peoples' belief in *Unhu*/Ubuntu, starting at pre-school level and incorporating diverse cultures for national identity. *Unhu* should be the energising spirit in education, the family, in nation building

285

and in international relations. That the new philosophy should focus on a holistic education which:

- incorporates diverse cultures because we are a multi-cultural society.
- fosters a holistic education for survival; that is, head, heart, hand, and health to produce a balanced citizen.
- encourages the transmission of selected values with special consideration to what comes through information and communication technologies.
- inculcates values like, hard work, respect for others, honesty, good morals and patriotism.
- prepares learners to be adaptable, self-reliant, creative, and self – directed.
- affirms that education is a right for all in accordance with the 1990 Jomtien commitment.
- is an empowering tool for competitiveness in a global environment in the information and globalisation age?
- is people-centred, promoting the family and is based on a cultural foundation and with a community-based approach?
- gives serious consideration to the mother tongue for use as medium of instruction in our schools, on the grounds that it is the vehicle for culture and transmits people's experiences gathered over many centuries.

The Commission recommended that the following be the characteristics of the product of an education system:

- a person who is honest and accountable to society.
- a person who has morality and ability to learn from the philosophy of *unhu*/Ubuntu.
- a person imbued with ideals of freedom, equality, and tolerance and social responsibility.
- a person who has skills of communication, negotiation, and ability to resolve conflicts peacefully.
- a person who is creative, innovative, self-motivated, and personally accountable.
- a person who cherishes and upholds a team spirit.
- a person who respects other people.

286

- a person who has self-respect and respects property.
- a person with respect for knowledge and appreciation of all cultures of Zimbabwe.
- a person with a good work ethic and who strives to work hard for his own good and for the good of the family and the country.
- in this information age the products of our schools should have skills to gather, sift, analyse and make critical judgement (p. 33).

Nziramasanga went further to recommend professional, practical, technical, and environmental education and adequate support for marginalised groups – particularly those with disabilities and girls.

Paulo Freire's theory of education and decolonisation (Freire, 2000)

Paulo Freire was a Brazilian educator and philosopher. His ideas contribute significantly to social work education, teaching, training, learning and practice and more generally to decolonisation.

- Emancipatory learning – learning should empower students, people or communities to challenge, overturn and liberate them from oppression and colonialism.
- Learning should be transformative.
- Education should conscientise people and make them aware of their oppression, leading to acting against oppression.
- Critical pedagogy, learning, reflection, understanding, and awareness are all important, they lead to emancipation which leads to liberation.
- Teaching and learning should involve respectful dialogue and acknowledge the humanity of each other.
- Educators should not treat students as empty vessels (it is dehumanising) that they fill with the knowledge but rather learn together at the same pace (the banking concept of teaching, where students are fed with knowledge to digest later, is wrong).
- Unjust systems dehumanise people, and those dehumanised should pursue a process of humanise themselves (to become truly humans).
- For liberation to occur, those facing injustice must use their own language to define their world and the injustice they face.

287

- Liberation needs revolutionary leaders, who use dialogue with people to develop a common understanding of their injustice, and then plan actions together.

Different levels of training

Training permanently and holistically happens in families and communities. It also happens in primary, secondary and tertiary educational instructions, temporarily and fragmentedly.

Family and community training and socialisation

Each family and community has mechanisms to train its members to provide each other with support, welfare and care when needed. There are specialised roles for parents, siblings, aunts, uncles, grandparents, and friends. Training usually happens through socialisation in everyday life but also through ceremonies, rituals, rites of passage, camps and internships. This training includes work, trades, life, spiritual, religious, environmental and cultural training.

Primary and secondary education

Training for social services happens at primary and secondary schools, starting with building the capacity to prevent social problems. This work is done by teachers as part of extra-curricular and curricula activities. Curricula activities are embedded in the educational syllabus, usually provided by the government but can also be private. Subjects that contribute to social services and form a basis for tertiary qualifications include:

- Social studies
- History
- Geography
- Religious education (focusing on Africa religion)
- Moral education (focusing on Africa culture)
- Sociology
- Psychology
- Languages

288

- Society and culture
- Art
- Humanities
- Family studies
- Community studies
- Agriculture
- Environmental studies
- Health studies
- Business and entrepreneurship

Tertiary training

Tertiary qualifications come from undergraduate or post-graduate training. The programs that contribute to social or human services are:

- Social Work
- Social Welfare
- Social Development
- Social Services
- Community Work
- Development Work
- Social Administration
- Disability Work
- Psychology
- Sociology
- Public Health
- Mental Health
- Human Services
- Geriatrics/Older People Studies
- Gender Studies
- Community Police Studies
- Child Protection Studies
- Family Studies
- Agriculture Development
- Environment Development
- Counselling
- Entrepreneurship
- Research, Monitoring and Evaluation

Undergraduate training

- Certificate
- Diploma
- Associate degree
- Bachelor's degree
- Bachelor Honours Degree

Postgraduate training

- Graduate Certificate
- Graduate Diploma
- Master's degree (Coursework)
- Masters Philosophy Degree (Research)
- Master's degree Integrated (Coursework and Research)
- Doctoral Degree (Coursework)
- Doctoral Philosophy Degree (Research)
- Doctoral Degree Integrated (Coursework and Research)
- Associate/Assistant Professor (not a degree but an award)
- Professor (Full) (not a degree but an award)
- Senior Professor (not a degree but an award)
- Emeritus Professor (not a degree but an award)
- Distinguished Professor (not a degree but an award)

Components of tertiary training

1. Government
2. Library
3. Teachers
4. Administrators and recruiters etc.
5. Community
6. Peers
7. Regulators
8. Accreditors
9. 'Support' staff
10. Employers
11. 'Indigenous' 'indigenous' authority

290

12. Buildings – classrooms
13. Plan
14. Artwork
15. Identity – names, colours, graduation wear
16. Committee of advisors
17. Policies
18. Alumni
19. Students

Key aspects when developing a syllabus

Each program must have goals from where subject learning outcomes are derived. It is important to ensure that the goals of decolonising and indigenising training are prominent. This is achieved by using local philosophy, values, ethics, knowledge, methods, practices, and literature. The library plays an important role in training because it contains the literature that supports the syllabus. An important aspect is language because it affects how people philosophise, value, theorise and act. Because of the high levels of poverty in Africa, syllabus must develop the productive capacity of individuals, families, community, and society. This is called a developmental approach.

An academic program can adopt different training directions or philosophy as follows:

1. Practice-based
2. Field-based
3. Theory-based
4. Development-based
5. Needs-based
6. Experience-based/Practice-based
7. Best practice-based
8. Evidence-based
9. Ubuntu-based
10. Indigenous/local-based (opposed to western or colonial based)
11. Strengths-based vs deficit-based

Continuous professional development (CPD)

CPD is self-led knowledge enrichment by people who are already qualified. Its goal is to keep up to date with knowledge and to develop new skills for practice. The activities that qualify as CPD are many, and they include:

1. Writing, reading, or reviewing a journal article, book chapter, book, report or policy.
2. Attending, participating or organizing an indaba, seminar, tour, webinar, conference, community development event, volunteer activities, advocacy or social action activity.
3. Creating a website, database, blog, newspaper and newsletter
4. Starting or participating in a family project, village project, trust, CBO, NGO or PVO.
5. Reflecting on your work as a social worker.
6. Planning and reviewing your CPD for each year.
7. Designing, running, reviewing, or attending a course or program of training in-class or online.
8. Supervising, mentoring or coaching trainee or qualified social workers.
9. Researching including collecting, analysing and reporting primary or secondary data.

It helps to create a CPD plan at the beginning of each year and evaluate it at the end of the year. Below is an example of a CPD plan.

CPD planning template

Template 6: Continuous professional development (CPD) planning tool

	CPD Category	How you meet category 1 and name the evidence that you have
1	Writing, reading, or reviewing a journal article, book chapter, book, report or policy.	
2	Attending, participating, or organizing a seminar, tour, webinar, conference, community development event, volunteer activities, advocacy or social action activity.	
3	Creating a website, database, blog, newspaper and newsletter.	
4	Starting or participating in a family project, village project, trust, CBO, NGO or PVO.	
5	Reflecting on your work as a social worker	
6	Planning and reviewing your CPD for each year.	
7	Designing, running, reviewing or attending a course or program of training in-class or online.	
8	Supervising, mentoring or coaching trainee or qualified social workers.	
9	Researching including collecting, analysing and reporting primary or secondary data.	
10	Other activities as deemed fit for CPD.	

Domains of training in social and development services

The four domains and eight methods of training and fieldwork are (Mugumbate et al, 2023) as follows:

1. Understanding, Developing and Protecting Families
   a. Work with Individual Family Members.
   b. Family Work.
2. Understanding, Developing and Protecting Communities

293

      a.   Community Work.
3.   Understanding, Developing and Protecting Society and Nations (Socially, Economically, Politically and Spiritually)
      a.   Social Development.
      b.   Economic Development.
      c.   Political Development.
      d.   Spiritual Development.
4.   Understanding, Utilising and Protecting the Environment.

Assessing training

During training, students are assessed to demonstrate attainment of learning outcomes. Assessment also assesses if students can decolonise and apply knowledge in real life context. Other reasons for assessing are to assess ability to evaluate evidence, evaluate communication and reporting skills and assess student's ability to receive and use feedback. Assessing students should not cause anxiety on them and their families. Lecturers should do all it came to make assessments an ordinary aspect of learning. Below are some basic rules.

- Assessments must reflect the social and developmental challenges, issues or problems of the communities or country.
- Assessments must align with what students will do when they qualify.
- Assessments offer an opportunity to solve social and developmental challenges, issues, and problems They are not done for passing to get a certificate, diploma, or degree.
- There must be an opportunity for feedback.
- Feedback must be timely.
- There must be an opportunity to discuss feedback.
- Must be suitable for the level and time.
- Expectations must be made clear e.g. through a written assessment rubric or discussion before assessment is done.
- Assessments should have due dates for submission and return of feedback.
- Assessment can be under exam and non-exam conditions.
- The work must be done by the student.

There are many types of assessments. These include classroom-based assessments which happen in the classroom or exam room; community-based assessments which happen in the community including at home or school, agency-based assessments which happen at an organisation providing social work and development services; field-based assessments – happen in the field, outside homes and offices (for example, at an irrigation site, dam construction site, cultural event or cultural site); laboratory-based assessments which can happen in a laboratory (simulation laboratory or a simulation work room); and placement-based assessments which happen during student placement under the supervision of a qualified social worker or development practitioner.

Written or text-based assessments

- Creating a bibliography.
- Creating a case study.
- Writing an essay – the most popular assessment but it doesn't offer students many skills.
- Filling a workbook.
- Creating a portfolio.
- Creating a plan of action.
- Completing a multiple-choice quiz (a few questions or many questions) – another popular assessment but it doesn't offer students many skills.
- Completing a test with short answers (sentences or paragraphs) – doesn't offer much.
- Watch a video then write deep thoughts or reflections about lessons learnt.
- Create a poster, brochure, flier, travel guide and cultural guide
- Write a policy, policy paper or brief.
- Write or review a decolonisation document.
- Create a timeline.
- Create a budget.
- Write a letter, briefing note, notice or memoranda.
- Write a social assessment report or any other report.
- Translate content to local language.
- Creating a diary of events, views, observations, or reflections
- Note-taking.
- Write a biography.
- Write a poem or song.

295

Research-based assessments

- Writing a proposal or protocol for research or project.
- Doing research project and writing a short report.
- Writing an ethics application.
- Research and write a thesis or dissertation (long report).
- Publish a journal article.
- Reviewing orature and literature and writing a report.
- Filling a workbook.
- Evaluating orature or literature.
- Analyse a policy gap.
- Do an experiment and report or show results.
- Research orature (proverbs, maxims, idioms etc) and applicable to social work and development.

Oral assessments

- Debate with one or more people.
- Interview a community member or a teacher or another student in-class.
- Individual presentation of a topic or poster.
- Group presentation.
- Oral examination – ask questions orally for oral responses.
- Telling a story or sharing an experience.
- Singing a song.
- Reciting a poem.

Simulation-based assessments

- Dramatise childcare practices in Africa with your classmates as community members.
- Address a community meeting with your classmates.
- Dramatise a family meeting with classmates as family members.
- Dramatise a court session.
- Poster presentation.
- Simulation of a case conference in a hospital.
- Teamwork (process).
- Demonstrate how to enter the Chief or King's compound.
- Simulate a home with dolls and utensils.

Creative assessments

- Design a community centre.
- Create a visual artefact.
- Curate an exhibition.
- Create a group project or program.
- Write a book chapter or book.
- Creating a training program.
- Conceptualising, planning or facilitating a conference.
- Create and execute a social action project or program.

Community-based assessments

- Visit a community and assess their needs.
- Attend a community meeting and address or participate.
- Fieldtrip and writing a report afterwards.
- Attend a village development meeting or court.
- Observe the environment.
- Attend a spiritual event or activity.
- Door to door awareness, consultation, or education.
- Doing a needs assessment for a group project.
- Plan or organise a seminar, *indaba, dare* or webinar.

Digital assessments

- Create a website.
- Create a blogpost.
- Create a digital portfolio.
- Record a podcast.
- Make a social media post (text, video or audio).
- Computer based presentation e.g. PowerPoint presentation.
- Create a film.

Placement-based assessments

- Visiting an agency for observation and guidance.
- Short-time shadowing of a social or development worker (one hour to one week). This involves observing and learning from an experienced social worker.

- Volunteering at an agency for short (one hour to one month), medium (two months to five months) or long term (six months to one year). Usually there is less or no supervision.
- Supervised placement (attachment) for short, medium, or long term.

More development-focused assessments

- Create a community development plan.
- Create a decolonisation plan.
- Create an indigenisation plan.
- Evaluate a community intervention.
- Create a development committee or taskforce.
- Review a policy, strategy or law.
- Design a project to generate income or food.
- Create a resource mobilisation campaign.
- Create a prevention strategy.
- Doing comprehensive needs analysis or assessment for a family or community.
- Creating a social work group or club.

Becoming a published author

The literature that is used is training shapes the outcomes of the training, therefore, the literature must be the most appropriate. Literature comes from a process called publishing, which involves identifying a gap in literature, writing to fill the gap, choosing a medium to publish (journal article, book chapter, book, internet page, audio file, presentation or other), publishing and dissemination. Below is a list of journals related to social services in Africa.

Table 10: Social services journals and other publications in Africa

	Publication	Details	Comments
1	African Journal of Social Work	Published by the National Association of Social Workers – Zimbabwe.	Publishes six times a year.
2	Social Work/Maatskaplike Werk	Published by Dept. of Social Work, Faculty of Arts and Social Sciences, Stellenbosch University.	Publishes four times a year in March, June, August and October.
3	Journal of Social Development in Africa	Published by the Midlands State University, School of Social Work, Zimbabwe.	Publishes two times a year.
4	The Egyptian Journal of Social Work (EJSW)	Published by the Faculty of social work, Helwan University, Egypt.	Publishes two times a year.
5	African Journal of Disability	Published by CRS, AfriNEAD and CEDRES.	Publishes one volume a year. Articles are published as soon as they are accepted.
6	People Centred – The Journal of Development Administration	Published by the of Institute of Development Administration, Zimbabwe.	Publishes four times a year.
7	Africa Development / *Afrique et Développement*	Published by the Council for the Development of Social Science Research in Africa (CODESRIA),	Published four times a year until 2018. Bilingual – English and French.

299

		Pan-African research organisation headquartered in Dakar, Senegal.	
8	Southern African Journal of Social Work and Social Development	University of South Africa Press, South Africa.	Published three times a year until 2016.
9	African Journal for the Psychological Study of Social Issues	Department of Psychology University of Ibadan Ibadan, Nigeria.	Published three times a year.
10	SAHARA: Journal of Social Aspects of HIV/AIDS	The Social Aspects of HIV/AIDS Research Alliance (SAHARA).	Publishes one issue per year through Taylor and Francis.
11	Nigeria Journal of Social Work Education	University of Ibadan, Nigeria.	Published once yearly in June.
12	Rwanda Journal of Social Sciences, Humanities and Business	University of Rwanda.	Publishes four issues, one volume per year (four times a year).
13	Gender and Behaviour	Department of Psychology Obafemi Awolowo University Ile-Ife Nigeria.	Publishes two times a year.
14	Journal of Sustainable Development in Africa	Clarion University of Pennsylvania, USA.	Published outside Africa. Published four times a year in Fall, Winter, Spring and Summer.
15	Benin Journal of Social Work and	Department of Social Work,	Published three times a year beginning 2020.

		Community Development	University of Benin, Nigeria.	
16	Journal of Social Work in Developing Societies	Published by Department of Social Work, University of Nigeria, Nsukka, Nigeria.	Published once a year.
17	Journal of Sociology and Development	St. Augustine University of Tanzania, Department of Sociology.	Once a year.
18	The Zambia Social Science Journal	Southern African Institute for Policy and Research, Zambia.	Published two times a year. last published in 2018.
19	Institute of Social Work Journal	Institute of Social Work, Tanzania.	Publishes two times a year. No single article verified. Publishes several fields in one journal – Social Work, Human Resource Management, Business Administration, Labour Relations and Public Management and other business-related fields.
20	Journal of Ubuntu	Published by the of Institute of Development Administration, Zimbabwe.	Publishes continuously, beginning August 2024.

The process of publishing in a journal is not hard. It starts with reading the journal policy to enable selection of the best journal, formatting your article to meet the journal guidelines, and submitting to the journal. The journal editor will screen your manuscript for suitability. If suitable, it is peer reviewed by about two other people knowledgeable about the topic. You are not told who these people are, and they will not be told who the writer is. The two will not know each other. When you get the feedback from peers, the editor will tell you if they are accepting your manuscript or not, and any revisions needed. After revising (in other cases several times), it is accepted for publication. After it is published, it changes from a manuscript to an article or literature, and you change from a writer to an author whose published literature can be cited. The most appropriate publications value and use local knowledge: philosophy, values, theories and ethics, written or oral.

Publishing books follows the same process as a journal, only that you can be published as a chapter writer in an edited book, or you publish your own book. There may be a cost involved in publishing a book but in some cases, publishers recover the cost from sales. Self-publishing has become an important part of literature development, that is, the role of the publisher is skipped. Technology to write, review, publish, disseminate and market has become readily available, making it possible for people to publish books and internet material on their own. Internet publishing includes books, web pages or blog posts.

Fieldwork

Learning in Africa, as is in many if not all parts of the world, involves observation and doing. For example, aunts or uncles pass on knowledge about mentoring by allowing young people to observe them, and to practice while they watch. The 'interns' learn to think and act like their aunts or uncles. Theory and practice are integrated. The African theory of education (ATE) and African philosophy of education (APE) came from the philosophy described above. There are several other African theories that support fieldwork or experiential learning.: Pan-Africanism, Afrocentrism, developmental social work, Ubuntu and Indigenization, Decolonisation. African orature (oral literature) contributes significantly to the need for learning by doing e.g. proverbs.

ATE teaches us that education should not only be academic, but it must also serve a relevant purpose and must be relevant and useful to our communities. APE teaches us that our communities have a role to play in education, in fact, before modern day education, learning was happening

302

in our communities, especially experiential learning. Both ATE and APE emphasize Ubuntu, that is, education is not only about the learner, but their interaction and interdependence with their family, community and society at large. Fieldwork provides an opportunity for learners to use knowledge gained in the classroom to test and improve their skills through experience. In the process, they gain more knowledge, gain confidence by working with clients and confirm their skills. In professional social work, every trainee social worker needs to undergo this ritual of field placement.

Fieldwork is also known as practicum, internship, field placement, field practice, industrial attachment, field learning or experiential learning. Usually done face to face, but remote or online placements are possible and increasing. Fieldwork is when a student uses knowledge gained in their education or coursework for practice training. Learning happens through (1) observing and doing work with qualified social workers, usually in an agency (2) observing and doing work with another professional (3) observing and doing work with the community (4) observing simulated activities (5) independently working on a creative social work project. Placements can be combined with other subjects in one semester (concurrent) or they can happen in a semester without other subjects (block). From the definition, it is clear fieldwork has five basic components, there are **SISSCR**:

- **S**tudent.
- **I**nstitution of training.
- **S**upervisors.
- **S**ervice provider - agency providing social services.
- **C**ommunity – the community where field education, innovation or activism takes place.
- **R**egulator – this is the institution, body, committee responsible for setting guidelines, regulations and standards.

The three forms of fieldwork placements suitable for Africa are:

1. **C**onventional social work placements
   - Include placements in clinical social work, welfare and charity settings, usually urban focused, non-preventive and individually focused.
   - Can include classroom or laboratory-based simulations.

- Work well where there are enough experienced social workers and adequate resources to support students on placement, not usually the case in Africa.

2. **C**ommunity and **d**evelopmental social work placements
   - Involve communities, villages, remote and rural areas – these are community focused or bottom-up placements.
   - Student can be placed in an agency that has no social workers or placed within a community instead of an agency.
   - Work in communities that have no access to agencies, social workers or are remote.
   - Promotes equitable development because without their involvement, the communities will never benefit from social work.
   - The focus is to reduce poverty, empowerment and prevention of social challenges.
   - More than 75% of people in Africa are poor, with no access to social workers, social work agencies or training institutions making these placements relevant.
   - Student can create or contribute to a social laboratory, which is an initiative to research social issues with the community and experiment solutions.

3. **C**reative social work placements
   - This model views social work students as innovators, contributors, creators, curators, activists, advocates or researchers.
   - Social work as an art, using individual talents and strengths to solve social challenges.
   - Working with other disciplines or communities where there is no social work supervisors or where social work is not usually there.

Together, 1-3 are referred to as the CCdC model. It is important for students to have experience from at least 2 types of placements. 2 and 3 work very well in Africa where there is a shortage of supervisors, by involving communities and other professionals there will be checks and balances. After the placement, the student writes a comprehensive report that includes potential roles of social work in the community of placements. 2 and 3 allow us to learn from our communities and contribute new

304

knowledge to social work. 1 has numerous limitations in Africa that can be solved by using 2 and 3.

Process of fieldwork

1. Student is enrolled in subjects that allow them to gain knowledge of the social work in general and skills relevant to their preferred fieldwork objectives.
2. Student does fieldwork subjects or seminars to prepare them for fieldwork, this helps them acquire necessary skills and knowledge and to link their skills and interests to the agencies or communities for fieldwork.
3. Institution gives students fieldwork guidelines, regulations, standards, community engagement protocols and forms.
4. Students submit fieldwork form specifying their preferred options for fieldwork.
5. Fieldwork coordinators contact agencies to find available places for students and inform students of dates, supervisors etc.
6. Student draws a draft fieldwork plan for the fieldwork that fieldwork lecturer will review or mark.
7. Student is interviewed by agency or community and if accepted they discuss fieldwork plan and improve it. A fieldwork contract is signed by the student, agency, agency supervisor and the school.
8. Student starts fieldwork with regular supervision from agency or community and supervisors Supervisor can be individual observation and meetings, small group meetings or whole class workshops or seminars. Initial report is submitted.
9. Meetings of supervisors and agency to discuss progress. Mid-term report is submitted.
10. Student submits end of fieldwork report, all outcomes must be listed and discussed.

Length of fieldwork

After studying three social work institutions in Tanzania, Zimbabwe and Lesotho, Dhemba (2012) recommended 960 hours of placement time. In Zimbabwe, most institutions offer field placement in 3rd year for 8 months, 20 workdays a month, 160 workdays. Each working day has 8 hours, so this translates to 1280 hours placement time for a 4-year bachelor's degree. Some South African institutions have first year placements of 40 – 320 hours plus 4th year placements of 480 – 800 hours, giving a potential maximum of 1120 hours.

Supervision

Supervision can be done face to face, by phone or online, one to one, or in groups. The academic supervisor can have weekly contacts of about 30 minutes via phone, online, individual or group meeting. A physical visit to student on site in the middle or end of placement or both is important. This visit involves speaking with a student and the agency representative or supervisor, together, separately, or both. The academic supervisor or field educator can organise regular supervisor seminars for students. The agency supervisor needs constant contact with the student including (1) daily check-ins or observations (2) weekly briefings (3) monthly meetings. Types of supervisions include:

- Observation.
- Discussion with student or agency supervisor or both.
- Discussion with service users or community or both.
- Report assessment.
- Daily or weekly journal checking.
- Peer feedback.
- Creative work e.g. exhibition or content assessment.
- Community work e.g. community mobilisation event or content assessment.
- Oral presentation to an audience with questions and comments.

Placement objectives and activities may include:

- Development work tasks.
- Community work tasks.
- Group work tasks.
- Casework or individual work tasks.
- Family work tasks.
- Administrative tasks or leadership objectives.
- Research tasks.
- Professional development tasks.
- Communication skills tasks.

306

- Collaboration tasks.
- Theory or ethics tasks.
- Creative task.
- Indigenising or decolonial objectives.
- Advocacy or activism objectives.

Assessing field learning

There are several ways to assess or mark fieldwork. Some types of assessments are given below, with examples of grading or marks. Not all assessment types provided below are used, and whatever combination is used, the grading should add up to the total required, for example 100%, by direct addition or by weighting.

- Pre-fieldwork seminars attendance (5%, that is, weighing 5% of total fieldwork marks).
- Fieldwork plan (10%).
- Fieldwork agency or community mark (50%).
- Observation of student working (25%).
- Assessment of creative outcomes (50%).
- Oral report back at school (30%).
- Initial report (10%).
- Mid-term report (20%).
- Final report (50%).
- Adverse circumstances can result in a student getting an instant failure e.g. breaking ethics, laws or gross lack of professional judgement or practice (-100% or minus 100%).

The student will create, collect, and keep records such as journal notes, meeting minutes, copies of communications, reflection notes and activity notes. Student could be asked to provide these reports to both supervisors, which can be narrative, creative or community-focused with more visuals than text:

- Placement initial report.
- Mid-term report.
- Fieldwork plan evaluation report.
- Final report or creative works.
- Oral report, presentation, or exhibition.

Placement settings

- Communities for creative, developmental placements or political/radical social work.
- Government departments providing social work e.g. Department of Social Development.
- Non-government agencies providing social work services.
- Community based organisations.
- Health centres.
- Charity or religious centres.
- Development agencies.
- Research centres and institutes.
- Corporate companies.
- Consultancies.
- Local government and municipalities.
- Community centres.
- International settings.
- Classroom, laboratories, or simulation rooms.

Fieldwork outcomes

Each field placement must have placement outcomes. Outcomes are end results, including benefits to the student, school and community but can also be negative. Examples of positive outcomes include: fieldwork report for community or library, creativity work e.g. exhibitions, policy change from advocacy, community organisation or group started or strengthened, income, production capacity enhanced, infrastructure improved, community development plan adopted, research report or publication, student passing their fieldwork subject, practice skills and knowledge gained and families strengthened. Examples of negative outcomes include raising community expectations, ending projects prematurely, cultural humiliation, conflict in families or community, exposure to political persecution, planting colonial ideas, trauma or student failing fieldwork subject.

Common mistakes in training and fieldwork

- Copying philosophies, outcomes online.
- Asking outside consultants to design the courses for you.
- Huge numbers.
- Not aligning numbers with local needs.
- Staffing.
- Training for brain-drain.

Guidance: Using Ubuntu in training and academic fieldwork

Education and training must be relevant to the prevailing social issues and aspirations. If you teach cattle how to survive in water, when most of the time they spend their time on land, you are training them to die. Cattle need grazing not swimming lessons.

- When starting a training or education institution, find it on Ubuntu.
- When designing an educational and training program, base it on Ubuntu.
- When recruiting, seek students who are able to address most if not all levels of Ubuntu – family, community, society, environmental and spiritual, do not focus on academic merit when recruiting but focus on potential to address all levels.
- When designing courses and subjects, have learning outcomes centred on Ubuntu.
- Use Ubuntu to decolonise history that you teach to students.
- Emphasise what Ubuntu offers the world, instead of its shortcomings.
- Use Ubuntu to make training objectives relevant to addressing local social needs.
- Use alternative assessments and moderation methods that value Ubuntu.

Summary

- Training can happen at the family and community level, and in society. This training is usually continuous and lifelong and not paid for.
- Training continues in primary, secondary and tertiary institutions.
- Social services training should be seen as continuous, begging in the family and community, and then made more specialised in schools and colleges but all intended to provide skills to solve social challenges.
- An important part of training is observation and mentoring, and this happens at all levels.
- More structured observation and mentoring is called fieldwork or placement, and this involves a student working in an agency to practice skills under supervision.
- Assessment for all training must be relevant, and appropriate to local social challenges.
- Publishing literature improves access to local knowledge, and this happens when written work is published in books and journals but also on websites.
- A common mistake made in training and fieldwork design include copying training guidelines and materials from context that are different from your own. Other mistakes are failure to resource and evaluate training adequately.

Further and advanced knowledge

- What are the shortcomings of social service education in Africa? How can this be addressed? What role can you play?
- What are the main goals of training at family and community level?
- What challenges usually result from inappropriate methods and content of training? How can this be addressed?
- Research planning and evaluation for social and development programs.
- Fieldwork planning and evaluation for social and development programs.
- Planning and delivering higher degree research programs.

Questions for in-class assessments and examinations

- Draw a poster showing the four domains and 8 methods of social services training?
- Create a CPD plan for a social worker who left college 10 years ago.
- Create a fieldwork plan with potential agency, domain of practice, objectives, activities and timeline.
- Create a blog post about tips for fieldwork.
- Identify guidelines of two journals of your choice and compare them.
- Attend a village community meeting when you come back make a presentation about 'Involving the community in university education.'
- Debate on what is more relevant: CPD or postgraduate training?
- Debate on what is more relevant: fieldwork or bringing the community as guest lecturers?

Potential questions for research

The four domains of social services training (Mugumbate et al, 2023) are:

1. Understanding, Developing and Protecting Families.
2. Understanding, Developing and Protecting Communities.
3. Understanding, Developing and Protecting Society and Nations (Socially, Economically, Politically and Spiritually).
4. Understanding, Utilising and Protecting the Environment.

- Using a literature review or group discussion, identify current training needs of students and practitioners for each domain.
- Pick a domain of your choice and develop five outcomes and methods of training. Use a document analysis for this task. The documents you can analyse are university handbooks and course outlines.
- Select five research methods from the list below and explain how they can be used to research the environmental domain or economic sub-domain.

- o Stories approach
- o Orature review
- o Experiential method
- o Auto-ethnographic method
- o Diaries
- o Notes
- o Art
- o Dare or indaba method.
- o *Baliano* (plural is *mabaliano*) method.
- o Decolonised interviewing
- o Insider research method
- o Side-by-side approach or collaborative research
- o Narrative approach
- o Self-praise or self-poetry or praise poetry
- o Griot approach
- o Community projects
- o Stories research approach (SRA)
- o Tree of life approach
- o Dialogue approach.
- o Action research
- o Visual methods
- o Social media reactions (sentiments) approach
- o Work party research
- o Task method
- o Walks method
- o Prayer method
- o Experimental approaches
- o *Kuumba* (creativity) method
- o Social laboratories (social labs)
- o Mixed methods

Fieldwork ideas

Fieldwork is an important component of social work training. It involves a student practicing to do social work under the guidance of supervisors, who are usually social workers. Usually, one supervisor is academic, and the other is a practitioner. Fieldwork also involves families or communities where social work happens. We will collectively call these participants (not clients or service users). So, basically, fieldwork involves the student, two

312

supervisors and the community although other people are involved as you will learn later. What do you think will happen if each of those people involved have a different philosophy of life? Can you truly practice social work when you share a different philosophy with the participants? Can you truly train a student social worker when your philosophies are different? On the side, how effective can social work be when those involved have a common philosophy?

Key terms and their meanings

Assessment – a measure of learning.

Assessment – the process of checking if learning outcomes are being or have been achieved.

Bachelor's degree – a qualification that has at least 24 courses and is the first degree before one acquires other degrees.

Certificate – a training program that has four or more courses or equivalent to six months of study.

Colonial – based on the philosophy of foreigners and forced, directly or indirectly.

Community education – learning provided by members of the community, including relations.

Community-focused learning – learning more from communities.

Counsellor – a person who is trained or experienced to work with individuals and families to address their psychological, spiritual, therapeutic and social challenges.

Course – a collection of topics and activities for a single study area contributing to a qualification.

Cultural education – learning provided by figures and institutions of culture, including the family.

Cultural services worker – a person who is trained or experienced to work with individuals, families, community and society to address cultural issues.

Cummunityness – the level of community focus, involvement or presence.

Decolonising – rebasing on your philosophy.

Decolonising worker – a person who is trained or experienced to work with individuals, families, community and society to address political, cultural, indigenous and decolonising issues.

Degree – a training program that has 24 or more courses or equivalent to three years of study.

Design – creating a subject, course or program.

Development worker – a person who is trained or experienced to work with families, community and society to address development challenges.

Diploma – a training program that has 12 or more course or equivalent to two years of study.

Dissertation – a report of an academic research course, usually at undergraduate level.

Doctor of philosophy degree – a higher or postgraduate degree made up of a block of research study equivalent to at least three years.

Doctoral degree – a higher or postgraduate degree equivalent to 30 courses studied over at least three years.

Education – form of training which involves developing an educational philosophy, developing a training program, developing training methods, gathering training resources, selecting of trainees, delivering the training, assessing skills and knowledge gained and graduating.

Education philosophy – the main values, theories and ethics of an educational program.

314

Environmental education – learning that happens when people interact with the environment which benefits yourself or is shared with others, contemporarily or inter-generationally.

Family education – learning provided by relatives, including family, extended family and tribal members.

Family worker – a person who is trained or experienced to work with families to address family issues.

Fieldwork – learning from families, community, society or environment, away from the classroom.

Fieldwork, placement or attachment – a skills building method where trainees go to the field to observe, learn and perfect skills. A student uses knowledge gained in their education or coursework for practice.

Higher degree – a degree above bachelors, including postgraduate certificate, postgraduate diploma, masters and doctoral.

Indigenous – based on your philosophy.

Indigenous worker – a person who is trained or experienced to work with individuals, families, community and society to address cultural, indigenous and decolonising issues.

Institution of training – a school, college or university that provides a certificate, diploma or degree.

Knowledge – oral or written philosophy, values, theories, ethics or research.

Learning philosophy – the main values, theories and ethics of a learner.

Lecture – a teaching and learning format where a person with the required knowledge shares with a large group of learners.

Librarian – a person trained to research appropriate literature, order it and curate a space to store, display, borrow and read.

Literature – oral or written mediums of knowledge. Literature is used in training and research. It shapes the outcomes of the training, therefore, it must be the most appropriate.

Master of philosophy degree – a higher or postgraduate degree made up of a block of research study equivalent to at least two years.

Master's degree – a qualification that has at least 6 courses or equivalent to one and half year of study.

Moderation – a process of reviewing and assessing marking and grading.

Practice-centred – based on roles.

Program – a collection of courses that make up a qualification.

Psychologist – a person who is trained to work with individuals, families and groups to address their psychological, spiritual, therapeutic and social challenges.

Publishing – a process that involves identifying a gap in literature, writing to fill the gap, choosing a medium to publish (journal article, book chapter, book, internet page, audio file, presentation or other), publishing and dissemination.

Reciprocity – giving as much as you give as an individual, family, community or society.

Redesign – improving or creating a subject, course or program.

Regulator – an entity that oversees a professional training, practice or both.

Religious education – learning provided by figures and institutions of religion, including Africa religion.

Research – a process of identifying a knowledge gap, creating or collecting information to fill the gap and reporting the process and findings.

Research – a process of setting a knowledge generation philosophy, identifying knowledge gaps, creating research methods, implementing the methods, collecting data, analysing, reporting, using the findings and reviewing it.

Research project – a program of identifying a knowledge gap, creating or collecting information to fill the gap and reporting the process and findings.

Service provider – agency or community providing social services.

Social administrator – a person who is trained or experienced to manage social development programs.

Social development worker – a person who is trained to work with individuals, families, community and society to address social and development challenges.

Social scientist – a person who has a bachelor's degree after studying society in detail.

Social welfare worker – a person who is trained or experienced to work with individuals and families to provide or direct them to resources.

Social worker – a person who is trained to work with families, communities and society to address social and development challenges in empowering ways.

Sociologist – a social scientist with a bachelor's degree who studies and interprets society.

Spiritual education – learning provided by figures and institutions of culture and religion and the environment.

Student – a person who is learning.

Student-centred program – focused more on the student or learner.

Subject – a collection of topics and activities for a single study area contributing to a qualification.

Supervisor – a person who oversees and mentors' fieldwork learning of a student.

Teaching philosophy – the main values, theories and ethics of a teacher or group of teachers.

Thesis – a report of an academic research course, usually at post graduate level.

Training – imparting knowledge and skills.

Training philosophy – the main values, theories and ethics of a training program.

Tutor – a teacher whose role is to support learning of specific aspects of the topic.

Ubuntu-led training program – training inspired by Ubuntu philosophy.

Work-focused learning – learning more form workplaces.

References and recommended readings

Amadasun, S (2020). Is signature pedagogy still worthwhile? An empirical study of field practice experience among social work students in Nigeria, *Social Work Education*, DOI: 10.1080/02615479.2020.1771300

Mugumbate, J. R. (2020). Fieldwork in Social Work. African Social Work Network (ASWN), Available at www.africasocialwork.net/academics

Dhemba, J. (2012). Fieldwork in Social Work Education and Training: Issues and Challenges in the Case of Eastern and Southern Africa. *Social Work and Society, (10) 1*, online.

Freire, P. (2000). *Pedagogy of the oppressed* (30th anniversary ed.). Continuum.

Okala, U., Ijeoma U., Okechukwu E. and Ebue, M. (2014). A Critical Appraisal of the Relevance of Field Work Practice in Social Work Education in Nigeria. *Mediterranean Journal of Social Sciences. 5. 10.5901/mjss. 2014.v5n27p1328.*

Jönsson J. H and Flem A L (2018). International field training in social work education: beyond colonial divides, *Social Work Education*, *37:7*, 895-908, DOI: 10.1080/02615479.2018.1461823

Lombard A. (2015). Internationalising Social Work Education. The South African Experience. *Indian Journal of Social Work, 76(1)*, 1-16

Mugumbate R., Mupedziswa R., Twikirize J. M., Mthethwa E., Desta A. A. and Oyinlola O. (2023). Understanding Ubuntu and its contribution to social work education in Africa and other regions of the world, *Social Work Education*, https://doi.org/10.1080/02615479.2023.2168638

Nziramasanga C. T. (1999). The Presidential Commission of Inquiry into Education and Training. Nziramasanga Commission, Zimbabwe.

Omona, A. M. (1998). *Sociology of Education*. Kampala: Department of Distance Education, Makerere University.

Schmidt, K. (2014). A Qualitative Evaluation of Social Work Field Instruction offered by Universities in The Eastern Cape, South Africa. Master of Social Science Social Work Thesis, University of Fort Hare

Schmidt, K., and Rautenbach, J. V. (2016). Field instruction: is the heart of social work education still beating in the Eastern Cape? *Social Work, 52(4)*, 589-610. https://dx.doi.org/10.15270/52-2-532.

Appendices

Appendix 1: Ubuntu

Ubuntu is Africa's overarching philosophy. A philosophy contains a society's deep thoughts and ways of looking at life. It shapes how people think about the family, community, society, environment and spirituality. It shapes how people think about reality, existence, reason, knowledge, religion, truth, race, values, mind, behaviour, justice and language. In the chain of knowledge, a philosophy sits above theories. Theories are derived from philosophy. A society usually has one philosophy. Basically, each continent has its one overarching philosophy.

Ubuntu has strengths but also shortcomings. However, most of the 'shortcomings' are a result of misconceptions about Ubuntu. In the sections below, misconceptions will be clarifying first, followed by weaknesses then strengths.

Should you capitalise Ubuntu when writing? Should I write it in italics? When referring to the African philosophy, capitalise Ubuntu. Do not put it in italics. When referring to *Ubuntu* in specific countries use a small letter u. This distinguishes it at the two levels - national e.g. South Africa and continental Africa.

Definitions of Ubuntu

Ubuntu is the worldview of Black people of Africa from where they derive relational, communal, societal, environmental and spiritual knowledges, values and practices *(Mugumbate, Mupedziswa, Twikirize, Mthethwa, and Oyinlola, 2023).*

What happens to the individual happens to the whole group, and whatever happens to the whole group, community or country happens to the individual. People, country, environment and spirituality are intricately related. The individual can only say: 'I am because we are and since we are, therefore, I am' *(Mbiti, 1969).*

Ubuntu synonyms

- Angola (*gimuntu*)
- Botswana (*muthu, batho*)

321

- Burkina Faso, Cote d'Ivoire, Equatorial Guinea, Guinea, Gambia Liberia, Sierra Leonne and Mali (*maaya*)
- Burundi (*Ubuntu*)
- Cameroon (*bato*)
- Congo (*bantu*)
- Democratic Republic of Congo (*bomoto, kimuntu* or *bantu*)
- Ethiopia (*medemer*)
- Ghana (*biako ye*)
- Kenya (*utu, munto, omundu* or *mondo*)
- Malawi (*umunthu*)
- Mozambique (*vumuntu*)
- Namibia (*omundu*)
- Nigeria (*mutunchi, iwa, agwa, omwayaonyamo*)
- Rwanda (*Ubuntu*)
- South Africa (*Ubuntu, ubundu* or *botho*)
- South Sudan (*nhiar-baai*)
- Tanzania (*utu, obuntu* or *bumuntu*)
- Uganda (*obuntu, obuntubulamu*)
- Zambia (*umunthu*)
- Zimbabwe (*unhu, hunhu, Ubuntu, ibuntu*)

Levels of Ubuntu

1. Individual
2. Families (*ukama*)
3. Village
4. Community (*ujamaa*)
5. Societal (Cultural, Economic, Political and Global) (*ujamii*)
6. Environmental (*imvelo*)
7. Spiritual (*uroho*)

Principles of Ubuntu

- Communality as the basis of society
- Environmentality as the basis of survival
- Dialogue and consensus building as building blocks for cooperation
- Respect as the basis of human interaction

- Spirituality or religiosity as the foundation of relationships between living and deceased members, the environment and God

Ubuntu maxims and proverbs

- *Umuntu ngumuntu ngabantu* (South Africa) – collectivity, communalism
- *Ndiri nekuti tiri* (Zimbabwe) – collectivity, communalism
- Onye aghana nwanne ya (Nigeria) – don't leave anyone behind
- *Mambo vanhu* (Zimbabwe; Samkange, 1980) – people-centred leadership
- *Chikuru upenyu* (Zimbabwe; Samkange, 1980) – valuing life
- *Motho ke motho ka batho* (Botswana) – collectivity
- *Mwana ndewemunhu wese* (Child belongs to the village) – collectivity
- *Umoja ni nguvu* (Swahili) – collectivity
- *Ndi nii tondu wanyu* (Kenya) – collectivity
- *An dhano nikeche wantie* (Kenya) – collectivity
- *Musha mukadzi* (Zimbabwe) – valuing women
- *Miti upenyu* (Zimbabwe) – valuing the environment
- *Mhosva hairovi* (Zimbabwe) – valuing justice
- *Munhu munhu nekuda kweVanhu* (Zimbabwe; Samkange, 1980) – we are human through others.
- *Ibu anyi danda* (Nigeria) – carrying a load together means no one is feeling the burden.
- *Munno mu kabi ye munno ddala* (Uganda) - a friend or partner in difficult times is your real/genuine friend/partner.
- *Agbajo owo la fin soya ajeji owo kan ko gbe eru de ori* (Yoruba, Nigeria) - solidarity
- *Nwa ora* (Igbo, Nigeria) - children belong to the whole community.
- *Ofu aka ruta mmanu, o zuo aka ni ile* (Igbo, Nigeria) - if one finger is stained with oil, the oil will spread to other fingers.
- *Ibu anyi danda* (Igbo, Nigeria) - no task or load is insurmountable for *danda* (type of an ant), meaning bigger things are achieved when you work together.
- *Onye aghana nwane ya* (Igbo, Nigeria) - no one should leave their neighbor behind
- *Isandla sihlamba esinye* (Xhosa, South Africa) - one hand washes the other.

323

- *Mmua lebe oa bo a bua la gagwe* (Tswana, Botswana)- everyone has a right to a say, for even what might appear like a bad suggestion helps people to think of better ideas.
- *Molemo wa kgang ke go buiwa* (Tswana, Botswana) - the good on the conflict is discussion.
- *Ntwa kgolo ke ya molomo* (Tswana, Botswana) - greatest fight is by mouth.
- *Se wo was fi na wosankofa a yenkyi* (Akan, Ghana) - not wrong to go back for that which you have forgotten; reflect.
- *Ubuntubulamu* - being humane.

Appendix 2: Umoja waAfrica (African Union)

Website: https://au.int

Agenda2063: https://au.int/en/agenda2063/overview

Background

"The African Union (AU) is a continental body consisting of the 55 member states that make up the countries of the African Continent. It was officially launched in 2002 as a successor to the Organisation of African Unity (OAU, 1963-1999). In May 1963, 32 Heads of independent African States met in Addis Ababa Ethiopia to sign the Charter creating Africa's first post-independence continental institution, The Organisation of African Unity (OAU). The OAU was the manifestation of the pan-African vision for an Africa that was united, free and in control of its own destiny and this was solemnised in the OAU Charter in which the founding fathers recognised that freedom, equality, justice and dignity were essential objectives for the achievement of the legitimate aspirations of the African peoples and that there was a need to promote understanding among Africa's peoples and foster cooperation among African states in response to the aspirations of Africans for brother-hood and solidarity, in a larger unity transcending ethnic and national Differences. The guiding philosophy was that of Pan-Africanism which centred on African socialism and promoted African unity, the communal characteristic and practices of African communities, and a drive to embrace Africa's culture and common heritage."

Purpose of the AU

- To promote the unity and solidarity of the African States
- To coordinate and intensify their cooperation and efforts to achieve a better life for the peoples of Africa
- To defend their sovereignty, their territorial integrity and independence
- To eradicate all forms of colonialism from Africa; and
- To promote international cooperation, having due regard to the Charter of the United Nations and the Universal Declaration of Human Rights

Departments

- Agriculture, Rural Development, Blue Economy and Sustainable Environment (ARBE)
- Economic Development, Tourism, Trade, Industry, Mining (ETTIM)
- Education, Science, Technology and Innovation (ESTI)
- Infrastructure and Energy
- Political Affairs, Peace, and Security (PAPS)
- Health, Humanitarian Affairs and Social Development (HHS)
- Women, Gender and Youth
- Civil Society and Diaspora
- Legal Affairs
- Agriculture, Rural Development, Blue Economy, and Sustainable Environment (ARBE)
- The Department of Agriculture and Food Security
- Rural Economy
- Rural Development
- Sustainable Environment and Blue Economy (SEBE) Directorate
- Structure of the Health, Humanitarian Affairs and Social Development (HHS) Division of AU
- The Department of Health, Humanitarian Affairs and Social Development (HHS) works to promote the
- Humanitarian Affairs Division
- The AIDS Watch Africa (AWA) Secretariat
- Directorate of Social Development, Culture and Sports
- Labour Employment and migration Division
- Social Welfare, Drug Control and Crime Prevention Division
- Culture and Sport Division

Regional agreements

- Agenda2063 implemented by the New Partnership for Africa's Development (NEPAD)
- Common Market for Eastern and Southern Africa,
- African Continental Free Trade Area (AfCFTA)

326

Principal decision-making organs

- The Assembly of Heads of State and Government
- The Executive Council
- The Permanent Representatives Committee (PRC)
- Specialised Technical Committees (STCs)
- the Peace and Security Council and
- The African Union Commission
- Pan-African Parliament
- Economic, Social and Cultural Council (ECOSOCC)

Organs on judicial, legal matters and human rights issues

- African Commission on Human and Peoples' Rights (ACHPR)
- African Court on Human and Peoples' Rights (AfCHPR)
- AU Commission on International Law (AUCIL)
- AU Advisory Board on Corruption (AUABC)
- African Committee of Experts on the Rights and Welfare of the Child.

The AU is also working towards the establishment of continental financial institutions.

- The African Central Bank
- The African Investment Bank
- African Monetary Fund

The Regional Economic Communities (RECs) and the African Peer Review Mechanism are also key bodies that that constitute the structure of the African Union.

Anthem

The African anthem was composed by Ethiopian poet Tsegaye Gabre-Medhin as a poem. In 1986, it was adopted as the African anthem by the Organisation of African Unity (OAU), the predecessor of the AU. In 2002, at the formation of the AU, the anthem was continued. The music was composed by Arthur Mudogo Kemoli, a Kenyan, in 1986. It tells the

African history of struggle, independence, liberation, labour, unity, justice, and hope.

How to cite it:

African Union (AU) (2002). Let us all unite and celebrate together. Anthem. Addis Ababa: AU.

Gabre-Medhin, T. (1966). Proud to be African. Poem. Addis Ababa: Tsegaye Gabre-Medhin

Anthem in Swahili (audiovisual with lyrics)

Agenda2063

"As an affirmation of their commitment to support Africa's new path for attaining inclusive and sustainable economic growth and development African heads of state and government signed the 50th Anniversary Solemn Declaration during the Golden Jubilee celebrations of the formation of the OAU /AU in May 2013. The declaration marked the re-dedication of Africa towards the attainment of the Pan African Vision of *an integrated, prosperous and peaceful Africa, driven by its own citizens, representing a dynamic force in the international arena* and Agenda 2063 is the concrete manifestation of how the continent intends to achieve this vision within a 50-year period from 2013 to 2063. The Africa of the future was captured in a letter presented by the former Chairperson of the African Union Commission, Dr. Nkosazana Dlamini Zuma."

Aspirations

The agenda is the plan of the AU for 50 years from 2013 to 2063. The agenda has seven (7) aspirations that respond to Africa's problems as follows:

1. A prosperous Africa based on inclusive growth and sustainable development
2. An integrated continent politically united and based on the ideals of Pan-Africanism and the vision of African Renaissance

328

3. An Africa of good governance, democracy, respect for human rights, justice, and the rule of law
4. A peaceful and secure Africa
5. Africa with a strong cultural identity common heritage, values, and ethics
6. An Africa whose development is people-driven, relying on the potential offered by the African people, especially its women and youth, and caring for children
7. An Africa as a strong, united, resilient, and influential global player and partner

Email from the future

Email from the future (English):
https://au.int/sites/default/files/documents/33126-doc-02_email_from_the_future.pdf

Email for the future (French):
https://au.int/sites/default/files/documents/33122-doc-02_email_from_the_future_french.pdf

Flagship projects

https://au.int/en/agenda2063/flagship-projects

The AU has social programs and therefore employs or uses the services of social workers. A social worker working with the AU is basically doing continental social work. The continent is divided into regions, with regional institutions where social workers are also employed. A region includes a collection of countries that are geographically connected.

Regions of Africa

Africa is divided into five regions: East, South, West, Central and North. The regional organisation for all these regions is the African Union (AU) with 55 countries.

East Africa: Tanzania, Kenya, Uganda, Rwanda, Burundi, South Sudan, Djibouti, Eritrea, Ethiopia, and Somalia

Southern Africa: Angola, Botswana, Lesotho, Mozambique, Namibia, South Africa, Eswatini (which decolonised it name from Swaziland in 2018), Zambia, Zimbabwe

West Africa: Benin, Burkina Faso, Cape Verde, Côte D'Ivoire, Gambia, Ghana, Guinea, Guinea-Bissau, Liberia, Mali, Mauritania, Niger, Nigeria, Senegal, Sierra Leone, and Togo.

Central Africa: Angola, Cameroon, Central African Republic, Chad, Congo Republic – Brazzaville, Democratic Republic of Congo, Equatorial Guinea, Gabon, and São Tomé and Principe.

North Africa: Algeria, Egypt, Libya, Morocco, Sudan and Tunisia

Regional economic communities (RECs)

There are regional economic communities (RECs) and regional mechanisms (RMs).

- Arab Maghreb Union (UMA)
- Common Market for Eastern and Southern Africa (COMESA)
- Community of Sahel–Saharan States (CEN–SAD)
- East African Community (EAC)
- Economic Community of Central African States (ECCAS)
- Economic Community of West African States (ECOWAS)
- Intergovernmental Authority on Development (IGAD)
- Southern African Development Community (SADC)

Appendix 3: Research approaches, designs, and methods for Africa

Research designs

- African research methodology (ARM) (e.g. Khupe and Keane, 2017)
- Afrikology (Nabudere, 2011)
- Indigenous research methodology (IRM) (Chilisa et al, 2017)

Research approaches

- Ubuntu research approach
- Community-centred approach
- Sankofa methodology
- Collective research approach
- Cultural safety approach (CSA)
- African-centred or Afrocentric research
- Empowerment or capability research approach
- Responsible research approach (RRA)
- Developmental research (DR)
- Household, family or community-oriented research (HOFACOR)
- Participatory Action research (PAR)
- Environmental approach:
- Relational research approach or paradigm
- Environmental approach
- Mixed approaches
- Creative approaches
- Collaborative approach

Research methods

- Stories Approach
- Orature review
- Experiential method
- Auto-ethnographic method
- Diaries

- Notes
- Art
- Dare or indaba method.
- *Baliano* (plural is *mabaliano*) method.
- Decolonised Interviewing
- Insider research method
- Side-by-side approach or collaborative research
- Narrative approach
- Self-praise or self-poetry or praise poetry
- Griot approach
- Community projects
- Stories research approach (SRA)
- Tree of life approach
- Dialogue approach
- Action research
- Visual methods
- Social media reactions (sentiments) approach
- Work party research
- Task method
- Walks method
- Prayer method
- Experimental approaches
- Social laboratories
- *Kuumba* (creativity) method
- Mixed methods

Abbreviations

ACARTSD	African Centre for Applied Research and Training in Social Development
AfCFTA	African Continental Free Trade Area
AfCHPR	African Court on Human and Peoples'
AEC	African Economic Community
AIDS	Acquired Immunodeficiency Syndrome
AJSW	African Journal of Social Work
AMU	Arab Maghreb Union
ANC	African National Congress
APE	African Philosophy of Education
ARBE	Agriculture, Rural Development, Blue Economy and Sustainable Environment
ARM	African research methodology.
ASASWEI	Association of South African Social Work Educational Institutions
ASD	African Social Development
ASF	Association Solidarité Féminine
ASSWA	Association of Schools of Social Work in Africa
ASWDNet	Africa Social Work and Development Network
ASWEA	Association of Social Work Education in Africa
ATE	African theory of education.
AU	African Union
AUABC	AU Advisory Board on Corruption
AUCILAU	Commission on International Law
AWA	The AIDS Watch Africa
BSA	British South Africa
BSW	Bachelor of Social Work
BUSE	Bindura University of Science Education
CA	Community Association
CAMFED	Campaign for Female Education
CBO	Community Based Organisation
CEN-SAD	Community of Sahel–Saharan States
CODESRIA	Council for the Development of Social Science Research in Africa
COMESA	Common Market for Eastern and Southern Africa (
COVID	Corona Virus Disease
CPD	Continuous Professional Development
CSA	Cultural safety approach
CSWSD	Consortium for Social work and social development

CSWZ	Council of Social Workers Zimbabwe
DCO	Development Coordination Office
DESA	Department of Economic and Social Affairs
DNA	Deoxyribonucleic Acid
DOI	Digital Object Identifier
DR	Developmental Research
DRC	Democratic Republic of Congo
DSD	Department of Social Development
DSW	Department of Social Welfare
EAC	East African Community
EASS	Egyptian Association for Social Studies
ECA	Economic Commission for Africa
ECCAS	Economic Community of Central African States
ECE	Economic Commission for Europe
ECLAC	Economic Commission for Latin America and the Caribbean
ECOSOCC	Economic, Social and Cultural Council
ECOWAS	Economic Community of West African States
EJSW	The Egyptian Journal of Social Work
ePUB	Electronic Publication
ESCAP	Economic and Social Commission for Asia and the Pacific
ESCWA	Economic and Social Commission for Western Asia
ESTI	Education, Science, Technology and Innovation
ETTIM	Economic Development, Tourism, Trade, Industry, Mining
FAO	Food and Agriculture Organisation
FDMP	Food Deficit Mitigation Programme
GASOW	The Ghana Association of Social Workers
GBM	Green Belt Movement
HABITAT	United Nations Human Settlements Programme
HF	Human Factor
HHS	Health, Humanitarian Affairs and Social Development
HIV	Human Immuno Deficiency Virus
HOFACOR	Household, Family or Community Oriented Research
HSCT	Harmonized Social Cash Transfers
HTML	Hypertext Markup Language
IAC	International Association for Counselling
IACD	International Association for Community Development
IASSW	International Association of Schools of Social

334

IBRD	International Bank for Reconstruction and Development
ICCPR	International Covenant on Civil and Political Rig
ICESCR	International Covenant on Economic, Social and Cultural Rights
ICRMW	International Convention on the Protection of the Rights of All Migrant Workers and Members of Their Families
ICSD	International Consortium for Social Development
ICSW	International Council on Social Welfare
ICT	Information Communication Technology
IDA	International Development Association
IFC	International Finance Corporation
IFSW	International Federation of Social Workers
IGAD	Intergovernmental Authority on Development
IIAG	Ibrahim Index of African Governance
IIF	Individual-in-Family Theory
ILO	International Labour Organisation
IMF	International Monetary Fund
INGO	International NGOs
IOM	International Organization for Migration
IRM	Indigenous research methodology
ISBN	International Standard Book Number
ITC	International Trade Centre
JDA	Journal of Development Administration
MAE	Made in Africa Evaluation
MFS	Machobane Farming System
MSW	Master of Social Work
NASOW	Nigeria Association of Social Workers, pages 21
NASWZ	National Association of Social Workers Zimbabwe
NDA	National Development Agency
NEPAD	New Partnership for Africa's Development
NGO	Non-Governmental Organisation
NPO	Non -Profit Organisations
OAU	Organisation of African Unity
OCHA	Office for the Coordination of Humanitarian Affairs
PAPS	Political Affairs, Peace and Security
PAR	Participatory Action Research
PDF	Portable Document Format
PRC	The Permanent Representatives Committee
PTSD	Post-Traumatic Stress Disorder
PVO	Private Voluntary Organisation
RDC	Rural District Council

REC	The Regional Economic Communities
RRA	Responsible Research Approach
SAASWIPP	South Africa: South African Association for Social Workers in Private Practice
SACSSP	South African Council for Social Service Professions
SADC	Southern African Development Community
SAHARA	The Social Aspects of HIV/AIDS Research Alliance
SAP	Structural Adjustment Programs
SASSA	South African Social Security Agency
SDC	School Development Committees
SDF	Sanga Development Foundation
SDG	Sustainable Development Goal
SEBE	Sustainable Environment and Blue Economy
SG	Secretary General
SMART	Sustainable, Measurable, Achievable, Results Based and Time-bound
SME	Small and Medium Enterprise
SRA	Stories research approach
SWOT	Strengths, Weaknesses, Opportunities and Threats
SWPCNA	Social Work and Psychology Council of Namibia
UDHR	Universal Declaration of Human Rights
UK	United Kingdom
UMA	Arab Maghreb Union
UN	United Nations
UNAIDS	Joint United Nations Programme on HIV/AIDS
UNDP	United Nations Development Programme
UNEP	United Nations Environment Program
UNESCO	United Nations Scientific and Cultural Organisation
UNFPA	United Nations Population Fund
UNHCR	High Commissioner for Refugees
UNHHR	United Nations High Commissioner for Human Rights
UNICEF	United Nations International Children's Emergency Fund
UNIDIR	United Nations Institute for Disarmament Research
UNITAR	United Nations Institute for Training and Research
UNRISD	United Nations Research Institute for Social Development
UNSSC	United Nations System Staff College
UNU	United Nations University
URL	Uniform Resource Locator

USA	United States of America
UZ	University of Zimbabwe
VIDCO	Village Development Committee
WADCO	Ward Development Committee
WB	World Bank
WHO	World Health Organisation
WTO	World Trade Organization (WTO
YWCA	Young Women Christian Association
ZAMFI	Zimbabwe Association of Micro Finance Organisations
ZOIC	Zimbabwe Opportunity Industrialisation Centres

Index

339

C

Cameroon Association of Social Workers · *118*

Caribbean · *63, 154*

case study · *28, 53, 54, 55, 250, 274, 282, 295*

case study · *27, 28, 52, 53, 190, 274*

CCdC model · *304*

Central Africa · *147, 330*

Chama Cha Wataalamu wa Ustawi wa Jamii Tanzania · *119*

Chief · *52, 143, 150, 160, 207, 216, 220, 249, 296*

child protection · *xvii, 191, 218, 269, 274, 279, 280*

child protection committees · *218*

child responsibility · *217*

children · *6, 41, 52, 53, 56, 106, 113, 139, 153, 155, 179, 192, 213, 218, 235, 239, 243, 264, 270, 274*

Chilisa · *32, 34, 58, 89, 331*

Chinua Achebe · *16*

Christianity · *7, 12, 13, 15, 22, 26, 31, 74, 75, 194*

Collectivism theory · *263*

collectivity · *xxiv, 55, 68, 186, 323*

colonial · *xxiii, 4, 7, 8, 10, 17, 24, 25, 33, 48, 52, 54, 74, 76, 77, 78, 79, 82, 92, 93, 97, 98, 99, 106, 107, 117, 123, 140, 141, 142, 143, 144, 145, 151, 152, 155, 156, 166, 170, 173, 215, 217, 224, 229, 232, 233, 308, 319*

colonial missionaries · *92*

colonial philosophy · *10, 25*

COMESA · *147, 207, 330*

communal philosophy · *9, 10*

communalism · *17, 323*

community association · *237, 333*

community committees · *215*

community development · *xvii, 115, 142, 143, 150, 194, 195, 196, 197, 200, 201, 202, 203, 204, 205, 206, 207, 208, 209, 211, 212, 213, 215, 216, 221, 224, 225, 227, 229, 232, 234, 235, 236, 237, 238, 239, 241, 242, 245, 246, 251, 252, 253, 254, 257, 292, 293, 298, 308*

community enterprises · *210*

community level · *81, 137, 159*

community needs assessment · 205

Community of Sahel–Saharan States (CEN–SAD) · *147, 330*

community work · *iv, 5, 98, 182, 184, 196, 200, 201, 202, 203, 204, 205, 207, 208, 213, 216, 219, 223, 225, 227, 234, 235, 236, 237, 238, 239, 241, 242, 246, 250, 251, 252, 253, 254, 255, 257, 306*

community workers · iii, 150, 186, 202, 206, 217, 224, 227, 229, 232, 237, 239, 240

communityhood · 24

continental level · *137, 159*

counsellors · *iii*

county or district level · *137, 159*

CPD · *117, 126, 292, 293, 311*

Creator · *58*

cultural

culture · *xxv, xxvi, 17, 29, 34, 56, 83, 138, 140, 141, 142, 143, 144, 145, 149, 151, 153, 156, 178, 198, 239, 313, 314, 322, 327, 331, 333, 334, 335, 336*

cultural teachers · *140, 141*

culture · *5, 6, 8, 16, 17, 19, 27, 28, 30, 31, 43, 53, 66, 67, 71, 74, 75, 77, 82, 105, 127, 131, 138, 143, 150, 165, 166, 167, 168, 169,*

340

institutionalisation · *54, 56*
Intergovernmental Authority on
   Development (IGAD) · *147, 330*

J

Jairos Jiri · *31, 65, 102, 103, 135*
Jember Teferra · *113*
Joshua Nkomo · *107, 109, 110*
journal · *22, 83, 124, 128, 129,*
   130, 292, 293, 296, 298, 301,
   302, 306, 307, 316
Journal for Social Work
   Education in Africa · *124*
Journal of Social Development in
   Africa · *135, 179, 299*
Journal of Social Work in
   Developing Societies · *301*

K

Kaseke · *79, 80, 89, 98, 135, 182,*
   196, 197, 207, 258, 281
Kaunda · *15, 29, 30, 34, 59, 64, 89,*
   105, 106
Kenya · *4, 15, 17, 35, 67, 90, 105,*
   112, 115, 118, 147, 198, 208,
   209, 214, 256, 257, 322, 323,
   329
Kenya National Association of
   Social Workers · *118*
kintu · *19*
Kofi A. Annan · *152*
kuntu · *19*
Kwame Nkrumah · *18, 65, 79*

L

Lesotho Social Workers'
   Association · *118*

M

Mabvurira · *99, 267, 282*
machobane · *204, 223, 335*
Madagascar Association of Social
   Workers · *119*
Mame Seck Mbacké · *114*
Maripe · *iii, xviii*
marriage · *xxiv, 11, 12, 23, 43, 72,*
   150, 207, 212, 218, 231, 232,
   271
Maxeke · *100, 135*
Mbigi · *15, 29, 30, 35, 77*
mental health · *230, 266, 267, 281*
migration · *7, 24, 77, 79, 93, 143,*
   148, 217, 225, 226, 259, 260,
   261, 264, 265, 269, 273, 274,
   278, 279, 282, 326
Mitri Widad · *113*
Mokgatlho wa Badiri ba Tsa
   Selegae mo Botswana · *118*
morality · *42, 58, 60, 64*
Moroccan Association of Social
   Workers · *119*
motho ke motho ka batho · *323*
Mugumbate · *iii, xvi, 74, 89, 90, 96,*
   103, 135, 168, 172, 179, 197,
   198, 248, 257, 258, 267, 269,
   271, 281, 282, 293, 311, 318,
   319, 321
mukando · *209*
muntu · *19*
Mupedziswa · *74, 90, 98, 123, 134,*
   166, 168, 179, 183, 198, 319,
   321
Musodzi Chibhaga Ayema · *102*
mutual assistance · *208*
Muzondo · *iii, xix, 198*

N

Nabudere · *20, 32, 35, 267, 282,*
   331

344

345

347

Kanimambo | Zikomo kwambili | Murakoze | Maita basa | Asante sana |Abarrka Urakoze cyane | Twa totela | Twa tota | Twa lumba | Wafwako | Twa sakidila | Aksanti | Merci | Mwebale nyo | Jerejef | Abarrka | Au jarama | Osoko | Ese gan | Nagode Da alu | Likpakpanl | Konkomba | Anilituln | Aw ni tchié | Baarka | Takuta Mwapicita | Mwaita basa | Tatenda | Obrigado | Choukran | شكرا | Kathaalne |Yin aca l